Recentering Pacific Asia

The Pacific Rim of Asia – Pacific Asia – is now the world's largest and most cohesive economic region, and China has returned to its center. China's global outlook is shaped by its regional experience, first as a premodern Asian center, then displaced by Western-oriented modernization, and now returning as a central producer and market in a globalized region. Developments since 2008 have been so rapid that future directions are uncertain, but China's presence, population, and production guarantee it a key role. As a global competitor, China has awakened American anxieties and the US-China rivalry has become a major concern for the rest of the world. However, rather than facing a power transition between hegemons, the US and China are primary nodes in a multi-layered, interconnected global matrix that neither can control. Brantly Womack argues that Pacific Asia is now the key venue for working out a new world order.

BRANTLY WOMACK is Senior Faculty Fellow at UVA's Miller Center and Emeritus Professor of Foreign Affairs at the University of Virginia. He is the author of *Asymmetry and International Relationships* (Cambridge, 2015), *China among Unequals: Asymmetric International Relationships in Asia* (World Scientific Press, 2010), and *China and Vietnam: The Politics of Asymmetry* (Cambridge, 2006).

Recentering Pacific Asia

Regional China and World Order

BRANTLY WOMACK
University of Virginia, Charlottesville

With commentaries by

WANG GUNGWU
National University of Singapore

WU YU-SHAN
Academia Sinica, Taipei, Taiwan

QIN YAQING
China Foreign Affairs University

EVELYN GOH
Australian National University

Shaftesbury Road, Cambridge CB2 8EA, United Kingdom

One Liberty Plaza, 20th Floor, New York, NY 10006, USA

477 Williamstown Road, Port Melbourne, VIC 3207, Australia

314–321, 3rd Floor, Plot 3, Splendor Forum, Jasola District Centre, New Delhi – 110025, India

103 Penang Road, #05–06/07, Visioncrest Commercial, Singapore 238467

Cambridge University Press is part of Cambridge University Press & Assessment, a department of the University of Cambridge.

We share the University's mission to contribute to society through the pursuit of education, learning and research at the highest international levels of excellence.

www.cambridge.org
Information on this title: www.cambridge.org/9781009393812

DOI: 10.1017/9781009393867

© Brantly Womack 2023

This publication is in copyright. Subject to statutory exception and to the provisions of relevant collective licensing agreements, no reproduction of any part may take place without the written permission of Cambridge University Press & Assessment.

First published 2023

A catalogue record for this publication is available from the British Library.

A Cataloging-in-Publication data record for this book is available from the Library of Congress

ISBN 978-1-009-39381-2 Hardback
ISBN 978-1-009-39383-6 Paperback

Cambridge University Press & Assessment has no responsibility for the persistence or accuracy of URLs for external or third-party internet websites referred to in this publication and does not guarantee that any content on such websites is, or will remain, accurate or appropriate.

Contents

List of Figures	*page* viii
List of Table	ix
Author and Commentators	x
Acknowledgements	xii
Note on the Cover Map	xvii

	Introduction	1
	The Outline of the Book	15
1	Continuities in China's Pacific Asian Centrality	23
	Beyond Imperium and Hierarchy	24
	Situational Elements of China's Centrality:	
	Presence, Population, Production	29
	Asymmetric Perspectives	33
	Managing Relationships	37
	Connectivities: Thin, Sharp, and Thick	40
	Asymmetric Agency	42
2	Thin Connectivity: Traditional Chinese Centrality	45
	The 3 Ps	46
	Presence	46
	Population	49
	Production	51
	Asymmetric Perceptions of Centrality	53
	Asymmetry: Normal but Neither Static nor Uniform	53
	The View from the Center	55
	The View from the Periphery	58
	Thin Connectivity as Practice and as Policy	60
	As Practice	60
	As Policy: The Tribute System	62

A Different Situation from the West	64
A Liquid Center in the West	65
Zheng He and Afonso de Albuquerque Compared	68
Commentary: Wang Gungwu	71

3 Sharp Connectivity: Western Modernization and
   De-centered Pacific Asia 77
   Colonial Sharp Connectivity in Pacific Asia 80
      The Splintering of Pacific Asia 81
      Colonial Transformations 82
      Chaos in China 84
      The Japanese Exception 87
   Integrated Globalism and the American Imperium 88
      New Leadership, New Institutions,
         and New Sovereignties 89
      Independence and Re-association in Pacific Asia ... 91
   Asymmetric Perceptions of Western Centrality 93
      From Above 94
      The View from Below 95
   China's 3 Ps Transformed 96
      Presence 97
      Population 100
      Production 102
   Conclusion: Westernization, Modernization, and the
      Pacific Asia Region 104
   Commentary: Wu Yu-Shan 107

4 Thick Connectivity: The Re-centering of Pacific Asia ... 113
   The 3 Ps 116
      Regionality beyond Hegemony 116
      Presence 118
      Population 122
      Production 124
   Relationships 126
      Thick Connectivity 127
   Asymmetric Perceptions of Recentering 131
      From Above 131
      From Below 134
   China's Soft Return 136
   Stepping on Toes with Larger Feet 137

	Conclusion: The Era of Re-centering Regional Relationships	144
	Commentary: Qin Yaqing	148
5	China, Pacific Asia, and Reconfiguring a Multinodal World	153
	The Rise of the Rest	156
	The Ironies of Being Left Behind	156
	Demographic Power v. Wealth Power	158
	A Multinodal World	161
	Not Balance of Power	168
	Partnerships Rather than Alliances	169
	Pacific Asia as a New Global Region	172
	Global Significance of Pacific Asia	173
	Pacific Asia's Economic Cohesiveness	174
	Pacific Asia's Problematic Political Cohesiveness	176
	China's Ambiguous Identity	177
	China–Japan as the Key Relationship	179
	China and the World	180
	China as Developmental Alternative	181
	Global Presence	183
	Conclusion: China, Pacific Asia, and Multinodal Governance	189
	Commentary: Evelyn Goh	191
6	Global Power Rivalry, Pacific Asia, and World Order	200
	Asymmetric Parity	201
	Parity in Center Court	202
	Asymmetric Parity	207
	The Texture of the Multinodal Matrix	212
	China's Regional Challenge	214
	The Global Challenge of the United States	217
	Risk Reduction	222
	Military Dangers	224
	Mutual Risk Reduction	225
	Global Leadership in a Multinodal World	226
	Principles of Multinodal Order	226
	Challenges Facing the Primary Nodes	228
	Beyond the Primary Nodes	229
	Conclusion: What If?	230
Bibliography		233
Index		250

Figures

4.1	Pacific Asia's percentage of global GDP	*page* 118
4.2	Pacific Asia's GDP per capita	119
5.1	GDP of developing countries as percentage of GDP of developed countries	158
5.2	GDP of US and Pacific Asia as percentage of rest of world	173
6.1	China's GDP as percentage of US GDP	208

Table

5.1 Top global value chain partners for Pacific Asia   *page* 175

Author and Commentators

Brantly Womack is Professor Emeritus of Politics at the University of Virginia and Senior Faculty Fellow at the Miller Center. His interest in the general dynamics of Chinese domestic development and international relationships has led to a number of books, including *Asymmetry and International Relationships*, *China among Unequals: Asymmetric International Relationships in Asia*, *China's Rise in Historical Perspective*, and *China and Vietnam: The Politics of Asymmetry*. Most recently his research has focused on China's re-emergence and its implications.

Commentators

Chapter 2: **Wang Gungwu** is a legendary historian of China and its external relationships. He began his studies with research on the evolving structure of power between the Tang and Song dynasties, and his later research encompassed the Chinese diaspora, and the linkage of traditional and contemporary notions of China's role. Recent publications include his two-volume autobiography which relates his personal experience of growing up as an overseas Chinese in Southeast Asia, and the book *China Reconnects: Joining a Deep-rooted Past to a New World Order*. Wang is the founding director of the East Asia Institute of National University of Singapore and is University Professor there. Before moving to Singapore he was Vice-Chancellor of Hong Kong University, and prior to that Director of Australian National University's Research School of Asian and Pacific Studies.

Chapter 3: **Wu Yu-Shan** is Academician and Distinguished Research Fellow of Taiwan's Academia Sinica and founding director of its Institute of Political Science, as well as Professor of Political Science at National Taiwan University. He is a leading scholar on comparative political development in Asian politics, European communism, and cross-Strait politics. Recent books include *The Chinese Models* *of Development: Global, Local and Comparative Perspectives* and *Resurgence of China: A Dialogue between History and International Relations* (in Chinese).

Chapter 4: **Qin Yaqing** is Emeritus President of China Foreign Affairs University, Chancellor of the Diplomatic Academy, and one of China's pre-eminent theorists of international relationships. He is a member of the Foreign Policy Advisory Group of the Chinese Ministry of Foreign Affairs. Qin translated Wendt's *Social Theory of International Politics* into Chinese. His book, *A Relational Theory of International Politics*, was published by Princeton in 2018. Qin is particularly interested in the globalization of international relations theory.

Chapter 5: **Evelyn Goh** is the Shedden Professor of Strategic Policy Studies and Director of Research at the Strategic and Defence Studies Centre at Australian National University. She is a leading expert on the changing political and diplomatic contours of East Asia. Her work on the hedging strategies of China's neighbors is well known. Goh recently co-authored (with Barry Buzan) *Re-thinking Sino-Japanese Alienation: History Problems and Historical Opportunities*, and current projects include *"Strategic Diplomacy" in the 21st Century*.

Acknowledgements

This book is the result of fifty years of learning from Asia scholarship, and from interaction with Asian friends in Asian contexts as well as with American and European friends. It is not predictive, since one of the basic lessons of the past fifty years has been that China, Pacific Asia, and their relationship to the world have changed, sometimes dramatically and unexpectedly. China's domestic developments have encompassed the pragmatism of Deng Xiaoping, the trauma of Tiananmen, the institutionalizing efforts of Jiang Zemin and Hu Jintao, followed by the de-institutionalizing personalism of Xi Jinping – what is next? In terms of foreign affairs, we have witnessed China's admission to the UN and general diplomatic normalization, the shift of Taiwan policy from liberation to peaceful reunification, followed by the transition in Taiwan to democracy and Taiwanese identity, not to mention the intertwined mushrooming of the Chinese and Pacific Asian economies and regional reconfiguration since 2008. Anyone who has lived through these transformations knows better than to simply assume the present and to expect more of the same.

Despite the unpredictability of these transformations, none of them were random accidents. Each one, in retrospect, was related to the prior massing of both resources and problems, and to the perceptions of populations, elites, and leaderships regarding their situations and options. Not only were the leaders sometimes surprised and disappointed by these developments, but even the success of a project like Deng Xiaoping's "reform and openness" would lead to new situations and new challenges. As the history of the Association of Southeast Asian Nations (ASEAN) shows, continuity requires adaptability. It is tempting to fall back on the familiar distinction of "continuity and change," but, in fact, continuity and change are inextricably intertwined in the actions of the present, in what is attempted, and in what actually succeeds.

The premise of this book is that we are in the long present of a new era. Although I date the beginning of the era at 2008, that is to say fifteen years before my current writing, it is such a massive change in the world order that we have yet to grasp its implications. The United States remains the leading power in economics, politics, and security, but clearly it is not in control. The developing world, with China as its avatar, is not replacing the developed world, but it is displacing the massiveness of its presence. The era of Western modernization is shading into something else, with Pacific Asia playing a major, and possibly a leading, role. And with China already risen, Putin's invasion of Ukraine splitting Eurasia, and the Cold War mentality in the United States, we may already be moving into Act Two of the twenty-first century's reconfiguration.

The dynamics and questions regarding the Pacific Asian region help shape the agenda of the global prospect, and this book is an attempt to rethink the elements of the past and present that shape its real options. Of course, China, Pacific Asia, and their new global roles are not the only factors shaping world order, but they are important, and they are the ones that I know best. A rethinking is necessary for all concerned. For China, the return to regional pre-eminence has resonances with its traditional centrality, but not the Empire as sanitized and glorified by Chinese popular memory. What were the extent and limits of traditional centrality? How was centrality lost? What does it mean to again become central to a modernized and international region? What to do about Greater China? For Pacific Asia, how to relate to a peacefully risen, but very, very large, China? And how to relate regionally to a China now in global rivalry with the United States? For the United States, China certainly presents challenges to America's global role and to its self-confidence, but is China a challenger? Is proportional change in the global political economy necessarily threatening? Is American leadership adaptable, or is it condemned to a retro mentality of making itself great again? For the rest of the developing and developed world, what difference does greater connectivity and agency make in a world that again has two global powers? If these questions are not rethought, the default answers are likely to be a confusion of backward steps from the present into a misunderstood future, steps shaped by the changing ground on which they tread, but as likely to stumble as to make progress.

What I am offering are rethinkings rather than answers, and my first debts are to the four preeminent scholars who have contributed their thoughts to the volume. Wang Gungwu is probably everyone's favorite historian of China; certainly he is mine. Wu Yu-Shan is the founding director of the Institute of Political Science at Academia Sinica in Taipei, and we have had a long collaborative relationship. Qin Yaqing is China's pre-eminent theorist of international relationships, and we have enjoyed many wide-ranging discussions of philosophy and contemporary foreign policy. Evelyn Goh is a leading researcher of the international relationships of Pacific Asia whose analyses of current developments are particularly valuable. Together, they bring a diverse Pacific Asian reality to these rethinkings.

My next level of debts is to those who made possible the original lecture series at the University of Virginia during the fall of 2021. Heading the list is Dorothy Wong, the Director of the East Asia Center, without whose enthusiasm and support the project would not have been launched. Then come the people who made it happen: Jamie McConnell, who funded the Center's lecture series, and Brian Murphy, who mastered the mechanics of hybrid presentations before present and virtual audiences. Steve Mull, Harry Harding, Len Schoppa, and Amitav Acharya each chaired one of the four sessions and added their own insights. And the large and persevering audiences gave me confidence to proceed to authoring the book. The Miller Center, UVA Global, and the Politics Department also supported the series.

As its six chapters rather than four lectures suggest, the book is a much expanded project. To have presented the big ideas in the lectures was important for my own thinking, but the book's more formal and deliberate explication was a major task. I was aided by indefatigable friends who commented on each chapter. A cluster of my former students, now professors in their own right, were most helpful: Paige Tan, Alice Ba, Kate Kaup, Shino Watanabe, April Herlevi, and Prashanth Parameshwaran. And other friends also provided their encouragement and comments: John Brandon, Ren Xiao, Wei Ling, Clemens Ostergaard, Harry Harding, and Shirley Lin. I also profited from discussions with Chas Freeman, Ed Luce, Josh Eisenman, Julie Chen, Allen Lynch, Dale Copeland, Tayyab Safdar, John Robinson, Dongryul Kim, CC Kuik, Shaun Breslin, and Mike Lampton. While no one but me is to blame for the result, any particular good idea or nuance is likely to show their influence.

Acknowledgements

While none of the chapters have appeared elsewhere, the ideas were a long time in gestation, and they benefited from colleagues and audiences around the world. I would like to thank the New Zealand Contemporary China Research Centre in Wellington; Sydney University; the German Institute of Global and Area Studies (GIGA), Hamburg; the Institute for Defence Studies and Analyses (IDSA), New Delhi; Duisburg University; the Diplomatic Academy of Vietnam; Vietnam National University of Humanities and Social Sciences; the Institute of Political Science of Academia Sinica (IPSAS), Taipei; Manchester University; Jilin University; China Foreign Affairs University; China University of Politics and Law; Chinese University of Hong Kong, Shenzhen Campus; Consejo Mexicano de Asuntos Internacionales (COMEXI), Mexico City; Xi'an Jiaotong-Liverpool University (XJTLU), Suzhou; East China Normal University, Shanghai; the Central Compilation and Translation Bureau; China Academy of Social Sciences; Peking University; University of Montevideo; ThinkChina, University of Copenhagen; Instituto Superior de Relaciones Internacionales, Havana; the China Institute at the University of Alberta, Banff; colleagues in Addis Ababa and at University of Mozambique, Maputo; and finally, on the eve of the Covid lockdown, Helsinki University, the Finnish Institute of International Affairs, and the University of St. Petersburg. In the United States I am grateful for ideas from meetings of the American Political Science Association (APSA), the International Studies Association (ISA), the Association for Asian Studies (AAS), and several conferences at University of Texas at Austin. In Charlottesville, besides meetings at the University of Virginia, the Charlottesville Committee on Foreign Relations has been a welcome venue. The following journals have published some of my exploratory ideas: *China Journal of International Politics, International Affairs, Journal of Contemporary China, Pacific Affairs, Journal of Chinese Political Science*, and *China: An International Journal*.

This is my fourth book with Cambridge University Press, and it was a pleasure to work with John Haslam, Carrie Parkinson, Robert Judkins, Sarah Norman, and Amala Gobiraman. I also deeply appreciate the support of the two anonymous external reviewers.

Always last but never least, the support of my family was and remains essential. The project consumed my waking hours and my energies, and my retirement from teaching in June 2021 merely concentrated my focus. Without the love and aid of my wife Ann, my daughter, Sarah, and, at a greater distance, David, Alice and Otto, I would have either given up or starved to death.

But back to my initial acknowledgements. As China and Pacific Asia were transformed over the past half-century, I was transformed as well. Whatever value these rethinkings have is owed to those who made possible my contact with Pacific Asia. The years of Covid have been a painful reminder of how important personal experience and travel are to one's life and thinking. I hope that connectivity will return, for me and for all.

Note on the Cover Map

The map on the cover is the earliest map of the Pacific Asian region. It was painted at the beginning of the seventeenth century, possibly to decorate a merchant's villa as a display of his routes of trade. The main routes are here highlighted in red by Dr. Hongping Annie Nie, and they show an intricate pattern of regional trade reaching from Japan and Korea to the Indonesian islands, with one heading westward through the Malaccan Strait, including directions as far as Aden and Hormuz. The Fujian trading metropolis of Quanzhou is shown with eighteen routes connecting to sixty ports.

The map is transitional in every respect. It demonstrates the diminishing ability of the Ming Dynasty to control regional relationships with the tribute system. However, its focus on intraregional trade is about to be supplanted by the splintered globalism of Western modernization. Regional relationships have returned in the current era, but as a distinctive part of a changing world order.

The map was donated to Oxford's Bodleian Library in 1659 by John Selden, and remained unnoticed until its rediscovery by Robert Batchelor in 2008. Since its rediscovery it has been considered one of the most important premodern Chinese maps.

Introduction

China has again become the central presence for its neighbors in East and Southeast Asia – Pacific Asia – and, taken as a whole, the regional economy is now greater than the American and EU economies combined.[1] While China has become a global power as well as a regional center, the cohesiveness of Pacific Asia will be the major determinant of larger global roles for China, and the region itself has a newly central role in the dynamics of the global economy. Currently regional economic connectivity is impressive, but China's growth and economic centrality amplify deep concerns among its neighbors about regional politics and security intentions. Meanwhile a higher dimension of uncertainty is added to the region and to the world by the emerging great power rivalry between the United States and China.

Given the unknowns of the global future and the novelty and importance of China's global role, it is tempting to concentrate on China as a global actor, and especially on its rivalry with the United States. Because China is now a global presence, every global event, whether Putin's invasion of Ukraine, or even the failure of US diplomacy at the 2022 Summit of the Americas in Los Angeles, has an important China angle. China's role as a regional power is viewed, not only as secondary, but also assumed to be derivative from the bigger picture. The "global first" focus is also common in China as well as in the rest of the world. The actions and gestures of the two major players of the new "Great Game," as well as their presumptive ambitions and worries, have become the center of attention, while the rest of the world is seen through the lens of their competition.

The general problem with such a global fixation is best illustrated with examples from the Cold War, the previous Great Game. For the

---

[1] In terms of purchasing power parity (PPP). In dollar value, Pacific Asia was 73 percent of combined US and EU production in 2021. China was 62 percent of Pacific Asia's total production. Calculated from International Monetary Fund (IMF), *World Economic Outlook*, October 2022.

United States, "Vietnam" became a war, not a country, a place to contain the spread of Communism and to prevent vulnerable dominoes from falling. Meanwhile, China's initial fraternal (though big brotherish) support for Vietnam in the 1950s was radicalized in the 1960s into its own version of global politics. China tried unsuccessfully to pressure Vietnam into joining China's crusade against Soviet revisionism. The end result was terrible destruction for Vietnam, wasted lives for the United States, and for China, the alienation of a neighbor. What did Vietnam want? As Ho Chi Minh put it, "Nothing is more precious than independence and freedom."[2] Despite global involvement, Vietnam eventually prevailed.

The fundamental lesson of great power failures in Vietnam, in Afghanistan, in Iraq, and in many other intrusions is that the global field of play is an interactive one, with diverse and located situations, interests and strengths. The great game is played with living pieces that make their own moves as well as responding to others. In the long term, the asymmetric relationships between the whole range of participants shape the outcome. Moreover, the texture of the matrix of asymmetric relationships – not only with regards to security, but in economic, historical, and cultural realms as well – sets the very uneven ground upon which states interact, rise, and fall.

The root cause of the anxieties about China among developed countries, and especially in the United States, is the change in the proportions of relative global mass evident since the Global Financial Crisis of 2008. Ever since the Industrial Revolution the West has shaped the world in its own image, and in its own interests as well. After the Cold War the US became accustomed to being the only superpower. China now raises the prospect of a different world order. The natural impulse of incumbent powers, especially the United States but also the West more generally, is to preserve existing advantages by containing China. But that involves two questionable assumptions. First, that containment is possible, and second, that cooperation is not possible. On the first, China's rise is part of a general change of proportions between the developed and developing worlds, and digging in

---

[2] Ironically, Ho coined his most famous slogan while in China in the summer of 1966 as the guest of honor at a mass demonstration of Red Guards in support of Vietnam. Brantly Womack, *China and Vietnam: The Politics of Asymmetry* (New York: Cambridge University Press, 2006), p. 178.

one's heels to stop history is a dubious enterprise. On the second, the "rise of the Rest" is occurring within the liberal economic order, not outside its pale. It is premised on the mutual advantage of trade and investment, rather than on conquest. To counter China by relying on decoupling and sanctions to preserve one's diminishing advantages is more likely to be self-isolating in the long run than to be effective.

The ground has been shifting beneath the stage of global political theater since 2008. Despite the emerging asymmetric parity of the United States and China, the situation is fundamentally different from a power transition between an incumbent power and a rising power. As Evelyn Goh has put it, it is an order transition rather than a power transition.[3] Global value chains have displaced simple bilateral trade, creating networks of economic interdependence. Globalization appears threatened by decoupling and nationalism, and de-globalizing counter measures are likely to encourage regional networks at the expense of global rules and institutions. As the salience of localized resilience increases, so does China's status as the regional center of Pacific Asia. China's rise is a major global phenomenon in this new order, but China has not risen alone.

But if China is here to stay, and the global configuration is changing as well, then developed countries, and especially the Anglophone world, need to rethink assumptions that are deeply embedded in its era of preeminence. As Shaun Breslin has colorfully put it, with China's rise, the old ghost of the Yellow Asian Peril has blended with the newer one of the Red Communist Scare to form the current specter of the Orange Threat of Chinese Communism![4] Even a colorless interpretation of China's rise tends to picture a reverse mirror image of the Western imperial cycles – the Thucydides' Trap.[5] But, as presented below, China's traditional centrality in Pacific Asia was fundamentally different from the mortal competition of empire-eat-empire that was typical of the West. Certainly the world of the twenty-first century is quite different from that prior to the Opium War of 1840,

---

[3] See Goh's contribution to this volume. See also Evelyn Goh, *The Struggle for Order: Hegemony, Resistance and Transition in Post-Cold War East Asia* (Oxford: Oxford University Press, 2013).
[4] Shaun Breslin, *China and the Global Political Economy* (Basingstoke: Palgrave Macmillan, 2013), p. 1.
[5] Most famously Graham Allison, *Destined for War: Can America and China Escape Thucydides's Trap?* (New York: Houghton Mifflin, 2016).

but memories count. More than that, there are some basic similarities between China's present regional situation and the past. It is still a big country, centrally located, with a major role in regional economic connectivity. The content of its regional centrality has changed, but one could say that the most fundamental change between traditional and contemporary Pacific Asia is its relationship to the rest of the world.

But in Pacific Asia, and at the present time, it is particularly important to view global reality from the bottom up rather than from the top down. Not only do the individual countries have more agency than ever before, but at the same time they face new uncertainties at both the regional and global levels. The Pacific Asian region has evolved over the past fifty years because of opportunities of regional economic cooperation in the global marketplace, but also because of shared concerns about vulnerability as secondary players in the global political economy. China's rise as well as regional prosperity has enhanced the region's global presence, but at the same time the reconfiguration of the region around China raises new concerns. Intra-regional and extra-regional tensions are inversely related. Global uncertainties highlight the importance of regional connectivity and cohesiveness; regional uncertainties add salience to relationships beyond the region. Part of the distinctiveness of the Pacific Asian region is its dense and dynamic interweaving with the world beyond.

The argument of this book is that China's regional identity is crucial to understanding its diplomatic culture, its economic success, and its continuing political challenges. But what is China's region? Regions are notoriously difficult to delineate.[6] Often the designation is done by outsiders for their own convenience. The term "Middle East" came to prominence in the hands of Alfred Thayer Mahan, the famous proponent of maritime geo-politics, to denote the region between the Near East and the Far East.[7] The origins of the term "Southeast Asia" are even more convoluted, due to the different purposes to which its mainland and island parts were put by European colonialists. The global South might be a candidate for China's region, in terms of politics

---

[6] Barry Buzan and Ole Wæver, *Regions and Powers: The Structure of International Security* (Cambridge: Cambridge University Press, 2003); Peter Katzenstein, *A World of Regions: Asia and Europe in the American Imperium* (Ithaca, NY: Cornell University Press, 2005).

[7] Clayton Koppes, "Captain Mahan, General Gordon, and the Origins of the Term 'Middle East,'" *Middle Eastern Studies* 12:1 (1976), pp. 95–98.

and economics, but it is a vague and non-contiguous grouping. Not only is the Indo-Pacific similarly dispersed, but it seems to have gained political currency in order to exclude China rather than to provide it with a region. Kent Calder has made a strong argument that the region including China is Eurasia as a whole.[8] Certainly both the historical relations that he describes and the current realities of connection are important, but Paris and Shanghai are seven thousand miles apart, and even further apart in terms of culture. A region should be cohesive, and, as Vladimir Putin has forcefully demonstrated, Eurasia is not. As the invasion proves, Eurasia does not have the regional cohesiveness of Pacific Asia, nor a thick enough relationship to Pacific Asia to be included in a macro-region.

My claim is that China's external identity and prospects are inseparable from what I am calling "Pacific Asia": Northeast Asia (the Koreas, Japan), Greater China (Mainland China, Hong Kong, Macau, Taiwan), and Southeast Asia (Brunei, Cambodia, Indonesia, Laos, Malaysia, Myanmar, Philippines, Singapore, Vietnam – the members of the Association of Southeast Asian Nations ASEAN). Admittedly, "Pacific Asia" is a novel term, and I am an outsider. But it is better than the alternatives. The World Trade Organization (WTO) has called Pacific Asia "Factory Asia" for good reason. Pacific Asia's intraregional trade exceeds that of "Factory Europe" and "Factory America."[9] But Pacific Asia is more than a factory, and it has a regional history. Within Pacific Asia itself the whole region is now commonly called "East Asia." But outside of Asia, "East Asia" usually refers to Northeast Asia (including mainland China), leaving out Southeast Asia and the rest of Greater China. The more common term used by outsiders that covers Pacific Asia is "Asia Pacific," but that typically includes both sides of the Pacific. For example, APEC, the "Asia Pacific Economic Cooperation," includes the United States, Canada, Chile, Peru, and Russia. Thus, I propose to inconvenience both insiders and outsiders with a new name. Pacific Asian insiders should realize that the global importance of their region requires a term clearer to outsiders than "East Asia." Outsiders should accept that, while Pacific

---

[8] Kent Calder, *Super Continent: The Logic of Eurasian Integration* (Stanford, CA: Stanford University Press, 2019).
[9] World Trade Organization, *Technological Innovation, Supply Chain Trade, and Workers in a Globalized World* (Geneva: WTO, 2019).

Asia deals with the Americas, Europe, Africa, and the rest of Asia, it does have a distinctive regional coherence.

China's important relationships are not limited to Pacific Asia. The innumerable infrastructural projects of China's Belt and Road Initiative (BRI) have the potential of transforming both China's connectivity and that of the developing world. Meanwhile Asia as a whole is becoming "more continental than sub-continental."[10] The Shanghai Cooperation Organization now includes, as members or observers, almost every Asian country except for the Arab Middle East and the rest of Pacific Asia. Moreover, China's relationship with Russia is especially important, and with the Russian invasion of the Ukraine it is currently at the center of attention in global diplomacy. The development of Central Asia, connecting through Russia to Europe, is a major effort at Eurasian connectivity currently derailed by the invasion. While China's relationship with India is important, and the "Maritime Silk Road" traverses the Indian Ocean, the Indo-Pacific is a rather broad and vague concept with little regional cohesiveness. Indeed, it is precisely the existing internal divisiveness of the South Asian region that adds a special concern to China's new presence there.

The magnitude and gravity of the transformation of the Pacific Asian region and more generally of the post-2008 global order require a reassessment of everyone's basic framing of regional and global dynamics. The world is now well beyond a situation of unquestioned American leadership, and a transformational "rising China" has morphed into a more troubled "risen China." While China is the largest obstacle on the American horizon, the two are not lone, symmetric boxers in a ring, but rather rivals with very different assets and challenges. Both are in broader, interactive environments with other decision makers, but the texture of their environments is quite different.

China is primarily a regional power, and Pacific Asia is its region. Coping with the diverse political and economic challenges of Pacific Asia is China's most immediate challenge. Mao's China failed in both dimensions of its regional challenge. Especially in contrast to Mao, Deng Xiaoping's "second revolution" of reform and openness was successful. Since Deng's death in 1997, economic integration has snowballed, but regional political problems have become more acute.

---

[10] Evan Feigenbaum, "Why America No Longer Gets Asia," *The Washington Quarterly* 34:2 (2011), p. 27.

The hardening of Xi Jinping's attitude toward Taiwan creates a vortex of uncertainty in the middle of the region. China's regional economic centrality heightens concerns about its political leadership. China cannot afford to ignore the concerns of its neighbors.

While "regional power" might sound demeaning – "*only* a regional power" – Pacific Asia has become key to the prospects of the global economy as well as the key to China's global success. China's global prospects depend on continuing its regional economic integration and stabilizing its role in regional politics. In 2022 Asia's growth rate exceeded China's, demonstrating thereby that the future of China's growth engine rests on the momentum of its regional train. India is a cautionary example of the importance of regional relationships to global ambitions. Only 5 percent of South Asia's trade is intra-regional. It is 20 percent cheaper for India to trade with Brazil than with its neighbor Pakistan.[11] Although India is not the sole cause of its own isolation within its region, despite its size and potential India has not been able to leapfrog its region into global preeminence. If the focus of China's regional relationships shifted from mutual economic advantage to hegemonic security, it would break the chain of mutual advantage. China's self-containment would gravely undermine its global influence.

The United States is primarily a global power, with strategic challenges quite different from China's regional ones. The US has been global in its outlook from its beginnings, and it has been the major global power for more than a century. Its political and economic destiny was set in the mid-nineteenth century by its success in the Civil War and by tying its two coasts together with the transcontinental railroad, followed by the Panama Canal. Successive technological revolutions in transportation and communication strengthened the salience of American global centrality. The United States remains central to the familiar global configuration, but it is no longer able to control the global political economy. The United States might seek to contain what it cannot control, but the root of the "China threat" is not China's enmity, but its success. If China does not contain itself by alienating its neighborhood, then containment efforts motivated by American hegemonic nostalgia are likely to lead to US self-isolation. Thorough economic decoupling would deprive the United States of a

---

[11] World Bank, "Why #OneSouthAsia?" accessible at www.worldbank.org/en/programs/south-asia-regional-integration/trade.

middle-class market half again its own size. The US would risk becoming a boutique economy, weakening the dollar's salience as a global currency. Further militarization would divert resources from economic growth and popular welfare. Pressure on allies is not likely to make them enthusiastic supporters, even if they comply. Just as China's strategic de-regionalization could lead to self-inflicted disaster, so could American de-globalization.

Thus, the rivalry between China and the United States is asymmetric in every respect: situation, dynamics, and resources. On the optimistic side, it is certainly possible that both will pursue strategies appropriate to their situations. China would give credible assurance of the autonomy and well-being of its neighbors, and the United States would adjust its still-central global role to the requisites of a multinodal, post-hegemonic world. Still optimistically, one side could steadfastly pursue an appropriate strategy while the other eventually learns from its mistakes. More realistically, each is likely to make mistakes in interaction with the other, and then each either learns from the mistakes or is sufficiently weakened by them to reduce the general risk. More pessimistically, an unstable and ambiguous global frontier develops as the result of zero-sum rivalry between the global powers. This could result in the de-regionalization of Pacific Asia and a de-globalization of world order. Most pessimistically, the militarization of global rivalry overwhelms political and economic concerns. Even in that case neither can destroy the other without risking its own destruction. For either side, victory is not an option.

It is reasonable to ask whether the era of post-hegemonic globalization is approaching its end as an indirect consequence of US-China rivalry and of global economic disruptions. I am writing in the sixth month of Russia's invasion of the Ukraine, and China's unwillingness to condemn the invasion plus the extent of US sanctions against Russia suggest a new division of the global political economy into two camps. This is a possible outcome, but it is more likely that while the texture of regional versus global relationships will become increasingly important, the massiveness and economic cohesiveness of Pacific Asian production and markets will prove irresistible to Western wealth and financial interests. Meanwhile, Pacific Asia is viscerally committed to global inclusiveness and to the familiar global system underpinned by the dollar. The sanctions against Russia are themselves the best evidence of the toughening of globalization rather than its fragmentation. Despite the egregiousness of Russia's action, vital products are exempted, and the governments of the majority of the world's population abstained from the UN resolution to condemn the invasion.[12] The strategic blowback of general sanctions against China would be more severe by orders of magnitude.

The major task facing the United States is not to counter China's centrality in Pacific Asia, but rather to understand both China and its region. As a global power, the United States tends to derive its regional tactics from its global grand strategy, and currently it lumps China and Russia together as its antagonists in a new Cold War. While the Russian invasion of the Ukraine stirs the Cold War fires of Europe, the situation is quite different in Asia. Moreover, the old Cold War had its share of mistaken regional applications, headed by the "small war" in Vietnam, and that lens is even less appropriate for the post-2008 world. Europe is certainly concerned about Russia, and from its own history Europe brings to Pacific Asia its assumptions about competitive balance of power as well as its memories of colonial relationships. But Pacific Asia is a different place, with different realities and different memories. Pacific Asia is a group of successful states with a variety of thick but problematic relationships among themselves and with a non-revolutionary party-state as its central economic power. In some contrast to the Cold War era, and in great contrast to the colonial period, each state in the region now has agency. They value their relationship with the United States, but they will avoid an either-or choice between global powers. If the United States does not attempt to understand the situation of a reconfigured Pacific Asia, its initiatives will be either non-starters, failures, or disasters.

It is not only the United States and other outsiders that need to adjust to a reconfigured Pacific Asia. In this century the changes in the regional and global configurations are so profound that everyone – including China and the other countries of Pacific Asia themselves – needs to rethink the broadest and most basic frameworks of their international relationships. This requires a rethinking of the historical continuities and discontinuities of the region. Before the Opium War in 1840, traditional China was certainly central, in some sense, to its region. Its location, its population, and its production gave it a societal

---

[12] Edward Luce, "The West is Rash to Assume the World is on its Side over Ukraine," *Financial Times*, March 24, 2022.

mass at the region's geographical center. Traditional China was sometimes in chaos, sometimes conquered, and always in a tense relationship with pastoral nomads to the north, but it remained a resilient point of central attention for the region. With the arrival of Western imperialism China ceased being a focal point for Pacific Asia. By 1880 China was not the principal concern of any of its neighbors. The region became a part of a global picture, but splintered among different colonial empires. Europe, despite its internal disunity and wars, became the first global center of attention. Upon decolonization and a US-centered world order, Pacific Asia became less splintered and more global, but the region itself remained decentered – separate spokes on the American hub. For Southeast Asia, the formation of the Association of Southeast Asian Nations (ASEAN) in 1967 began a tentative process of coordination. However, beginning in 2008 the contrast between China's continued growth as well as uncertainties about American leadership led increasingly to a centering of regional attention on China – both hopes and fears – and to a relative de-centering of the global order despite the continuing, though no longer dominating, central presence of the United States.

The two previous eras, namely China's traditional centrality and the forced globalization of Western modernity, are the major templates that Pacific Asia itself brings to the understanding of its current prospects. These are fundamentally different templates than the ones the West might bring, the former because it happened within the region before the triumph of Western imperialism, and the latter because the West held a very different end of the relationship. The default assumptions of external observers tend to be shaped by their own experiences, and therefore can be fundamentally misleading in gauging the regional interactions of others. To take Pacific Asia seriously – in its own terms, since it has agency – its historically informed consciousness must be understood as well as its current situation.

But in a new era even national memories can be misleading. Many Chinese see China's re-centering of Pacific Asia as a return to past glory and prestige. That is a distortion of both the past and the present. The current recentering is not a return to the past, and in any case the imagined past is quite different from its reality. By contrast, other Pacific Asians are concerned about China as a new regional hegemon analogous to the colonial hegemony they once experienced. In the past many lost their autonomy, and they do not want to lose it again. But they now have an agency that they did not have in the previous era, and while China's influence is increasing, if China attempted to impose hegemonic control it would undercut its own economy, its regional prospects, and its global aspirations.

The purpose of this book is to rethink China's relationship to Pacific Asia, and then to consider Pacific Asia's global significance and the challenges posed by US-China rivalry. We go back to basics concerning relationships in Pacific Asia and their implications for the global order. We begin with a search for elements of continuity and difference between the three eras, traditional, modern, and current, then consider the general situation and relationships of each era, and discuss changes in the global configuration and the significance of Pacific Asia for global dynamics. We conclude by analyzing the asymmetric rivalry between the United States and China.

Because we concentrate on the basics, much of the argument may seem obvious to the informed observer. But that is exactly the point. If we can frame the dynamics of Pacific Asia in terms sufficiently broad to be generally acceptable, then our rethinking will not become simply one more contrary strand of interpretation to be picked out and isolated from its context, and then added to the contradictory and bewildering variety of threads already available. And as Sherlock Holmes constantly noted to Dr. Watson, the "elementary" is obvious only after it is pointed out. Of course, Mr. Holmes had an easier task than we do, because all of his elements led in one direction. Pacific Asia's history lends itself to many interpretations, and the region's future holds a broad spectrum of possibilities. Holmes had merely to see and think about the elements, but we must rethink them, and invite our commentators and readers to rethink them as well. If we bring the obvious into conscious consideration, we are then observing the general framing of reality that otherwise could pass unnoticed. This is a crucial task in a changing era. If the framework is shifting in fundamental ways but the shift is not observed, then its new parameters can become unseen walls, surprising and frustrating our expectations and action.

Another important reason for rethinking the generalities of Pacific Asia is that each political community sees its history and its future prospects from its own vantage point. Reality as seen from South Korea will be different from reality as seen from Japan – it is reality "with Korean characteristics" versus reality "with Japanese characteristics." National constructions of reality are not simply self-serving inventions, though they are usually more critical of others than they are of themselves. It is impossible that history, the present, and the future would look the same to Korea and to Japan because they have had different histories, face different options, and must judge their own different future prospects. The realistic goal of their interaction is not that they come to a common agreement on these things, but that the interactive management of their different perceptions reduces uncertainties and leads to mutually beneficial results.

Each political community in Pacific Asia has its own unique national characteristics, and the immediate task of each in the new era is to figure out its own situation and options. But to a very large extent these will be shaped by interaction with others. To be sure, the best way to adroitly interact with others is to understand their different vantage points. As the military philosopher Sun Zi famously put it, "know your enemy." But in a new era, in an increasingly interconnected region, in a globalized world, it is necessary to rethink webs of relationships, not just bilateral ones. This requires rethinking history in a framework broader than one's own national memory. For regional dynamics, a regional history is necessary. China's centrality in premodern Pacific Asia is not something to be argued for or against, but to be understood in its reality and limits. Likewise, the vast differences of regional experiences during the era of Western modernization need to be considered in order to contextualize the experiences of each. Without reconsidering the general dynamic context that has shaped the present, the default temptation for both insiders and outsiders is to project one's own national outlook and to discount the possibility that others might think and act differently. While collisions of national outlooks and national interests are inevitable, they can be rendered less damaging and risky. One cannot expect mature, smoothly functioning relationships at the beginning of an era, but contextual understanding should make it possible to make the learning curve shorter and smoother.

No region is as intense or as diverse in its global interaction as Pacific Asia, and no state in the region would sacrifice its global opportunities just for the sake of regional cohesion. All in the region are deeply involved in developing their extra-regional relationships.[13] The acceptance of China's regional economic centrality is premised on China's role as part of a global framework and as a facilitator

---

[13] North Korea and Myanmar are current exceptions that prove the rule since their isolationism is regional as well as global.

of global connectivity. China's rise has changed the proportions of regional versus global involvement because of the relative speed of its development. But it would be impossible for China to sequester part or all of Pacific Asia, and it would hurt China's own global interests. While many of the infrastructural developments under the umbrella of China's Belt and Road Initiative (BRI) increase connectivity to China, they also increase the region's capacity for global participation. The economic integration of Pacific Asia is not in lieu of globalization, but integrally linked to globalization.

The rise of China is only part of a general convergence between "the West and the Rest." But China is the most prominent part. It is the largest manufacturing and trading nation, and has been the major contributor to global economic dynamism. Even if China had no intention of changing the global system, proportions would change, and proportional change has systemic effects. As Fred Bergsten points out, both the World Bank and the International Monetary Fund have in their 1945 charters that their headquarters would be located on the territory of the member with the largest quota, and by their own formulas of determining the quotas, China's is likely to exceed that of the United States as early as 2025.[14] Imagine the World Bank in Beijing and the IMF in Shanghai! And if China reaches the tipping point of the official quota and yet relocation is resisted by the US, who, then, is the revisionist?

Since 2008 the world has become too diffuse in its interrelationships to be controlled by the United States. The US remains the global central power in politics, economics, and security, although increasingly it shares the economic spotlight with China. However, "power" isn't what it used to be. When the United States was the hub of the global economy the others had no real alternative to its preferences. The Global Financial Crisis displayed American centrality, but also its loss of control, and China's continued development despite the crisis showed that there were dynamics that did not depend on the hub. China's continued rise has led to an asymmetric parity with the US, and this in turn to rivalry, but the world has become too diffuse for either global power to become hegemonic. The current global configuration is a multinodal matrix of located actors of different capacities. Power still matters, but the more powerful cannot simply dominate the less powerful. The

---

[14] C. Fred Bergsten, *The United States v. China: The Quest for Global Economic Leadership* (Cambridge, UK: Polity, 2022), pp. 3–5.

United States and China are the primary nodes, but there is a textured web of international relationships rather than bipolarity.

Since the United States is still at the center of the global order and China has become central to Pacific Asia as well as a global power, the increasing tension between them is particularly acute in Pacific Asia. The region already includes the two major security hotspots in the US-China relationship, Taiwan and North Korea, and the likelihood of long-term global rivalry deeply affects the outlook of all regional countries as well as the prospects of regional cohesiveness. Each country's options are different, but they share the dilemma of having China as their largest proximate concern and the United States as a key part of the configuration of their global interests. Therefore, evading a final choice between the rivals is a foundational strategy for other countries, though a primary diplomatic tactic is to leverage the greater attention they receive from both contenders. The surface texture of regional diplomacy reflects the global rivalry as each country pursues its own tactical advantages, but the strategic necessity of remaining both in the region and part of the global network grounds the desire to avoid an either/or choice. If one of the rivals presents an ultimatum, then that power becomes the proximate threat. If both rivals demand a choice, the prudent policy of others would be to develop ties outside the rivalry and, if necessary, to become an ally under duress, and therefore an unreliable ally.

Given the variety of national experiences within the Pacific Asia region, the importance of extra-regional influences, and the fundamental changes since 2008, a comprehensive rethinking is a challenging endeavor. What I am presenting is a rethinking that is intended to encourage other rethinkings, and other rethinkings are an integral part of the book. The initial format of the project was my four-part special lecture series at the University of Virginia in the Fall of 2021. The book is more developed and detailed than the lectures, and so the topics of the first and fourth lectures were each split into two chapters. Each lecture was followed by a virtual discussion by a distinguished Pacific Asian scholar presenting their own thoughts. The scholars were chosen because they are the people whose opinions I would most value, and I am delighted that they agreed to participate. Their brief biographies are presented elsewhere, and they are all well-known and top of their field: Wang Gungwu, Wu Yu-Shan, Qin Yaqing, and Evelyn Goh. They are active in Singapore, Taipei, Qingdao, and Canberra, respectively. They were invited not because of their reputations, but because of the quality and depth of thought that accounts for their reputations. They were asked for their thoughts on the topic of their respective chapters, not simply on the chapter itself. Readers will note that their points of emphasis sometimes differ significantly from mine, and perhaps even more from one another. I hope that readers will find stimulating the interplay between my analyses and their comments. Even more important, the presence of several divergent rethinkings rather than just my monologue should encourage readers to formulate their own thoughts.

The Outline of the Book

The first task is to clarify the general factors involved in Pacific Asian centrality and the consequences of China's centrality for regional configuration. Chapter 1 begins by questioning two presumptive prerequisites of centrality: hegemony and cultural superiority. While it is tempting to assume that China's regional centrality is due to its power, during the premodern era it remained the focus of regional attention even when its power was challenged, and in the current era its return to centrality is not the result of coercing its neighbors. Similarly, although it can be argued that China considers itself culturally superior, and traditionally most neighbors did accept a regional order centered on China, they were also quite skeptical of China's claims to virtue. Moreover, in the current era China's attractiveness, its "soft power," has declined even as China has become more prominent. It is therefore necessary to look for more enduring features that would explain both China's centrality in the premodern and current eras and at the same time its loss of centrality during the era of Western modernization.

I argue that China's centrality has three basic situational features: its interactive presence in the middle of the region, its population, always at least half of that of the region, and its production, which was key to regional commerce in the premodern and current eras. So, what happened to presence, population, and production – the "3 Ps" – during the era of Western modernization? The region became splintered by colonialism in the nineteenth century and absorbed into a Europe-centered (and later US-centered) world order. China did not disappear, but it was no longer a central presence. China's population became an inertial drag on its own modernization and of little military relevance, and its sophisticated but artisanal products were displaced by industrial production. In the current, post-2008 era, China's massive regional presence, organized population, and industrial production have again reasserted themselves.

A corollary to China's centrality in Pacific Asia is that the fundamental pattern of regional relationships is asymmetric. In each individual relationship, China has a different prospect of risk and of opportunity than its neighbor. The regional perspectives of China and its neighbors are therefore structurally different. The mix of opportunity and risk differed greatly across the region, but within each bilateral dyad, being on the China end and being on the peripheral end were significantly different positions. The situation became more complex in the modern era because China itself was marginalized. In traditional times and in the current era as well, the essential tradeoff in a normal asymmetric relationship was that the neighbor is deferential to China's central role while China acknowledges the neighbor's autonomy and core interests. But asymmetric relationships need time to acquire stability.

Without connectivity a region is simply a set of isolated units, but over the three eras the nature of connectivity changed fundamentally. The premodern era, the subject of Chapter 2, was characterized by *thin connectivity*. Of course, the volume of transactions was low between self-sufficient agrarian societies with limited transportation. But, especially for China, the stability of the system of traditional regional relationships was more important than commercial gain, so official relationships were controlled. Nevertheless, the region was structured around China's centrality, however distant from daily life, and the 3 Ps of presence, population, and production were essential elements of the configuration of regional order.

China was a remote presence in a diverse neighborhood, but, except at the southern and western sides of Southeast Asia where Indian and later Arab influence was prevalent, there was no comparable alternative. While fights among neighbors would of course be more urgent for those immediately involved, China was the central node of the regional order. For ambitious outsiders, the conquest and rule of China was the crowning objective, while for more settled states like Korea and Vietnam, China was a model of best practices. Anchoring China's presence was its preponderance of population. It was the solid population center of East Asia. China was roughly one-quarter of the world's population, until its population explosion after 1700 brought it to one-third of global population by 1820. In times of domestic cohesion China's population could sustain a formidable military force, but it also created a constant challenge of governance that could lead to domestic fragility and chaos. Even if the central government fell apart or if China was conquered, China's resilience as a state was founded on its population. Meanwhile China's scale allowed greater sophistication of premodern production, and so goods such as tea, ceramics, and silk could become essential components of regional connectivity.

The resulting asymmetric relationships were neither static nor uniform, but China's abiding interest in shaping thin connectivity was to preserve order by reducing uncertainty. This led to defensive policies such as the Great Wall and the prohibition on emigration, as well as to the control of official exchanges through detailed ritual. Of course, maritime trade was much more important to coastal areas such as Fujian and Guangdong, but the center tried to control official trade. If unofficial trade became too troublesome to be ignored, such as the opium trade in 1840, then the center tried to prohibit it. By the time of the Ming Dynasty in the fourteenth century, the asymmetric management of thin connectivity evolved into the tribute system. The rituals involved the neighbors' exchange of deference for China's acknowledgment of autonomy and the exchange of gifts. As far as Beijing was concerned, the politics of risk reduction outweighed the economics of trade.

There were fundamental differences between China's premodern centrality in Pacific Asia and Western empires, both traditional and modern. For China, tribute was primarily a means of controlling external risk by managing deferential relationships; for the West tribute was the spoils of victory. In Pacific Asia there was one asymmetric central power; in the West there were successive empires in mortal competition with one another.

In his commentary, the historian **Wang Gungwu** spans the course of Chinese centrality and its challenges from its beginnings to the present. He points out two factors that were integrative over space and time: the parallel river systems of the Yellow River and the Yangtze and the enabling of continuous historical identity by the Chinese writing system. China's centrality was assimilative, and the center-periphery relationship with nomadic groups was always problematic. Even in the modern era the inland Eurasian borders were a prime concern, and they remain so today.

Western colonialism was a different experience in every respect. As Chapter 3 describes, the management of thin connectivity by ritual was replaced by the forcing of *sharp connectivity* by imperialism.

Sharp connectivity was much more intense. It involved the restructuring of Pacific Asian societies to serve the interests of their respective European masters. In the process, Pacific Asia as a region was splintered, and its parts were reoriented toward global realities. Without a region, China was merely a fellow victim on the global periphery rather than a central presence; its population was seen as an inertial burden preventing domestic reform, and its artisanal production was overwhelmed by cheap industrial goods.

Although the picture changed after the founding of the People's Republic of China in 1949 and the emergence of the American world order, China remained at the periphery of a globalized Pacific Asia until 2008. Its initial political isolation and its concentration on economic self-sufficiency distanced it from its neighbors. When Deng Xiaoping adopted radically new policies in 1980, China's growth and engagement were welcome, but not until 1997 was China a significant regional actor. Meanwhile, Pacific Asia had passed from colonial splintering to becoming spokes around an American hub of globalization. Although Japan became the most important regional actor, there was no regional center.

Professor Wu Yu-Shan emphasizes the importance of power in his commentary. Power, made possible by technology and production, underwrote the success of Western imperialism. There were various modernization routes attempted in Pacific Asia, but liberalism was stillborn in the May Fourth Movement of 1919, and state socialism, "confused modernization," failed to thrive under Mao Zedong. The path that was followed in Taiwan after 1949, modernizing authoritarianism, was successful there, and subsequently in Deng Xiaoping's China from 1980. It is clear from these two examples that there are varieties within modernizing authoritarianism, and that different fates are possible.

Since 2008 China has again become the central concern of Pacific Asia. 2008 was a watershed year because the Global Financial Crisis shook regional confidence in the US-centered world order, while China continued to surge forward. Chapter 4 analyzes the transition of Pacific Asia to a China-centered region. It was not a return to the remoteness of traditional thin connectivity, nor was it a repeat of Western sharp connectivity. The current era's *thick connectivity* aims to maximize mutual benefit through increasing every dimension of contact between sovereign states. But as China has become the preponderant regional economy and the global order has become less certain, the concerns of the neighbors regarding China's centrality have become more acute.

Regarding the "3 Ps," presence, population, and production, while these have a different salience from the traditional era, they all have returned. China is a key player in the integrated regional economy. Its population has become the largest national market, and it has become the world's largest manufacturer and trading nation. There are some resonances with earlier eras. As in traditional times, China's overriding external strategy is one of avoiding risks. This is particularly evident in China's Covid strategy of minimizing contact. However, generally in a globalized environment with its resource dependencies and market fluctuations, China's strategy is one of diverse partners and multiple channels rather than targeting and controlling sources. Like the West in the era of modernization, China is involved in infrastructural projects designed to increase production and further globalize its partners, but its investment is based on mutual agreement rather than conquest. Nevertheless, the economic turmoil associated with the Covid years sharpened the differences of interest between investors and debtors.

China's basic challenge in the new era is to convince its partners that it respects their autonomy. China's intolerance of domestic diversity, intensified by Xi Jinping, spills over into its external policy in its treatment of Hong Kong and Taiwan. In imperial times and under the party-state, there was no acknowledgment of legitimate opposition, and while Deng Xiaoping's formula of "one country, two systems" appeared to promise systemic tolerance, Xi apparently regards this as merely transitional to unified control. Relatedly, China's ascendancy has bred an assertiveness and arrogance that rekindle neighbors' memories of their earlier subjugations by the West as well as traditional China's claims of superiority. China's practices of extolling its virtues and displaying its power are not reassuring to the region, even as its neighbors take advantage of the opportunities presented by trade, investment, and, until recently, tourism.

The international relations theorist **Qin Yaqing** makes three points in his commentary that may seem contrary or at least oblique to the main thrust of the book. First, he criticizes the notion of centrality as a fixed power hierarchy, preferring instead to see world order as a multinodal configuration. Second, he argues that global governance in today's world is one of horizontal, interactive relationships rather than hegemonic lines of command. Third, he argues that Pacific Asia will not center around China, arguing that the initiatives of ASEAN have been leading sources of regional order. The "nodes" of a multinodal system are defined by their relationships rather than their relative power.

Chapter 5 puts the reconfiguration of Pacific Asia into global perspective in four respects. First, in contrast to the divergence in power, wealth, and life chances between "the West and the Rest" that characterized the modern era, in this century there has been a multi-dimensional convergence between developed and developing countries. 2008 marked the first time since the nineteenth century that the production of the developing world was greater than that of the developed world.[15] This trend is due in part to greater population as well as to increased productivity, so a new type of power, demographic power, has arisen. China is the most prominent example, but by no means the only case. Second, the unipolar world order of the post-Cold War has shifted to a multinodal world order. It is not a bipolar order because more than the rise of China and the relative decline of the United States is involved. With global integration the options of all countries have diversified and the ability of global powers to coerce compliance has withered. Power remains important, but it is not necessarily decisive. The global order has become a matrix of interaction in which relative power attracts international attention but not necessarily obedience. However, the increase in the complexity and flexibility of international relationships increases the uncertainties of the world order.

Third, Pacific Asia has become a global powerhouse. In 2020 its GDP equaled that of the US and the EU combined, though its per capita GDP was only one-third of theirs. China is its economic and demographic center, but in terms of politics and security the divisions are sharp. China's greatest challenge is managing its regional relationships in Pacific Asia. Taiwan is the most acute challenge, but Japan poses special difficulties as well, and every country requires respect for its autonomy. Thus far, China's diplomatic progress not only lags behind its economic connectivity, but it also seems to lack a clear direction.

Fourth, China reaches beyond its region. The Belt and Road Initiative (BRI) and the Asia Infrastructure Investment Bank (AIIB) are the most

---

[15] IMF, *World Economic Outlook*. PPP attempts to compare actual production by correcting for the differences in purchasing power of different currencies. Since the currencies of developing countries are relatively undervalued, their PPP data is higher than data based on exchange value. Graham Allison makes a good case for using PPP data in *Destined for War*. Unless otherwise noted, my global GDP comparisons are based on purchasing power parity (PPP) data.

prominent among many initiatives. China's new presence in the world beyond Pacific Asia is supported by but does not depend on its regional role. Rather, China's global dynamic relies on the scale and dynamics of its growth and its active promotion of partnerships wherever possible. In most developing countries China's projects and financing present a welcome alternative to more expensive and more restrictive options. However, the honeymoon of the announcement of grand, transformative projects is often followed by problematic local implementation, changes in political wind, and problems of repayment. These natural political rhythms have been amplified by waves of pandemic, supply bottlenecks, and global tensions. In dealing with developed countries China is attractive as both a producer and a market, but the affinity of interests of developed countries with the United States creates a rift that could develop into a chasm. If a bipolar configuration develops, it is likely to differ from the Cold War camps by being closer to a developed/developing country split, with less unity of leadership on either side.

Evelyn Goh is well known for her emphasis on order transition rather than power transition in world politics, and in her commentary she stresses the compatibility of a multinodal framing that recognizes the continuing significance of power in a post-hegemonic context. While China's re-emergence is a key event for Pacific Asia, she cautions that regional centrality does not preclude global relevance, either for China or for the Pacific Asian region. China is not just regional, and neither is Pacific Asia. But becoming global implies new challenges of global governance and global responsibility. The overall tendency is toward "a multinodal Asia in a multinodal international system."

While China-centered Pacific Asia has become important globally, the emerging rivalry of the United States and China discussed in Chapter 6 deservedly gets attention as a major concern of world politics for the current generation. Together, the two global powers comprise one-third of the world economy. Not only is every other country concerned about its bilateral relations to each, but they are also concerned about the side effects of the rivalry. The rivalry is asymmetric. In the aggregate, China's economy is in the process of surpassing the United States, but it will not equal the US in per capita production or wealth in the foreseeable future. China has demographic power and the advantages of scale, but the United States is the large and wealthy country at the center of global finances and communications. Conflict is not inevitable in a post-hegemonic world, but long-term rivalry is unavoidable. But the rivalry, while competitive, is not necessarily zero-sum. China's core challenge is leadership in Pacific Asia. If it fails in its region, its global prospects will be dim. The United States faces the challenge of re-establishing its inclusive global leadership rather than concentrating on its alliance network to contain China. Both can succeed, and both can fail. If "winning" means the decisive defeat of the other at acceptable cost to oneself, then neither can win.

Risk reduction is a major problem in the rivalry because of the inevitable tensions between rising and incumbent powers, the contradictions between regional and global leadership, and faded existential memories of the horrors of war. Given the possibilities of accident, misinterpretation, and escalation, the focus of the military relationship should be on mutual risk reduction. Compared to climate change, thermonuclear war would be more sudden and probably more catastrophic.[16] Since some of the risks, for example, drones and cyber security, are not restricted to global powers, the United States and China could take the lead in more general risk reduction.

Beyond coping with the dangers of rivalry, earning deference in a multinodal world requires cooperation and respect. To translate power into influence when coercion is impossible, the powerful must be credible enablers of common purposes. Both global powers face challenges of coping with diversity, but of different sorts. The United States must respect system diversity, including that of the Chinese party-state. China must respect diversity below systems, starting with the autonomous and successful political communities in Greater China.

Fortunately, global order and even global leadership do not depend entirely on the global rivals. International organizations such as the UN, the World Bank, and IMF have a certain autonomy, and perhaps even more important are the efforts of inclusive regional integration pioneered by ASEAN and the EU. Also important are the efforts by non-governmental organizations to highlight specific issues of concern. For Pacific Asia, and perhaps for the rest of the world as well, the ongoing challenge is prudent agency and the encouragement of regional and global regimes that manage and secure mutual interests while reducing uncertainties. A new era will inevitably have a learning curve. Let us hope that its mistakes are correctable and its progress smooth.

[16] François Diaz-Maurin, "Nowhere to Hide," *Bulletin of the Atomic Scientists*, October 20, 2022.

1 | *Continuities in China's Pacific Asian Centrality*

China's traditional centrality in what I am calling "Pacific Asia" – East and Southeast Asia – has long been asserted and contested, and, despite China's marginalization from 1840 to 2008, some sort of regional centrality has now sufficiently emerged to again be asserted and contested. The primary mission of this book, and especially of this chapter, is to explore in what sense China might be considered central in premodern times and in the present, and to analyze how those factors of centrality fared during its era of marginalization. This is essential for understanding the role in the global order of both China and Pacific Asia.

The question of China's centrality – then and now – is an important one, because it is key to how one imagines the configuration of Pacific Asia. If the region, then and now, did not have a center but was essentially randomly associated interactors, then the calculi of all members would be the same. There would be differences of capacity among the members, but not fixed differences of position. Picture goldfish in a bowl. But if we assume that China is in some sense central, then there is a regional configuration as well as differences of capacity among the members. Part of each member's locational identity would be having China to the north, south, or west – or being China itself in the middle. While the contact with China might not be the most important to the member at any one time – it might be fighting with a fellow noncenter, for example – it would be the most significant direction for its overall regional orientation.

I argue that China was Pacific Asia's center of attention in the premodern era, that it lost that centrality in the era of Western modernization, and has been returning to regional centrality since 2008. Regarding the premodern era I am not claiming that China was always the predominant power, or that its neighbors accepted China as a cultural superior. But if not power hegemony or cultural hierarchy, what was China's traditional centrality? I argue that the situational factors of presence, population, and production, to be detailed below, accounted for China's centrality in regional attention, and in turn the configuration around China created characteristic asymmetries of perception and relationships. With the coming of Western imperialism, Pacific Asia was splintered between colonial powers and China became peripheral to the region's segmented globalization. After the Second World War, China remained on the periphery as Pacific Asia became less segmented but more global. With Deng Xiaoping's policies of reform and openness China gradually reentered the global and regional contexts, becoming a "significant other" to the region as a result of its actions in the Asian Financial Crisis of 1997. But only with the Global Financial Crisis of 2008 and China's undeterred continued growth did China again become the regional center of attention. Of course, regional attentiveness now is quite different from the traditional era. It is a changed China, a changed region, and a changed world. Nevertheless, China's presence, population, and production still matter, and the asymmetric relationships between center and noncenters are visible.

Beyond Imperium and Hierarchy

China certainly prided itself on its power and glory, and that remains the case today. A new version of the history of the Communist Party of China issued in November 2021 announces a new era.[1] While Mao Zedong established independence and Deng Xiaoping added wealth, Xi Jinping is claiming to introduce an era of "major-country diplomacy with Chinese characteristics" based on strength. What this means will be discussed in due course, but in descriptions of the traditional Chinese empire there is often the implication that China was central because it was the most powerful, if not all powerful. Indeed, the term "empire" derives from the Latin *imperium*, and the word was used to designate the power to command before it was used for the territory under Rome's control.[2] The idea that an empire was hegemonic, an area under one's control, is central to Western

---

[1] "Resolution of the CPC Central Committee on the Major Achievements and Historical Experience of the Party over the Past Century," *China Daily*, November 16, 2021, www.chinadaily.com.cn/a/202111/16/WS6193a693a310cdd39bc75b43.html

[2] Mary Beard, *SPQR: A History of Ancient Rome* (New York: Liveright Publishing, 2015), p. 196.

notions of empire. In the post-colonial world, the presumption that empire required hegemony remained in place despite the reluctance to make official claims of international power. It was somewhat nostalgic as well as exaggerated when, during the decline and fall of the Qing dynasty (1644–1911), traditional China began to be termed an empire in this sense.[3]

Certainly, there were times when China fit the model of an empire premised on preponderant power. Emperor Han Wudi (156–87 BC) expanded China by conquest to include an area larger than the Roman Empire at that time, and Emperor Qian Long's (1711–1799) extirpation of the Dzungars in 1757 resembled Western imperialism at its most ferocious.[4] Just as certainly, there were times when the central government of China was not the most powerful in the region, as the Mongol and Manchu conquests of China attest. Are there any underlying continuities in the configuration of a region that featured both conquering dynasties and conquest dynasties? Were the ethnic Chinese Ming dynasty (1368–1644) and the conquering Manchu Qing dynasty (1644–1911) as different as the Greek and Roman empires? After all, the Roman emperors prided themselves on their acquisition of Greek culture and Greek slaves, so there was some continuity there.

It would, however, be a bit far-fetched to claim that the Roman Empire was a continuation of the Greek Empire because of cultural continuities. It is impressive, however, that after the collapse of Alexander the Great's centralized control from Greece and Egypt to India in 321 BC, the eastern Mediterranean developed a shared Greek culture and commercial language despite emerging political divisions. Although there was no political center, the Hellenistic era created a regional identity that lasted almost three centuries and featured major cultural advances. Each part of the Hellenistic realm also adapted to local identities, most obviously the Ptolemies in Egypt. The Hebrew Bible was translated into Greek in Alexandria, Egypt, to make it available to Jews outside of Palestine. Evidently common culture can create a region. Perhaps cultural superiority, whatever that might mean, could create regional centrality?

---

[3] Krishan Kumar, *Empires: A Historical and Political Sociology* (New York: Polity, 2021), p. 33.
[4] Peter Perdue, *China Marches West: The Qing Conquest of Central Eurasia* (Cambridge: Harvard University Press, 2005).

In traditional Pacific Asia[5] there is strong evidence of regional identity in terms of shared cultural elements, and these had more continuity than central power. The Mongol and Manchu conquest dynasties adapted to the cultures of their preceding native dynasties. The influence of traditional Chinese high culture outside of China is most evident in Korea, Japan, and Vietnam, earning the subregion the name "Sinosphere,"[6] but China's material culture and political interactions reached well beyond these neighbors. Its reputation for greatness and riches – and some of its silks – reached as far as the Roman Empire.

The claim to China's centrality via cultural superiority can be understood in three ways. The first is simply that China's culture is better than everyone else's and therefore rightfully central. Many Chinese believe this, and it is implicit in many official paens, ancient and contemporary, to the length, depth and breadth of their civilization, that others cannot make similar claims and are therefore inferior. Moreover, China's "century of humiliation," when it was relegated to the periphery of the modern world, reflected more than the agony of victimhood and the loss of power suffered by China and its neighbors. Its humiliation was measured implicitly by its fall from its lofty self-conception and that fall's psychological as well as physical trauma.

The problem with this claim of cultural superiority as the ground of a claim to centrality is that superiority must be in the eye of the beholder as well. The deference shown to China in premodern times was not naïve wonder at China's superior attainments and glory. Rather, it was a pragmatic combination of diplomatic prudence and adaptation of best practices. China's self-glorification, like that of other large countries, ancient and modern, was viewed skeptically by outsiders, and as a symptom of either parochial narcissism or hypocritical pomposity. And certainly in the contemporary world such

---

[5] While I justify using "Pacific Asia" for the current era, for earlier times it is ahistorical as well as being an outsider's term, and China's northern relationships were more important and more troublesome than those with current Pacific Asian partners. Nevertheless, like most ahistorians, I struggle on, using terms meaningful to the present in order to include their past.

[6] See the rich exploration of literary aspects at Rice University's conference, "Reconsidering the Sinosphere" (March 2017). https://sinosphere.rice.edu/panels/

claims to superiority are alienating, and other cultures would expect that China would be as open to their attainments as it expects them to appreciate China's.

The second claim of cultural centrality is also based on superiority, but with a subtle difference. China claimed to rule "all under heaven" (天下 *tianxia*) because of its virtue (德 *de*). This was an ambiguous relational superiority. Its allusiveness could range from the Confucian notion of inducing good behavior in others by benevolence, to Sun Zi's dictum of "know your enemy," to a more Machiavellian notion of *virtù* as effective use of power. Certainly, relational skill was sometimes central to China's diplomatic success.[7] Moreover, the success of Deng Xiaoping's strategy in the 1990s of cooperating with neighbors and showing humility was certainly successful and could be called virtuous in several senses of the word.

But China was not always virtuous, in any sense, in dealing with its neighbors, and its diplomatic skill and success varied from ruler to ruler and from venue to venue. Soft power as well as hard power, both broadly defined, could be seen as the two handles of China's options in dealing with neighbors, but they concern how China should act from its central position rather than explaining centrality itself.

A third cultural explanation is argued by David Kang.[8] He contrasts the incessant wars of the modern West with the relative peace of Pacific Asia, and ascribes the difference to a cultural acceptance of hierarchy in Asia in contrast to the competitive individualism and national rivalries of the West. Although Kang's claim of peaceful acceptance of Chinese preeminence in the region has been energetically denounced by many historians, most of the evidence for their attacks is drawn primarily from China's interaction with nomadic groups.[9] By contrast, traditional China's relations with the Sinosphere have been more stable, if not necessarily benign, and the differences will be discussed in more detail in the next chapter. Nevertheless,

---

[7] Wang Zhenping, *Tang China in Multi-Polar Asia: A History of Diplomacy and War* (Honolulu: University of Hawaii Press, 2013), pp. 3–9.

[8] David Kang, "Getting Asia Wrong: The Need for New Analytical Frameworks," *International Security* 27:4 (Spring 2003), pp. 57–85; also Kang, *China Rising: Peace, Power, and Order in East Asia* (New York: Columbia University Press, 2007).

[9] Peter Perdue, "The Tenacious Tributary System," *Journal of Contemporary China* 24:96 (2015), pp. 1002–1014.

there are numerous problems with this cultural explanation even for the Sinosphere. The most obvious objection would point to China's persistent advantage in relative power vis-à-vis Korea, Japan, and Vietnam. But while the power asymmetry would account for the neighbors not attacking a more powerful center (although there are many instances of less powerful states starting wars with more powerful ones – Pearl Harbour comes to mind), why wasn't China more forceful in dominating its neighbors? However, although the Sinosphere neighbors rarely confronted China in a hostile manner, they were skeptical of China's cultural superiority, and there was not much lingering nostalgia about "Father China" after the West arrived in force. National resistance to colonialism did not look back to the good old days of the Chinese Empire, or show hierarchical submissiveness to the newcomers. Instead of pining for a return to the good old days of the Sinosphere, anti-colonial resistance looked forward to establishing new, modern national identities.

Most importantly for the "three eras" format of Chinese centrality discussed here, China's re-emerging regional centrality is clearly not a case of neighbors returning submissively to the cultural fold. Such an interpretation ignores the modern transformation of both China and its neighbors. It also devalues the agency of the neighbors in their relationships to China and downplays their anxieties and disagreements. While China's rise has been peaceful, and analogies to German or Japanese nationalism are far-fetched projections of Western anxieties, China's soft power has declined as its economic preponderance, military power, and national self-glorification have risen. To be sure, Chinese invocation of a harmonious past of *tianxia* is less threatening than Mussolini's evocation of the Roman imperium, but it is no less problematic.

Both the premise that China's once and future centrality was/ is based on power and the premise that its centrality is culturally accepted by its neighbors claim too much from the idea of centrality. They assume that for China to be central it must be in control, whether by force of arms or force of ideas. It is an easy assumption to make, since China was often in control and neighbors were often deferential. But I will argue for a more basic notion of centrality. Even for outsiders who conquered China, China was the center of regional attention. For example, the southern part of Mongolia that eventually became the Chinese province of Inner Mongolia (內蒙古)

is known as "Front Mongolia" (*öbör Mongol*) in Mongolian.[10] From China's standpoint it is its closest part, from the Mongolian vantage point it is the part facing the world; to the right was the west and to the left the east. In the case of raiders and conquerors China was the regional focal point of risk and opportunity – more opportunity than risk, especially in the case of conquest dynasties. Although each neighbor might be exposed to more proximate risks and opportunities with other neighbors or even from outside the region, these local concerns did not configure the region.

While regional centrality as (merely) centrality of regional attention might appear too soft and nebulous to be worthy of the name, the common exposure of members to a central venue configures the region in important ways. The relationships of the center to each peripheral member are asymmetric, and so the perspectives of center and periphery are structurally different. In most times and places the center is less at risk than its peripheral neighbor, but even when the neighbor harbors the power and ambition to best the center, it wishes to replace the current central authority in China with its own central authority – in China. The initial triumph of a conquest dynasty like the Mongol Yuan might disprove the notion of Chinese continual power, but the subsequent rule of the Yuan confirmed China's centrality in the regional configuration. There is a profound difference between the succession of dynasties in China and the succession of empires in the West. Dynasties replaced one another within the Chinese geographical and cultural space. Western empires conquered their predecessors and established new centers in different spaces. The task here is to understand China's resilient centrality of attention and its consequences for the regional configuration of Pacific Asia.

Situational Elements of China's Centrality: Presence, Population, Production

What, then, lies behind China's centrality in the premodern era, marginalization in the era of Western modernization, and return to centrality since 2008? Moreover, what notion of centrality could cover the variety of traditional China's relationships with both the

---

[10] Martha Avery, *The Tea Road: China and Russia Meet across the Steppe* (Beijing: China International Press, 2003), p. 102.

various nomadic groups – including ones that eventually conquered China – and with the Sinosphere? And what notion of centrality could find continuity between traditional and contemporary Pacific Asia and yet still be sensitive to the transformation of relationships? Lastly, are there structural differences between imperial centralities in the West (including American centrality) and Chinese centrality, traditional and contemporary? A tall order, and one that drives us back to basics.

Regional centrality requires as its foundation a configured field of relationships in which all peripheral members have in common a significant relation to the center, while they differ in their relationships to other members and to those beyond the region. Thus, the center has varied relationships with each member, but in their configuration they are all center-periphery relationships. Preponderance of power can augment centrality and it certainly affects interactions, but it is neither sufficient nor necessary. Europe in the nineteenth century was a global center as a region, but itself was a cockpit of competing states desiring to be (European) regional centers. Moreover, opportunity as well as fear can command attention. A bird feeder will be central to its avian neighborhood, and while the birds may fight for access they are not forced to feed. I will argue that China remained a center to its northern neighbors despite changes and precarious balances of power. Similarly, as we have seen with the Hellenistic world, cultural commonality does not necessarily imply centrality, while cultural superiority may be assumed by a center but is unlikely to be believed by the rest. So what could constitute a centrality for China that was enduring in the premodern era, absent in the subsequent long modern century, and is again emerging?

I will argue that there were three elements underlying China's centrality: presence, population, and production. They are interrelated but distinguishable. The salience of these elements was different in each era. In the premodern era they anchored regional relationships based on thin connectivity. Western imperialism forcibly reoriented China's neighbors toward Europe, and even in the post-colonial period, China's isolation prior to 1980 precluded a regional re-centering. With Deng Xiaoping's reform and openness China gradually became a "significant other" in the region, but it was not until after the Global Financial Crisis of 2008 that China again became a central presence in the region.

It may seem strange to argue that the effects of three such basic elements of China's centrality could change dramatically over the three eras. But it is the same logic that Ian Morris applies to his emphasis on geography: "Geographical differences do have long-term effects, but these are never locked in, and what counts as a geographical advantage at one stage of social development may be irrelevant or a positive disadvantage at another. We might say that while geography drives development, social development determines what geography means."[11] By the same token, the relational meaning of China's presence, population, and production underwent tectonic shifts over the three eras.

"Presence" is the bottom-line element for centrality. It can be understood in terms of China's position as the highest significant point of attention in Pacific Asia. Of course, location helps. Although presence is more than being in the middle, China's position in the middle of a vast inland area with a close maritime ring puts it in a quite different situation vis-à-vis its neighbors than other large polities. But being in the middle, while certainly helpful for centrality, is not sufficient. During the era of Western modernization China was marginalized but it never relocated, and only in the current era has it returned as the focus of regional attention. Central regional presence requires sustained attention from regional members, and there must be reasons why such attention is paid. Attention can be attracted either by opportunity or anxiety, or both, and these tend to be more vivid and varied in neighboring relationships than in distant ones. Presence does not require formal political subordination or hierarchy. It is not simply power. China was present to Genghis Khan (1158–1227), Toyotomi Hideyoshi (1537–1598), and Nurhaci (1559–1626) as their principal object of acquisition and control. Essentially, central presence is a persisting pattern of significant regional attention. It configures a region by providing a common relational focus.

"Population" gives substance to China's located centrality. According to Angus Maddison, China's population ranged between 22 and 27 percent of global population between the years zero and 1700, and it is a safe assumption that China's population has accounted for more than half of the Pacific Asia region's population for the past two

---

[11] Ian Morris, *Why the West Rules – For Now* (New York: Farrar, Strauss, and Giroux, 2010), p. 45.

thousand years.[12] The West has never had a comparable demographic center, although among its peers in the developed world the population of the United States has been essential to its relative strength in the twentieth century. By 1900 the US was almost as populous as Russia and clearly larger than Germany, France, or the UK. Currently China has 18 percent of the world's population and 62 percent of Pacific Asia's.

Demographic scale makes a difference. Although in 1820 China's GDP per capita was only 86 percent of Asia's average, its total GDP was almost half of the Asian total and 30 percent of the world's.[13] China's mobilized population could be formidable, whether for war or for production, but its size created a standing governance challenge of provision, organization, and control. At the time of Alexander the Great's conquests the armies fighting in China were much larger than his or the Persian armies, but the Chinese were fighting among themselves. Controlling China has never been easy. As the Sage King Yu lamented in the *Book of History*, "When I come before millions of the people, I feel as much anxiety as if one with rotten reins were guiding six horses. Thus, for one who is the people's superior, how can he dispense with respectful caution?"[14]

"Production" is the third element. The significance of China's production is particularly evident in the current era, but its scale and sophistication were also prominent in premodern times. Production enabled the spread of China's material culture especially its most notable products, tea, silk, and ceramics. These had the advantage of high value, portability, and longevity. They and the wealth that they helped create were targets of raids by nomadic groups. Production created an active dual centrality of outgoing trade, including imperial gifts, and incoming goods, silver, and raids. If we expand production to include books and ideas, production was the lifeblood of regional relationships. Eventually the West transformed the nature and scale of global production, sidelining China but also producing the global context in which China would re-emerge. Current Chinese production does not

---

[12] Angus Maddison, *China's Economic Performance in the Long Run*, 2nd ed. (Paris: OECD, 2007), p. 24.
[13] Ibid., p. 44.
[14] W. H. Medhurst, tr., *The Shoo King, or the Historical Classic* (Shanghai: Mission Press, 1846), pp. 122–123.

have the august reputation of its traditional high culture output – as the economist Arthur Kroeber put it, China's business model is "80 percent of the quality at 60 percent of the price" – but China has become the world's largest manufacturer.[15]

Presence, population, and production – the "3 Ps" – are deeply interrelated. Without the other two Ps China's presence would simply be a space on a map. The scale of China's population enabled the sophistication of its traditional production and at present the magnitude of its industrial production. And if we consider infrastructural improvements such as irrigation, production also facilitated population growth. Meanwhile, China's position as the center of regional attention enabled it to draw innovations and wealth from the periphery.

The problem of how China lost the 3 Ps during the era of Western modernization will be the subject of Chapter 3, but the short answer is that globalization de-regionalized Pacific Asia. The West did not arrive as a conquest dynasty, but rather as a new, global center of attention, this time with power playing a more pronounced role. It is easy to understand how the West might view China as a losing empire, but it was rather a center that lost its region. China was no longer a major concern of its neighbors. Its population retained the passive advantage of being too big for a single power to swallow, but it sank into chaos. The methods of its artisanal production were diffused by the world economy, and in any case their value was undercut by the scale and efficiency of industrial production. Thus, the demise of China's regional centrality can be described in terms of the withering of its 3 Ps, and its return in 2008, discussed in Chapter 4, can be described in these terms as well.

Asymmetric Perspectives

China has had a wide variety of neighbors, and itself has covered the full spectrum from chaotic vulnerability to ruthless power projection, so it is difficult to generalize about center-periphery relationships. However, some generalizations can be made about how regional perspectives are shaped by the 3 P configuration, and an ideal type can be described that best fits the traditional Sinosphere but

---

[15] Arthur Kroeber, *China's Economy: What Everyone Needs to Know* (Oxford: Oxford University Press, 2016), p. 58.

also has applications to nomadic relationships and to contemporary perspectives.

The most basic generalization is that while China occasionally faced neighbors who were its equal or superior in military power, the configuration of the interaction was always asymmetric. To take the limit case of the Manchu conquest as an example, what the Manchus wanted to do to China was different from what China wanted to do to the Manchus. The Manchus wanted to control the central, most populous, and richest place in its region, while the Chinese would have been happy if the Manchus had simply stayed in their place. It was not a symmetric interaction. To claim that China was (and is) among unequals does not mean that it was (or is) in control, but rather that the other actors, powerful and autonomous though they might be, were and are not other regional centers. The salience of centrality might increase or diminish depending on China's internal cohesiveness and external policies – and it disappeared with the coming of the West – but as long as there was regional cohesion and its presence, population, and production held, it was the center, and its relationships were those of center and periphery. After the Manchu conquest, the Manchus were in charge and they (as the Qing dynasty) had to deal with the challenges of centrality.

Asymmetry implies that the risk and opportunity faced by each side are different.[16] To the extent that attention and perception are shaped by exposure to risk and opportunity, each side of an asymmetric relationship will have structurally different perceptions of the other. In effect, both sides are seeing different things, and will interact according to their own perceptions rather than according to the intentions of their partner/opponent. Each side tends to project their perceptions of the relationship onto the other. Thus misunderstanding is built into the structure of asymmetric relationships. Hence Sun Zi's admonition to "know your enemy" is both obviously correct and constantly forgotten and renewed.

Of course, center-periphery asymmetry is not the only cause of international misunderstanding. Besides informational asymmetries, in which one side has better information than the other or there are incorrect estimates of relative strength, there will be differences of history

---

[16] This is elaborated in some detail in Brantly Womack, *Asymmetry and International Relationships* (New York: Cambridge University Press, 2016).

and expectations. If we consider current relations between Japan and China, they are fraught with mutual resentments based on history.[17] Moreover, center-periphery asymmetry is often interlaced with asymmetries of power, and cultural disjunctions as well as shared culture affect interactive behavior. Nevertheless, the configurative asymmetry of Pacific Asia deserves special attention. With regard to the interaction of China and Japan, it might be useful to try to distinguish how much of Japan's current concerns about China are due to China's rising power, and how much to the changing configuration of the region. How much of Japan's perception of "the China challenge" is due to China as a bilateral challenger, and how much is due to the difficulties in adjusting to China as center of a region that includes Japan.

Originally, my ideas of asymmetric international relationships evolved from analysis of relationships between China and Vietnam,[18] and while traditional relationships outside the Sinosphere were often quite different, the model is useful as an ideal type most clearly applicable to Vietnam and Korea but with comparabilities beyond, as well. Applied to center-periphery asymmetries, the model assumes that the center (C) has greater capabilities than the peripheral partner (P), but that P is capable of resisting C's coercion. An asymmetric relationship persists in which P is more exposed to its risks and opportunities, while C has more important domestic affairs and perhaps other, more challenging international relationships.

Given the difference in exposure, P is likely to be more alert to risks and opportunities, while C's attention will be distracted elsewhere. After all, C has many neighbors. Characteristic misperceptions will result from the projection of one's own situation on the other. In normal times C will make accommodations because of the trouble of focusing its attention and resources on P, though it will present concessions as graciousness, while P will try to shape the details of the relationship to its advantage. C will tend to view itself as magnanimous and to view P as manipulative and untrustworthy. For its part, P will view itself as clever and righteously defensive while viewing C as

---

[17] Barry Buzan and Evelyn Goh, *Rethinking Sino-Japanese Alienation: History Problems and Historical Opportunities* (New York: Oxford University Press, 2020).

[18] Brantly Womack, *China and Vietnam: The Politics of Asymmetry* (New York: Cambridge University Press, 2006).

hypocritical and malevolent. Of course, in good times they will smile at each other. When problems occur C will be interested in closure so that it can get back to more important matters, so it will try to bully P back into line. Meanwhile, P is likely to assume that C's bullying is a mortal threat and therefore to resist. Since C has only a limited interest in the conflict, P's resistance is likely to prevail despite C's greater resources. Thus, the hostile relationship is not really one of cat and mouse, though C might imagine it to be and P might fear it, but rather one of cat and hedgehog.

Since C cannot eliminate P and P cannot conquer C, the relationship is resilient. In a mature asymmetric relationship, C acknowledges the autonomy of P, and P shows deference to C as the regional center. The exchange of autonomy and deference is a delicate matter – neither is absolute. If C grants autonomy to P but P plans to challenge C's centrality, then C has nurtured a snake. If P shows deference to C but C tries to dominate, then P has surrendered its autonomy. The relationship remains a frontier of interaction, governed by mutual accommodations and ritual and reassured by its history of peaceful interactions. Faced with a periphery that it can't dominate, C has an interest in orderly interactions; and facing a center that it can't challenge, P also has an interest in order. But each will continue to pursue its own interests, and the dissonance of perceptual differences remains.

It is important to note that in an ideal typical asymmetric relationship a marginal increase in capacities by either side does not change the relationship. In a symmetric rivalry, being a step ahead of the other is most important, and so gain relative to that of the opponent is more important than absolute gain. But between China and Vietnam, for example, relative gain by either will not change the relationship because of the large degree of asymmetry. Vietnam will never be bigger than China, and China will never find it easy to dominate Vietnam. Thus win-win is a possibility, although – again because of asymmetry – the proportions of risk and gain will be different for each.

Another major difference between asymmetric and symmetric relationships is that while symmetric partners might achieve mutual understanding on the basis of similarity, in asymmetric relationships there will always be a difference of exposure and therefore differences of perception. Whether it is the United States and Canada or Germany and Austria, it is easy for the larger side to assume that the smaller is happily docile, but in fact the smaller will be alert to its opportunities and risks and resentful of the larger side's lack of appreciation of its situation and its occasional intrusions on the smaller side's autonomy. Asymmetric relationships are more a matter of the management of misperceptions than a melding of minds.

As a central power in a number of such relationships, C has the advantage of collective regional attention and therefore it is in the default position of regional leadership. It could assume a magisterial position of resolving conflicts in the periphery or correcting their perceived inadequacies, but regional policing if actively pursued can exhaust central resources and leave it vulnerable elsewhere, as well as causing fear and resentment. It could maximize its advantage of centrality and minimize its costs by providing a structure for center-periphery relations that institutionalized the exchange of deference for autonomy and served only as a court of last resort for problems on the periphery, with judgments that could be adjusted to evolving realities rather than rigidly enforced. This is how I understand the tribute system, especially as it crystallized in the Ming dynasty in the Sinosphere. The regular ritual obeisance and the granting of titles were the formalized exchange of the assurance that the periphery would not challenge the center and that the center would respect the autonomy of the periphery. As we will discuss in the next chapter, between China and the nomads the system did not quite work in the same way, but it had some similar elements.

Managing Relationships

Given the mutual structural misperception in asymmetric relationships, it may seem surprising that so many of them are long-term and peaceful. But it must be remembered that the interactions are resilient. If C bullies P, it is likely to become involved in a frustrating situation in which overcoming P's determined resistance costs more than victory would be worth. And P might learn that it is best to be publicly deferential while at the same time protecting itself from C and advancing its own interests in the relationship. After a mutually costly confrontation, both sides have reason to avoid a repetition. Moreover, the mutual failure demonstrates that domination is not in C's best interest and that for P, successful resistance is possible but costly. Thus, conflict can demonstrate through experience the wisdom and prudence of the exchange of C's recognition of P's autonomy in exchange for P's deference to C's regional stature.

A mature relationship is one that operates within the bounds of relatively stable expectations. Both the experience of costly and frustrating conflict and the more pleasant ones of peaceful coexistence create over time the expectation that both sides will weather future storms and take advantage of mutual opportunities. Habituation over time may solidify certain prejudices that each has about the other, but it also renders less likely that C will harbor illusions about its ability to successfully coerce P, and at the same time P realizes that life on the wrong side of C is likely to be even less happy than suffering its current irritants.

Given hundreds of years and multiple C to P relationships, regional habituation may take the form of a posture of benevolent rule on C's part and a culture of hierarchical submission on the part of P's, but its practical foundation lies in experience and continuity. When circumstances change, the common sense of habitual relationships can be upended by new developments. Moreover, in a new situation such as the re-emergence of China since 2008 it takes time for new habituations to develop. Mistakes by either side delay habituation, but they do not necessarily derail it. Memories accumulate of what worked and what did not.

While the common sense of the ongoing mature relationship suggests that what worked yesterday will work today and tomorrow, there are divergent public memories of previous conflicts lurking in the background for both sides. National histories are the cultivated self-consciousness of political communities. For example, C would not forget the time when P sided with a third power against it, and P certainly would not forget its heroic resistance to C's aggression in times past. National histories will feature the benevolent tolerance of C on one side, but the righteous resistance of P on the other. While the research of academic historians on both sides might modify the juxtaposition, sometimes at the historians' personal peril, each side finds satisfaction in reaching back to its own experience at the time and its embellishment in generational transmission. While the common sense of a working relationship holds, the national histories are in the background, but they can be foregrounded in times of crisis.

Habituation provides a passive reassurance in a mature asymmetric relationship, and diplomatic ritual provides an active and visible confirmation of the commitment of both sides to a smooth relationship. The basic significance of the "summit meeting," the ritual of public meetings of heads of state, does not lie in the "deliverables," namely, the agreements signed or commitments made, but rather in the mutual official acknowledgment of the legitimate representation of the other side by its political representative. The rituals of public meetings are more intense and valued more highly in Asia because of their special importance in asymmetric relationships. China needs to have its central position acknowledged, and the neighbors need reassurance that China will respect their autonomy. This ritual is the essence of the tribute system in traditional Pacific Asia and also the foundation for the current intensity of public meetings of state in the region. The public meeting is likely to be accented by gifts and agreements, but its primary significance is the demonstration of mutual respect.

As the next chapter will detail, the overall pattern of China's traditional centrality is quite different from the cycles of imperial power familiar in the West. Robert Gilpin provides the classic analysis of these Western cycles.[19] The empire expands due to its marginal power advantage over its neighbors, but as its territory increases the cost of managing further expansion approaches and then exceeds the advantages gained from the new territories. Ironically, then, success breeds collapse, especially since challenges can be mounted from the fringe. The cycles can be accelerated or delayed by technological advances or by quality of leadership, but the tragic flaw of hegemonic expansion is internal: eventually its reach will exceed its grasp.

China's 3 Ps created two basic differences in the imperial ebb and flow of Pacific Asia. First, while there were times and places when China's reach exceeded its grasp, China tended to be forced back rather than be replaced by a different empire located on its periphery. Thus China had a chance to learn from its own ebb and flow. Second, because it was the population and production center, China had less to gain from expansion. This did not prevent emperors from being greedy, but it raised the perceived cost of acquisition and lowered the anticipated relative value. Quite a contrast to the thirst for distant riches that drove Western expansion. Thus, rather than controlling its neighbors, generally China recognized their autonomy in exchange for

---

[19] Robert Gilpin, *War and Change in World Politics* (Cambridge: Cambridge University Press, 1981).

their deference. Self-restraint is a hard lesson for a superior power to learn, and sometimes it must be relearned, but China had the advantage of resilience. It gradually became more adept in the management of asymmetric centrality. It is not clear, however, that the 3 Ps would have the same moderating effect in the current era.

Connectivities: Thin, Sharp, and Thick

Regions are relational entities, so the intensity and nature of their connectivity matters. One of the major differences between the three eras of Pacific Asia has been the shift in connectivity. The premodern era was characterized by thin connectivity, Western colonialism by sharp connectivity, and the current era by thick connectivity. While changes in scale and direction of connectivity were important, the differences in connectivity policy by the central power were even more so.

The primary policy value in traditional China's external relations was stability, and therefore China restricted the official exchange of goods and the movement of people and occasionally clamped down on unofficial trade. *Thin connectivity* was safe and trouble-free connectivity. The exchange of goods during tribute missions was an important part of the stabilization of asymmetric relationships, but the quantity was controlled, and because China was the center, it was necessary that the gifts it dispensed should be of higher value than the gifts received. China was self-sufficient in basic goods, and although elite goods were desirable their trade was subordinated to security concerns. Migration was forbidden (though ineffectively) until the late nineteenth century.

The *sharp connectivity* of the era of Western colonization decentered and fragmented Pacific Asia. European competition over the trade and control of Asian products encouraged production, and by the nineteenth century colonial regimes were transforming Asian economies to better serve the global market and thereby profit their European owners. Colonists moved in and indigenous populations were moved about in service of their respective empires. With decolonization after the Second World War, the American imperium retained political sharpness under the bipolarity of the Cold War, but economic connectivity became more globalized and integrated.

In the current era, China's regional policy has been part of its global policy of *thick connectivity*. China's re-emergence in the region was premised on its entry into the global market, and its new policies of reform and openness served a central commitment to maximum economic growth. Like sharp connectivity, thick connectivity encouraged trade, and the infrastructure development sponsored by the Belt and Road Initiative (BRI) aims to transform economies. However, in a post-colonial era, China relies on cooperating with sovereign states rather than seizing control. And the new connectivity infrastructure is open-ended in its focus even though the network is China-centered.

It is tempting to elide the differences in connectivity between the eras with the evolution of technology, but the point here is the change in general policies of connectivity, not the capacity of contact. Certainly, a village in the premodern era had limited physical horizons, while the Industrial Revolution, with its concomitant transformations of military hardware and communication, laid the foundation for Western sharp connectivity. Similarly, container ships and the internet have removed physical horizons altogether, making thick connectivity possible on a global scale. But connectivity policy is not simply the passive superstructure of connectivity capacity. Although sharp connectivity could not produce a global system in the premodern era, it was certainly present. Thucydides' description of the Delian League shows precocious sharpness on Athen's part, while Barbara Tuchman's account of the fourteenth century in Europe has many instances of brutal subjection, before technology empowered its dissemination abroad.[20] On a happier note, the formation of modern states was the result of thickening connectivity as well as political consolidation. Of course, all of these things happened in Asia as well. The Yuan colonized and incorporated Yunnan, and Vietnam destroyed Champa on its march to the south. But China was central in a region that it did not have the incentive or means to dominate, and, with much trial and error, its policy of thin connectivity gradually emerged. Technological change did empower Western global modernization, but its sharpness vis-à-vis "the Rest" was a matter of policy. Lastly, thick connectivity as a policy best fits the capacities of globalization, but it can also be challenged by trends toward decoupling and segmentation.

[20] Barbara Tuchman, *A Distant Mirror: The Calamitous 14th Century* (New York: Knopf, 1978).

Asymmetric Agency

A final characteristic of centrality in Pacific Asia is the change in asymmetric agency in the three eras. Pacific Asia's experience was quite different from the Western model of *imperium*. If centrality is based on power, then one could imagine that the center-periphery relationship is a version of the principal-agent problem. Under the shadow of compellence, the subordinate periphery obeys. The center, as principal, expects the agent to do its bidding, at least within the range of subordination set by prior agreement or practice. An international system presupposes some degree of autonomy on the part of lesser powers (otherwise why would it be "international"?) but subordination can be specified in an agreement and can include privileges granted to the agent in exchange for a specified commitment to serve. Medieval European systems of vassalage were formalizations of these arrangements. With the emergence of sovereign states after the Peace of Westphalia (1648), systems of alliances replaced state vassalage, giving small states the apparent freedom to choose alignments, although these were constrained by their location and relative power.

China's traditional centrality, especially in the Sinosphere, was quite different from European vassalage. On the one hand, its relationship to peripheral states was not based on an exchange of privilege for obedience, but rather on an exchange of recognition of autonomy for deference. The periphery's requirement of deference was that of the "waifan" 外藩, "people beyond the hedge," and was not delimited by an agreement, but rather sustained by periodic rituals.[21] The autonomy granted by China was not a right that could be asserted against China on the basis of a contract. Rather, recognition of autonomy was a guarantee – ritualized in the tribute system and certified by the granting of titles to the ruler – that China would respect the located authority of the peripheral state to control its own affairs. If it were challenged by a peripheral state China might resort to an expedition of punishment. And if a ruler sanctioned by China were endangered by rivals China might send support. China's recognition of the legitimacy of the peripheral state was premised on deference. But given

---

[21] Joseph Fletcher, "The Biography of Khwush Kipäk Beg (d. 1781) in the Wai-Fan Meng-Ku Hui-Pu Wang Kung Piao Chuan," *Acta Orientalia Academiae Scientiarum Hungaricae* 36:1/3 (1982), p. 167.

that China's primary interest was in relational stability, typically the domestic autonomy of a tributary state was assured.

Under colonialism's sharp connectivity the agency of the colony was subordinated to the step-mother country, and the colonial government was an artificial implant imposed directly on the people of the colony, or indirectly through a subservient native client. Within the colony limited rights began to emerge, first for colonial expatriates, but the colony itself remained a possession without its own agency.[22] This subordination to the outside power became the primary target of national liberation movements. In the post-colonial world of the American imperium, sovereign agency was formally attained, but the necessities of adapting to the world market, the political pressures of the Cold War, and the tensions of new neighborhoods conditioned freedom of action. The general feeling in Southeast Asia of being at risk to external forces and internal challenges led to the formation of the Association of Southeast Asian Nations (ASEAN) in 1967.[23]

Chapter 5 will detail a general picture of current international relationships, arguing that since 2008 the global system has been *multinodal* rather than unipolar or multipolar. In a multinodal system domination and massive aggression are unlikely, but relative power still matters. The change is not disruptive for the general trend of Chinese foreign policy. In the 1950s China announced the "Five Principles of Peaceful Coexistence"[24] along with India and Burma, and these include non-interference in domestic affairs. The Five Principles remain key norms of Chinese foreign policy,[25] but in the current era China has taken a more active posture with slogans such as "human community with a shared future"[26] and cooperative programs such as

---

[22] Kumar, *Empires*.
[23] Alice Ba, *(Re)Negotiating East and Southeast Asia* (Stanford: Stanford University Press, 2009).
[24] These are: mutual respect for sovereignty and territorial integrity, mutual non-aggression, non-interference in each other's internal affairs, equality and mutual benefit, and peaceful coexistence.
[25] Brantly Womack, "China as a Normative Foreign Policy Actor," in Nathalie Tocci, ed., *Who is a Normative Foreign Policy Actor? The European Community and its Global Partners* (Brussels: Centre for European Policy Studies, 2008), pp. 265–299.
[26] Constitution of the People's Republic of China, as amended in 2018. Also rendered as "community of shared future for mankind." https://english.www.gov.cn/archive/lawsregulations/201911/20/content_WS5ed8856ec6d0b3f0e9499913.html

the Belt and Road Initiative (BRI, known initially as "One Belt One Road – OBOR). In September 2021 Xi Jinping proposed a "Global Development Initiative," a more multilateral effort than BRI.[27] All of these initiatives are based on the sovereign agency of partners, and they are also sensitive to the aspirations of developing countries. Moreover, China is a strong supporter of the UN and is engaged with other international governmental organizations. Regionally, it was a co-founder of the Shanghai Cooperation Organization and is involved in many projects with ASEAN. China's economic preponderance, however, leads to concerns about China's leverage, and these concerns are heightened by China's maritime sovereignty disputes in the East China Sea and South China Sea. But the deepest challenge to China's respect for agency are the questions of sub-sovereign autonomy in Taiwan, Hong Kong, and Macau.

---

[27] "Wang Yi Talks about the Importance of the Global Development Initiative." www.mfa.gov.cn/ce/ceus//eng/zgyw/t1909908.htm

2 Thin Connectivity
Traditional Chinese Centrality

Nothing stayed exactly the same from the founding of unified China in 221 by Qin Shi Huang (259–210 BC) to the Opium War in 1840. Dynasties rose and disintegrated. As the first line in China's most famous traditional novel put it, "The Empire, long divided, must unite; long united, must divide."[1] Capitals shifted within China from west to east, from north to south, and then back to north. Until the Opium War China's major security problems were always to the north, but the various nomadic groups presenting the threats each migrated westward toward Europe. Between the first millennium and the second, the population center of gravity moved from the wheat and millet fields north of the Yangtze to the land of fish and rice in the south. Rice demanded intensive farming and irrigation, but its yield was higher, and it supported a larger population and more cities. Population doubled between 1000 and 1300, and although it then dropped by a third due to Mongol depredations and bubonic plague, it tripled from 1700 to 1820. Increasing agricultural productivity enabled production per capita to be relatively stable, but China remained overwhelmingly agricultural.

With all these vicissitudes, what can we say about China's premodern centrality? Clearly we will have to make generalizations that will recall Hegel's retort to a nit-picking student: "Umso schlimmer für die Tatsachen!" – "So much the worse for the facts!" But the project here is not to find an iron law of reason or history that determines all. The centrality that we are exploring is not one of control, either by power or by culture, but rather the configuration of regional interaction. We are not explaining outcomes of interactions, but rather interpreting their patterns.

Key to the persistence and resilience of China's traditional centrality were its presence, population, and production – the "3 Ps" discussed

---

[1] Luo Guanzhong, *Three Kingdoms*, Moss Roberts, trans. (Beijing: Foreign Languages Press, 1995).

in the previous chapter. Each changed over time, but they generated characteristic asymmetric perceptions. China's general posture was one of cautious superiority. The attitude of the nomadic neighbors was quite different from that of the Sinosphere,[2] but all neighbors had in common a skeptical view of China's authority. Given the vulnerabilities of China to its neighbors, and vice versa, the thin connectivity of premodern Pacific Asia was a matter of prudent policy. The diplomatic practice and eventual institutionalization of tribute attempted to manage contact in order to minimize risk. This chapter concludes with an analysis of the major differences between Pacific Asia and the West, followed by Professor Wang Gungwu's commentary.

The 3 Ps

Presence

To call premodern Pacific Asia a region requires an uncomfortable amount of present-day hubris. It was not a subsystem of a global system, a region viewing itself as one among various regions. It was a region determined by its less than global horizons. The claim, "all under heaven," *tianxia*, might best be thought of as, from China's standpoint, "all that matters," a vista tapering off into the distance. It was shaped by climate in the north, as climate's ebbs and flows set the limits for agriculture and, further north, even for pastoral life. In the west the formidable deserts and mountains of Xinjiang added to the region's nomadic ring. In Southeast Asia beyond Vietnam, the cultural influence of India and later of the Arab world are more evident. To the east, Japan became part of the Sinosphere through the mediation of Korea but retained its confident insularity. The Tibetan plateau separated Pacific Asia from South Asia and created a high redoubt for Tibetans. Pacific Asia was thus a place, and China was in the middle of it. But its presence in the region was nevertheless defined by interaction.

As Wang Gungwu argues in his commentary, China was defined by its region as much as its presence defined the region. The nomadic threats required a defensive definition in that direction, symbolized by the Great Wall. China's agricultural wealth provided a constant

---

[2] The region of greatest Chinese influence in premodern times: China, Korea, Japan, and Vietnam.

temptation to northern pastoralists to enjoy the unwelcome connectivity of raids and pillage. While the Chinese could try to eliminate their opponents, the horsemen and their flocks and yurts were moving targets in a tremendous space. China's own center grew around its central plain (中原) where most of its capitals before the Southern Song (1127–1279 AD) were located. After the initial founding moment of the early Zhou dynasty (1046–771 BC) the relative flatness and fecundity of the central plain stimulated the harsh struggles of the Warring States period (475–221 BC). Like a bar-room brawl lasting two and a half centuries, the circle of contenders widened, and weapons became more deadly.

Vietnam provides a good example of the incremental spread of China's presence. A king of the Yue tribes in Guangxi (between the Chinese central plain and Vietnam) acquired advanced military skills as a mercenary in China's Warring States conflicts and conquered the disparate groups in the Red River delta, the heartland of Vietnam.[3] The trigger of the crossbow, the hi-tech infantry weapon of that era, became an important element in Vietnam's founding myth. The Guangxi Yue resisted Qin Shi Huang's brief incursion in 210 BC but were later incorporated, Vietnam included, into the independent southern kingdom of Nan Yue centered in Guangzhou. Finally Nan Yue itself was conquered and incorporated by the Han dynasty in 111 BC. And that is how Vietnam became part of China for a thousand years.

With the Han dynasty (202 BC to 220 AD), the primary interest of China's rulers shifted from the arts of war to the arts of governance. There were militarist exceptions, like the long reign of Emperor Han Wudi (186–57 BC), but their expansionism made governance problems more acute. In outlying areas like Vietnam the expansion of central governance amounted to a Chinese-style civilizing mission: iron ploughs, encouragement of monogamy, and bureaucracy.[4] As with later civilizing missions, the Chinese one led to resistance as well as change. The unsuccessful rebellion led by the Trung sisters (40 to 43 AD) became a core thread in Vietnam's long narrative of resistance to China.[5]

---

[3] Brantly Womack, *China and Vietnam: The Politics of Asymmetry* (New York: Cambridge University Press, 2006), pp. 98–101.
[4] Keith Weller Taylor, *The Birth of Vietnam* (Berkeley: University of California Press, 1983), pp. 27–47.
[5] Sarah Womack, "The Remakings of a Legend: Women and Patriotism in the Hagiography of the Tru'ng Sisters," *Crossroads: An Interdisciplinary Journal of Southeast Asian Studies* 9:.2 (1995), pp. 31–50.

Even though China at its base was a vast collection of mostly self-sufficient villages, its administrative unity was an important part of its external image. The emperor was in command, and laws, personnel, military, finances, and bureaucratic discipline were all centralized.[6] But while the hard lines of domestic authority were gathered in the capital, lower levels pursued their opportunities. Ultimately the emperor was in charge, but the field belonged to the localities. The challenge of domestic governance is suggested by the fact that indigenous dynasties controlled all of China for less than half the span of the traditional empire. There were long periods of chaos and division as well as the two conquest dynasties. Thus, as John Dardess pithily puts it, "The main business of China was China."[7] Most relationships beyond the domestic sphere were usually distractions from this main business, or threats to it.[8]

Perhaps the most important presence of China to its region was as a reservoir of best practices. For the Sinosphere, these began with the patterns and values of governance. Korea and Vietnam each had bureaucracies and an ethos of rule informed by Chinese classics (and each claiming to be superior to contemporary Chinese practice).[9] But best practices extended well beyond politics, and beyond the Sinosphere. China was present to neighbors in a way analogous to the global presence of the United States in the twentieth century. Surrounding elites were aware of what was going on there, skeptical of China's superiority, willing to adopt what appeared to be useful, and alert to any advantages or risks. Meanwhile, China adopted useful innovations from the periphery. The paddy rice that made China's shift to the south so productive was brought in by the Song emperor Zhen Zong (992–1022) from Champa, an Indianized polity that eventually became central Vietnam.[10] Perhaps the archetypal case of center-periphery interchange was the Forbidden City itself. One of

---

[6] Lin Shangli, 国内政府间关系 [Domestic Intergovernmental Relations] (Hangzhou: Zhejiang Renmin Chubanshe, 1997), pp. 265–297.
[7] John W. Dardess, *Governing China 150–1850* (Indianapolis: Hackett, 2010), p. ix.
[8] Alexander Woodside, "The Centre and the Borderlands in Chinese Political Theory" in Diana Lary, ed., *The Chinese State at the Borders* (Vancouver: University of British Columbia Press, 2007), pp. 11–28.
[9] Alexander Woodside, "Territorial Order and Collective-Identity Tensions in Confucian Asia: China, Vietnam, Korea," *Daedalus* 127:3 (1998), pp. 191–220.
[10] Randolph Barker, "The Origin and Spread of Early-Ripening Champa Rice: Its Impact on Song Dynasty China," *Rice* 4 (2011), pp. 184–186.

its key architects was Nguyễn An (1381–1453; in Chinese 阮安) who was taken from Vietnam to Beijing during the brief period of Ming occupation (1407–1427), made a eunuch, and later trained as an architect. In the nineteenth century the Vietnamese emperor Gia Long (1762–1820) built the Imperial City in Hue on the model of Beijing to become the center of newly unified Vietnam.[11]

Population

Although India's population is estimated to have been larger than China's until China's population explosion in the eighteenth century, none of the agricultural areas of Pacific Asia were comparable to China's. Japan in 1700 was closest, but only reached 20 percent of China's population.[12] Of the many ramifications of China's demographic centrality, those of sheer scale are the most basic. Every neighbor could appreciate the Cambodian saying, "where there is water there are fish, and where there is land there are Chinese." After their initial depredations, both the Mongols and the Manchus found it prudent to adapt to the traditional mode of rule. China could not be emptied or commanded; ultimately so many people had to be governed. Demographically, China was and is the solid center of Pacific Asia.

An agricultural population is limited by the physical frontiers of arable land. Although new crops and irrigation made the southern frontier a movable one, in the north and west the weather and aridity proved insuperable. A fundamentally different pastoral culture developed on the steppes, one based on extensive and mobile herding. When mounted archery was developed around the time of China's Warring States era, the stage was set for traditional China's most significant and persistent external security concern. The space available for nomad maneuvers was bigger than China itself.[13] As Owen Lattimore describes it in his classic, *Inner Asian Frontiers of China*,[14] it

---

[11] Alexander Woodside, *Vietnam and the Chinese Model: A Comparative Study of Vietnamese and Chinese Government in the First Half of the Nineteenth Century* (Cambridge, MA: Harvard University Press, 1971).
[12] Calculated from Maddison, *China's Economic Performance in the Long Run*, p. 24.
[13] The distance from Beijing to the Arctic Ocean is further than from Beijing to the southern tip of Vietnam – a long way to chase a nomadic foe.
[14] Owen Lattimore, *Inner Asian Frontiers of China* (first published by the American Geographical Society in 1940, later Hong Kong: Oxford University Press, 1988), p. 77.

was an enduring dialectic between mobility and wealth. Neither could be decisive. When mobility conquered wealth it became ensnared in the reticulated magnitude of the agrarian system. When wealth pushed back mobility, its frontier units had to cope with long logistics and continuing vulnerability or else to realign themselves against the center by colluding with the nomads.

One advantage of a large and relatively concentrated population is the capacity to mobilize large numbers for both military and infrastructural purposes. However, a sedentary empire could only recruit one in six men under wartime mobilization, or maintain an army of one in twenty men, whereas almost all nomads were fighters.[15] Although infantry tended to be ineffective in expeditions against the steppe nomads, its presence along and inside the Great Wall served to prevent most raids from becoming conquests, and to impress nomadic groups with the prudence of accepting diplomatic payoffs. More importantly, the army could forcibly underwrite the bureaucratic structure of domestic politics. But in times when domestic order was weak and the population desperate, localized popular mobilization confronting the dynasty could produce a "righteous uprising" (起义) claiming the transfer of the mandate of heaven (天命) to a new dynasty, and in the meantime creating chaos (大乱).

There were major demographic changes over the course of the Empire that deserve special attention. They are related to the already mentioned rapid development of population south of the Yangtze after the Tang dynasty (618–907). Rice made possible a southern population three times as dense as in the north. While the abundance of land and the shortage of farmers was a persistent problem in the north, the south developed a shortage of land. Especially after the population explosion of the eighteenth century, agriculture became more and more intensive, and the rice fields staircased up the mountainsides. More and more labor pursued less and less marginal gain, and with increasing maintenance costs as well.[16] By the nineteenth century the agrarian demography of traditional China was reaching the end of its

---

[15] Ian Morris, *Why the West Rules – For Now* (New York: Farrar, Strauss, and Giroux, 2010), p. 347.
[16] Mark Elvin, "The Environmental Impasse in Late-Imperial China," in Brantly Womack, ed., *China's Rise in Historical Perspective* (Boulder, CO: Rowman and Littlefield, 2010).

tether. In 1820 China was 82 percent of the population of Pacific Asia. By 1950 it had dropped to 64 percent.[17]

Production

Subsistence agriculture was the overwhelming economic activity in traditional China. The farmers fed China's cities, but crops were difficult to transport by land and they were not a major part of external trade.[18] The Empire was intensely committed to improving agricultural production. Moreover, the needs of agriculture stimulated broader and more sophisticated production. Farmers needed salt and tools, and the state's monopoly on salt and iron were important revenue sources.[19] In the Tang dynasty and even more so in the Song (960–1279) these ancestors of today's state-owned enterprises developed external markets. The tea fields and ports of Fujian flourished. In the year 1060 Fujian's tea output approached three and a half thousand tons.[20] Together with the salt pans on Fujian's coast, the state was indeed "plucking the mountains and boiling the seas" (摘山煮海). Around the state monopolies developed private operations, and foreign merchants became active in Guangzhou until they were massacred at the end of the Tang by a former salt smuggler.

The contrast of mobility and wealth between China and the nomads was not simply a matter of security. A group on the move must be self-sufficient in all basic needs. The nomads got everything from their animals, and kept them fed by moving on to new pastures. But mobility limited diversity of production. Lattimore gives the example of a nomadic blacksmith who must travel with his or her tools and materials. There was little besides horses that nomads could trade with China, and much in China that they did not need but was desirable nonetheless. And China wanted the horses. China's farmers were located and dependent on the state for the management of irrigation as well as for

---

[17] My calculations from the Maddison Project Database, www.rug.nl/ggdc/historicaldevelopment/maddison/releases/maddison-project-database-2020?lang=en.
[18] However, moving rice from south to north was a major aspect of domestic trade, and the reason for the Grand Canal.
[19] Mark Kurlansky, *Salt: A World History* (New York: Penguin, 2003).
[20] Martha Avery, *The Tea Road: China and Russia Meet Across the Steppe* (Beijing: China Intercontinental Press, 2003), p. 17.

necessities. They were also a large domestic consumer market for tea, ceramics and silk, the major products that also went abroad.

Roughly 5 to 7 percent of China's population lived in cities, around half of whom lived in cities of more than 10,000 residents. By the nineteenth century there were in China 310 cities of that size compared to 360 in Europe.[21] In contrast to their European cousins, however, China's urban elites were docile to their central bureaucracies. They lacked the formal autonomy necessary to the development of a bourgeois civil society. However, they provided major production and distribution nodes. China's major artisanal products were known and valued across Eurasia as well as in the region. Such wealth was tempting to the mobile, whether merchants, nomads, or pirates.

It should be noted that China's exports were not vital goods for the recipients. No one would freeze without silk, eat in the dirt without ceramics, or die of thirst without tea. However, especially in its second millennium, the Empire's products were attractive normal purchases for a broad range of consumers. And official control over much of the access sharpened the focus of regional centrality. Similarly, China did not depend on imports for its own vital needs. The exception that proves the rule was the importing of nomadic and Tibetan horses.[22] A constant resupply was necessary because pasture-fed horses were good for cavalry – to defend China against the nomads and the Tibetans. China ran what might appear to be a mercantilist trade economy except that its surplus of exports over imports was due simply to the greater market for Chinese goods abroad. Opium became a second exception to self-sufficiency, as the British tried to sell Indian opium to China to pay for their tea. Opium was banned and finally destroyed, creating the pretext in 1840 for the Opium War.[23]

The combination of population and production gave the centrality of China its resilience. Mobility might seize wealth, but it could not relocate its production, and China's scale put it beyond the transformational capacity of conquerors. A recognizable China would come back, phoenix-like, and it was still at the center. Moreover, its

---

[21] Maddison, *China's Economic Performance in the Long Run*, pp. 38–40.
[22] Paul J. Smith, *Taxing Heaven's Storehouse: Horses, Bureaucrats, and the Destruction of the Sichuan Tea Industry, 1074–1224* (Cambridge, MA: Harvard University Press, 1991).
[23] Stephen Platt, *Imperial Twilight: The Opium War and the End of China's Last Golden Age* (New York: Knopf, 2018).

production made it the center of attention as well as the geographical and political center. Traditional China was present to Pacific Asia, and visible more faintly beyond it.

Asymmetric Perceptions of Centrality

Asymmetry: Normal but Neither Static nor Uniform

International relations theory tends to focus on great powers and great wars. The problems of managing relationships with smaller powers are not major concerns. This is hardly surprising, since most theorists live and write for great powers, and the chief concern of great powers is war with other great powers. Hence the current increased concern about China's rise. Great power rivalries are assumed to be symmetric, since it takes a great power to challenge a great power, and so power asymmetries tend to be viewed as temporary disequilibria. However, in traditional Pacific Asia we are analyzing a situation in which an alignment of center-periphery persisted for two millennia, often but not always associated with a power asymmetry. Therefore, it is necessary to refocus our thinking on asymmetry as a normal condition rather than as a disequilibrium.

By a normal asymmetric relationship, I mean one in which both sides expect the current, familiar asymmetric situation to remain in place. Rulers change, and must adjust to one another, and each side views interactions from its own perspective, but neither is expecting that the periphery will become the center or vice versa. Within the uncontested framework of asymmetry each pursues its own ends, including both its prudential future as well as its immediate interests. A normal asymmetric relationship does not have to be institutionalized, but it does require a mutually accepted pattern. Each individual transaction will be interpreted within the expectations of the pattern.

This abstract idea of normal asymmetry can be illustrated by one of the most dramatic and important events in the history of premodern Pacific Asia, the failed Ming occupation of Vietnam from 1407 to 1427. It was an exception that proved the rule, and it involved the confrontation of two rulers, each of whom was bent on structural change.[24] In Vietnam, General Hồ Quý Ly (胡季犛, 1336–post 1407) overthrew the

[24] Womack, *China and Vietnam*, pp. 125–132.

existing Trần dynasty, named himself the founder of a new one, and renamed Vietnam Đại Việt (the Vietnamese Empire). When the Ming emperor sent a successor to restore the (recognized) Trần dynasty with an escort of 5,000 soldiers, Hồ massacred them. Meanwhile Yongle (1360–1424) had become the third Ming emperor by overthrowing his predecessor. Yongle attempted to establish a new, expansionist era for China. He is sometimes called the "second founder" of the Ming dynasty. His rule was personalist as well, since he was the second emperor to require the Jingdezhen porcelain works to put the reign period on the bottoms of porcelain. Expansion was only possible to the south, and Yongle's ambitions led him in two avenues, maritime and land. The maritime venture was more exploratory, with the seven voyages of Yunnanese Moslem eunuch Zheng He as the main venture. On land Yongle utilized Hồ Quý Ly's affront to the Empire's authority as a pretext to reclaim Vietnam as part of the Empire. His army of 250,000 soon defeated Hồ, and Hồ literally died in obscurity, one of the world's few rulers with a known birth year and an unknown demise.

Thus far it would appear that power prevailed, but the story becomes more interesting. Since service in Vietnam was the least desirable assignment in the Chinese bureaucracy it attracted the also-rans of the Empire, and since it was far from Beijing it offered opportunities for official plunder. Chinese presence became increasingly unpopular. A gifted guerilla leader emerged, Lê Lợi, who began his struggles against occupation in 1418. With many ups and downs, he finally defeated the Ming armies in 1427. In the meantime, Yongle had died and had been replaced by the more peaceable Xuande (1425–1435), who had decided that rather than annexing Vietnam it would be sufficient to go back to the previous mission of restoring the Trần dynasty. After his victories in 1427, Lê Lợi officially restored the Tran pro forma, sent back the defeated Ming army and their horses with an apology, and after a decent interval initiated his own dynasty in place of the Trần with renewed apologies and tribute missions. His rule was now recognized, and peace prevailed, more rather than less, for the next four centuries. Vietnam became the southern boundary stone beyond which China could not expand.

To put this narrative in the language of asymmetry, the problem began when Hồ demanded autonomy without deference, and Yongle tried to enforce deference. The mortal threat to Vietnamese autonomy stirred resistance that prevailed against the limited interests of China.

Then China backtracked from annexation to restoration in order to save face, and Lê Lợi pretended to restore the Trần and showed deference when his autonomy was recognized. Lê Lợi's prudence should be emphasized. If he had massacred the Ming armies and eaten their horses, the re-annexation of Vietnam would have been a mission of honor for successive Chinese rulers.

As this story demonstrates, a normal asymmetric relationship is not static. Rather, it is an interaction within an assumed asymmetric framework. There are other cases of Chinese aggression, successful resistance, apologies, and a resetting of the framework, especially in the Sinosphere. For China they were lessons of the wisdom articulated by Wei Xiang (?–59) in the early days of the Empire: "An action in which one party, relying on the superior size of its territory and boasting of the large number of its people, sets out to overawe its enemy by a show of force is called a campaign of arrogance, and it is doomed to annihilation."[25]

Because centrality is relational rather than simply a matter of unequal state power, it varies tremendously from one relationship to another. In traditional China the relationship was officially between rulers rather than between states.[26] The rulers, or their representatives, or occasionally the ruler's double,[27] led the tribute missions and were given titles and seals of office. Typically this was renewed for successors, but as the case of Lê Lợi shows, sometimes the empire adjusted to facts on the ground. Chinese external relations are best viewed, then and now, as a skein of particular relationships each with their own histories and expectations rather than as a grand strategy applied equally to all.

The View from the Center

China's view from the center of Pacific Asia was usually one of cautious superiority. Occasionally not cautious, as with Yongle's southern ventures; occasionally not superior, as with many anxious meetings of Tang emperors with threatening nomads and Tibetans.[28] But a view from the center is unique. In every direction the center sees attentive

---

[25] Quoted in Wang Zhenping, *Tang China*, p. 242.
[26] James Hevia, *Cherishing Men from Afar: Qing Guest Ritual and the Macartney Embassy of 1793* (Durham, NC: Duke University Press, 1995).
[27] Womack, *China and Vietnam*, p. 136.   [28] Wang Zhenping, *Tang China*.

eyes. All are attentive, though not necessarily friendly, and even if deferential they will pursue their own interests. While it encourages one's self-esteem to go the center of attention, it also implies that no bilateral action will be unnoticed by the rest. If China committed its forces in one place, as Tang emperor Gao Zu (566–635) did in Korea, it became more vulnerable elsewhere – on the western border with Tibet, in Gao Zu's case.[29] China's back was not against the wall, but rather against other vulnerabilities. The encirclement of centrality increased the need for a show of superiority as well as the need for caution. The architecture of Beijing's Forbidden City delivers a message of grand and stable centrality in order to discourage challenge, both domestically and externally.

China viewed its external interactions as governed by hospitality, generosity, virtue, and reciprocity. Above all, actions should be appropriate, *yi* (宜), fitting the actual circumstances of the relationship and the moment rather than rigidly applying general principles.[30] Hospitality required the emperor to treat tribute missions with respect as long as they were in turn respectful of the rituals of the audience.[31] Generosity was the expectation that the emperor, as superior power, would accommodate the needs of the visitor and give gifts of greater value than those received. The emperor did not bargain. He listened and graciously responded. China justified its actions in terms of Confucian virtue informed by precedents exemplifying virtue. Lastly, reciprocity was expected. Reciprocity was not symmetric. The Chinese emperor wasn't going to return the visit, and the visitor was expected to comply with imperial instructions. If not, an expedition of punishment might be necessary. In any case, situational appropriateness was key.

The above principles of China's self-understanding of its diplomacy often led to an official hypocrisy that was obvious to its partners and sometimes injurious to China's own interests. Chinese officialism was quite the opposite of rule-bound bureaucratism. Instead of always following the rules, it involved always reporting events as if they corresponded with the rules. A good example was the treaty

---

[29] Ibid., pp. 83–86.
[30] Qin Yaqing, *A Relational Theory of World Politics* (Princeton: Princeton University Press, 2018).
[31] Hevia, *Cherishing Men from Afar*.

of Nerchinsk (1689) establishing the China-Russia border.[32] It was pragmatically negotiated on the frontier with the help of Jesuit missionaries, but it was officially reported as an act of imperial graciousness to the ignorant Russians. The massaging of the facts to fit preconceptions was rife throughout the system. False but officially convenient reporting on the Opium War contributed to China's loss and to its failure to prepare for future confrontations.[33] Officials may have had greater flexibility in action than their Weberian counterparts, but they reported what Beijing wanted to hear. Officialism was the hypocrisy of hierarchy.

It would be a mistake to expect a consistency of behavior on China's part because of its overarching principles. Different emperors and different dynasties responded to different views of situational appropriateness. Consider how the behavior just described of Ming emperor Yongle toward Vietnam differed from the "Ancestral Injunction" of his father, the dynasty's founder:

The overseas foreign countries like Annan [Vietnam], Champa, Korea, Siam, Liuqiu [Ryukyu Islands], [the countries of the] Western Oceans [South India] and Eastern Oceans [Japan], and the various small countries of the southern *man* [barbarians] are separated from us by mountains and seas and far away in a corner. Their lands would not produce enough for us to maintain them; their peoples would not usefully serve us if incorporated [into the empire]. If they were so unrealistic as to disturb our borders, it would be unfortunate for them. If they gave us no trouble and we moved troops to fight them unnecessarily, it would be unfortunate for us. I am concerned that future generations might abuse China's wealth and power and covet the military glories of the moment to send armies into the field without reason and cause a loss of life. May they be sharply reminded that this is forbidden.[34]

Clearly the son viewed the world differently from his father.

---

[32] Joseph Esherick, "China and the World: From Tribute to Treaties to Popular Nationalism," in Womack, ed., *China's Rise*.
[33] James M. Polachek, *The Inner Opium War* (Cambridge, MA: Harvard Council on East Asian Studies, 1992).
[34] Ming Taizu, as quoted in Wang Gungwu, "Ming Foreign Relations: Southeast Asia," in *The Cambridge History of China*, vol. 8: *The Ming Dynasty, 1368–1644, Part 2*, Denis Twitchett and Frederick Mote, eds, (Cambridge: Cambridge University Press, 1998), pp. 311–312.

The View from the Periphery

Even the blandishments received from China looked different to the recipients. In the course of ten years (647–657) the first Tang emperor awarded to different Uighur chieftains the titles "Civilizing Generalissimo," "King of Righteousness," and "Qaghan of Benevolence."[35] The recipients might have wondered about title inflation and about the emperor's entitlement to entitle. But the more important tensions resulted from the rejection of subordination, cynicism regarding China's actions, and the need to establish a separate, non-Chinese identity.

The basic problem with subordination was that a leader showing deference to a regional center raised questions regarding his or her authority at home. The seal of office of the King of Annam (Southern Peace) were conferred in Beijing to someone who was known in Hanoi as the Emperor of Dai Viet. The seal was important. It was an implicit guarantee that Vietnam's northern border was secure. But domestic authority was even more important – it was all-important – and it could not be conferred by Beijing. Before the Ming invasion the Trần dynasty designated a child as the person to be approved by Beijing while the "senior emperor" was actually in charge.[36] Perhaps the most dramatic illustration of the contradiction between authority conferred and authority earned was the reaction of Toyotomi Hideyoshi (1537–1598), the unifier of Japan, to being named merely "King of Japan" by the Ming emperor. He flew into a rage and ordered a second invasion of Korea, aiming to conquer China.[37] Fortunately for both China and its neighbors, the absence of public media usually hid the tensions between ritual subordination in Beijing and unquestioned authority at home, but the problem of subordination and its acknowledgement was built into the system.

A second characteristic of views from the periphery was cynicism regarding China's motives and its superiority. The dramatic situation

---

[35] Wang Zhenping, *Tang China*, pp. 46–47.
[36] Nguyen The Anh, "Attraction and Repulsion as the Two Contrasting Aspects of the Relations between China and Vietnam," in *China and Vietnam: Historical Interactions. An International Symposium* (Hong Kong: Hong Kong University Press, 2001).
[37] Evelyn Rawski, "Chinese Strategy and Security Issues in Historical Perspective," in Womack, ed., *China's Rise*, pp. 63–88.

of the Athenian response to the Melians related by Thucydides was reversed. Instead of the Chinese saying, "Of men we know and of the gods we believe, that the strong rule when they can and the weak serve when they must," it was the neighbors who assumed that China's power and convenience lurked behind its mask of virtue. As to China's superiority, while it was certainly useful as a reservoir of best practices, the visiting scholars from the Sinosphere noted (with evident satisfaction) the defects and corruption of life in Beijing as compared with their own more faithful adherence to Confucian virtue at home.

The final characteristic of the view from the periphery is the most important one, and the one least appreciated by the center. Given the persisting regional alignment and China's occasional demonstrations of power, a fundamental element of becoming Korea, or Vietnam, or Japan – of creating an identity – was becoming a "not-China." The need was particularly acute under Chinese pressure. In 600 the Wa state in Japan sent a letter to the Chinese emperor hailing him as the "Son of Heaven of the country where the sun sets," while the Wa empress designated herself as the "Son of Heaven of the country where the sun rises."[38] The disruption of the Mongol fleets by the "divine wind" (kamikaze) in 1274 and 1281 strengthened Japan's confidence in its invulnerability.

Vietnam provides a particularly nuanced example of the interplay between center and periphery. On the one hand, resistance to Ming occupation brought the people and leadership together. As the great poet of the resistance Nguyễn Trãi (阮廌, 1380–1442) put it, in the voice of the leader Lê Lợi:

> Around our standard on a fragile bamboo pole
> I mustered forces from a scattered populace.
> As they drank my wine so I drank their water
> And we became like son and father
> Soldiers of one heart.[39]

However, the righteous solidarity against Chinese invaders was only the first half of the story. After the Chinese recognition of the Lê dynasty the golden age of Vietnamese Confucianism began, a trend

---

[38] Buzan and Goh, *Rethinking Sino-Japanese Alienation*, p. 207.
[39] John Whitmore, "The Development of the Le Government in 15th Century Vietnam" (PhD dissertation, Cornell University, 1968), p. 36.

that would have been unpatriotic earlier.[40] Moreover, with the northern border secure, Vietnam could defeat its rival Champa and begin the Vietnamese march to the Mekong.

Thin Connectivity as Practice and as Policy

Given China's overwhelming (and well-justified) concern with domestic prosperity and stability, given its general self-sufficiency, and given its centrality in presence, population, and production, China's primary strategic value in external relations was relational stability and security. This primary value did not preclude seizing opportunities and occasionally destroying opponents, nor did it exclude buying off threatening forces when it felt vulnerable. Moreover, the conquest dynasties, the Mongols and the Manchus, brought in different strategic values, in part because they were from different cultures, and in part because the very act of successful conquest of China demonstrated the possibility and attractiveness of expansion. But in general, cautious superiority required careful management of external relationships.

As Practice

China had many neighbors to deal with, and they were broadly different from north to south. In the north, the indigenous dynasties had to cope with nomadic groups that they could not eliminate, that shifted in their location and leadership, and that were usually in contact with China because of a desire for Chinese goods. As the famous Han historian (and historian of the Han) Ban Gu (32–92) described the pastoral problem:

They flee to dwell in the northern borderlands, in the cold and wet wasteland. They follow their herds across the grasslands and hunt for a living... Thereby both Heaven and Earth sever what is internal from what is external. Therefore also, the sage kings treated them as beasts and birds, did not make a treaty with them, and were not engaged in offensive expeditions. If you make a treaty with them, they will spend the gifts and then deceive you; if you attack them, the army will become exhausted and you will induce banditry. Their lands cannot be tilled for a living; their people cannot be treated as subjects; therefore they must be regarded as those who are external

---

[40] John Whitmore, "Literati Culture and Integration in Dai Viet, c. 1430–c. 1840," *Modern Asian Studies* 31:3 (1997), pp. 665–687.

and not internal, as strangers and not as relatives... When they arrive we must block and repel them; when they leave we must make preparations to be on guard against them. When they admire our righteousness and [send envoys to] submit tributes, we should accept them with courtesy; we should not sever the loose rein and should always leave them in the wrong. This is the constant Way applied by the sage kings to manage the foreigners.[41]

Diplomatic practice in the north and west was therefore a combination of defensive alertness and openness to contact. The Tang added the elements of careful study of nomadic internal politics, using groups against one another, bestowing generous gifts to pre-empt raiding, and building an elite cavalry on the nomadic model.[42]

As might be expected, the conquest dynasties had different relationships with their previous neighborhoods. Kublai Khan (1215–1294) had to deal with rival Mongol leaders who disapproved of his collaboration with the Chinese.[43] He used the wealth he gathered from China to defeat them. In other directions, toward Japan and Southeast Asia, he pushed, usually unsuccessfully, for their submission to his new dynasty, the Yuan. The Manchus dealt with their fellow non-Hans by incorporating them and their territories into an outer realm of control. In the Qing summer capital of Chengde, visiting Mongol leaders were made to feel at home in yurts, and the Dalai Lama and Panchen Lama could reside in replicas of home palaces, Potala and Tashilhumpo. The Puning Temple in Chengde, housing the world's tallest wooden Buddha, celebrated their common beliefs, in some contrast to Han Confucianism. But if the neighbors resisted they were destroyed. In dealing with the Ming-friendly Koreans the Qing insisted on the transfer of Confucian dynastic rituals to their dynasty and invaded when they resisted.

Diplomatic practice toward the south evolved more slowly since China itself was moving in that direction. The major population center beyond China was Vietnam's Red River delta, and that was the southernmost part of China from 111 to 960 BC. Since China was not threatened from this direction the main purpose of official contact was to confirm deference to China and autonomy of local rulers. Because the contact was with rulers rather than with states, change of leadership could involve questions of possible Chinese involvement, as we

---

[41] Quoted in Wang Zhenping, *Tang China*, pp. 243–244. [42] Ibid.
[43] Frederick Mote, *Imperial China 900–1800* (Cambridge, MA: Harvard University Press, 1999), pp. 444–516.

have seen with the Ming occupation of Vietnam. But with the victory of Lê Lợi, Vietnam became the southern boundary stone of Chinese national expansion.

As Policy: The Tribute System

With centuries of interaction recorded in dynastic histories, many neighbors, and the Confucian love of ritual, it is hardly surprising that a pattern would emerge in China's diplomatic practice. But over that length of time, and with such diverse neighbors and dynasties, the content of the rituals of diplomacy would vary considerably. Writing of Song dynasty diplomacy, Frederick Mote says:

> The Chinese did not spend much time formulating general statements of principle regarding interstate relations. Instead we find innumerable references to the implementation of ritual niceties in the form of communications between states, in the exchange of ceremonial gifts, in such courtesies as announcing imperial deaths and dispatching mourning envoys, in the adherence to sworn oaths of submission and allegiance, as well as in other details of ritual.[44]

When China itself was vulnerable, the forms could be maintained but might reverse the direction of deference. The same diplomatic patterns were used by the Song to show their submission to the Jin rulers in the treaty of 1141, whereby they lost their northern territories and paid tribute to the Jin. There was, as Mote puts it, "an East Asian community of shared procedures and common cultural patterns."[45] Or, as in Liam Kelley's great phrase, "a domain of manifest civility."[46] During the Ming and Qing dynasties the Sinosphere became more elaborate and institutionalized in its rituals.

At its core, the Ming and Qing tribute system was the ritual acknowledgment of a structured relationship of mutual but asymmetric benefit between rulers, with China as its center. The granting of titles of rule implied that China had the authority to grant them, but once granted the authority was then transferred. While envoys might be sent, there were no resident embassies in either direction. The gifts exchanged, the tributary *chao gong* (朝贡) and the imperial

---

[44] Ibid., pp. 380–381. [45] Ibid., p. 389.
[46] Liam Kelley, *Beyond the Bronze Pillars: Envoy Poetry and the Sino-Vietnamese Relationship* (Honolulu: University of Hawaii Press, 2005).

ci (賜), were to demonstrate the sincerity of the tributary ruler and the generosity of the emperor. The imperial gifts and the trading licenses associated with the mission were valuable, and sometimes China had to restrict the number of missions from a specific neighbor. The vast extent of China's international trade, while subject to official supervision and often involving state monopolies, was not directly connected to tribute missions.[47] A kowtow, kneeling and bowing to the ground before the emperor, was part of the court ritual, to the distress of Lord Macartney on his visit to Beijing of 1792.[48]

The existence or nonexistence of the tribute system has been the subject of recent acrimonious dispute, and as Peter Perdue, one of the disputants, has pointed out, "our views of Chinese history, like all historical interpretation, respond to the contemporary world."[49] Unfortunately the current tensions of the "contemporary world" may shed more heat than light, and may obscure the actual contribution that history and social science might make in contesting the background assumptions of both sides. What glimmers beneath the current heat, in my opinion, is the gulf between the perspectives of center and periphery on their relationship. China was proud of its central position, and saw its mode of diplomacy as the prudent ritualization of cautious supremacy. The periphery, north and south, resented China's officialism and claims to superiority, and especially in the north were quite aware of the opportunities offered by the variations in relative power. The major exception was Korea during the Ming dynasty, and that was because Japan posed the greater threat. Neither perspective is "correct," in some abstract sense. The appreciation of both is important to understanding the challenges of recentering in the contemporary world.

---

[47] The research group of the Chinese Academy of History divides the tribute system into four kinds of exchanges. First, the ritual exchange; second, the sideline exchanges of the mission; third, the occasional envoy exchanges, most notably Zheng He's voyages; and fourth, designated and managed market exchanges, such as the pre-Opium War "factories" in Canton. Of course, there were smuggling and piracy as well. 中国历史研究院课题组 [Research Group of the Chinese Academy of History] "明清时期'闭关锁国'问题新探" [A New Investigation of the "Closed Country" System of the Ming and Qing Eras], 历史研究 [*Historical Studies*] 3 (2022), pp. 4–21.

[48] Platt, *Imperial Twilight*.

[49] Peter Perdue, "The Tenacious Tributary System," *Journal of Contemporary China* 24:96 (2015), p. 1014.

The root principle of Pacific Asia's diplomatic practice and policy was the collective attempt to cope with mutual but asymmetric agency in a central configuration expressed in terms of personal relationships among located rulers. The Mongol Yuan dynasty was the exception that proved the rule, since it failed in its attempt to subjugate Japan and Southeast Asia. The implicit mutual acknowledgment of agency should be underlined because of its contrast to the following era of Western colonialism. The focus on ruler relationships rather than state relationships contrasts with the post-colonial era and with the current era. Contrasting with both subsequent eras is the reality of thin connectivity and China's policy of subordinating the possibilities of developing connectivity to its concerns with domestic stability.

A Different Situation from the West

In the above analysis I have avoided making contrasts with the West because the differences between Pacific Asia's situation and that of the West are too profound to be reduced to point-by-point distinctions. The West had different empires at different times, but they were defined by their shifting power to control rather than by the ballast of their presence, population, and production. Each empire in turn scanned its horizon for new conquests and new challengers. Pacific Asia's centric regional orientation focused attention on the middle rather than on the horizons, and the ritual management of asymmetric relationships of mutual agency were more common than victory, defeat, and subjugation. Regardless of relative power, there was an asymmetry of alignment and options in the north between the mobile and the settled, and to the south, China learned from Vietnamese resistance to require deference rather than subjugation.

There are many similarities between East and West, and Ian Morris's sweeping historical analysis, *Why the West Rules – For Now*, is as much about structural similarities as it is about differences of social development.[50] Two in particular stand out: the dynamic tension between civilizational cores and their peripheries, and the "paradox of development – the tendency for development to generate the

---

[50] Ian Morris, *Why the West Rules – For Now: The Patterns of History and What They Tell Us about the Future* (New York: Farrar, Strauss, and Giroux, 2010).

very forces that undermine it."[51] These are certainly true for both Pacific Asia and the West, but the fundamental differences in configuration produce different patterns. The resilience of China's central presence, population, and production gave an inward orientation to Pacific Asian dynamics. When nomads conquered China, they had to govern it. When nomads conquered Rome, the Empire disintegrated. Both cores were dynamic, but the Western core was configured by the power of its current hegemons, while the traditional Pacific Asian core was more deeply rooted in the 3 Ps.

If my broad descriptions of traditional Pacific Asian centrality smack of "orientalism," making Pacific Asia seem an exotic other, the following few pages on the West are likely to tip toward "occidentalism," the same kind of prejudicial stereotyping turned around. In a few pages it is hard to avoid stereotyping, and there are exceptions in both directions that do not "prove the rule" or disprove it, but rather make the rule uncomfortable and invite more pages. For example, the Mongol Yuan dynasty would seem to fit better on the non-centric Western side of the divide, while Egypt and perhaps Persia would seem to be more centered in their subregions. But this is a "big picture" venture intended to stimulate the rethinking of our general framing, and a big picture cannot be painted with a one-hair brush.

A Liquid Center in the West

The simplest contrast between traditional Pacific Asia and the West is that Pacific Asia had a Middle Kingdom, while the West had a Middle Sea, the Mediterranean. Pacific Asia had a solid center, and the West a liquid one.[52] Pacific Asia had a place, the West had a space. In time the North Atlantic became the new Mediterranean, but the basic situation of commercial contact and competition among multiple powers persisted despite changes in the major actors and technologies. By contrast, in Pacific Asia the presence of a demographic and agricultural solidity in its middle has continued to provide the deep context of its regional relationships. The consequences of this difference are

---

[51] Ibid., p. 284.
[52] R. Bin Wong has suggested that the Mediterranean region as described by Fernand Braudel has its analog in China's role in various Asian regions. Wong, "Entre monde et nation: les régions braudéliennes en Asie," *Annales. Histoire, Sciences Sociales* 56:1 (2001), pp. 5–41.

profound. Although too much can be made of contextual determinism, political communities must bloom where they are planted.

From the time of the Phoenicians by sea and the Celts and other wanderers by land, Western history has involved victory or defeat among potential challengers and trade with distant places. The major exception was Egypt, where the Nile provided a resource center and the desert natural barriers. But Egypt was not massive enough to anchor a broader regional pattern, and it was not maritime. Alexander founded Alexandria, its major port, in 331 BC and brought Egypt into the Hellenic world. Turkey was more typical: from earliest times it has been a palimpsest of the residues of peoples on the move by land and by sea.

The Phoenicians established trading colonies throughout the Mediterranean, followed by the Greeks and the Romans. Ironically (by Chinese standards), the success of Corinth and later of Athens was based on bad land and good commercial location. The glories of Venice, Genoa, Portugal, Spain, Holland, and England applied an ancient pattern of maritime ventures to new opportunities. Peripheral powers successively turned their liabilities into assets and re-oriented the Western core. There was an intense hunger for riches from abroad and a communal excitement about distant possibilities that never possessed China to the same extent. And on China's periphery, the gleam in the eye of Pacific Asian nomads was China itself.

Western empires arose in competitive environments. They were centers of relative power rather than natural centers of capacity. Some relied on raw power to demolish some opponents and to intimidate the rest; others reassured neighbors with tolerant policies and assurances of respect. In all cases, however, relative power was decisive not only for the fate of the ruler but also for the location and identity of the imperial center. Empires replaced empires, or subdivided in the case of Rome and Byzantium. Maritime control was vital because essential goods as well as riches came from elsewhere. The more control the Roman Empire acquired, the more dependent on distant resources – food and slaves – it became. These dependencies hastened its fall. Once fallen, it did not rise again. The Mediterranean was the central *space* around which armies contended and within which navies and pirates battled, but there was no resilient central *place*. It was the fate of Malta and Sicily, sometimes unfortunate, to be small and in the middle of the civilizational pond.

The West's fluid center brought with it a corresponding set of advantages and disadvantages. The advantages derived from competitive restlessness around a central space combined with access to distant lands. Ships and militaries were improved. The Western security curse was the decisive importance of relative power. The presumption of competitive challenge put a premium on being capable of defeating the others. This was true of land warfare with its risk of defeat and occupation, and of naval warfare, with its risk of ship destruction, commercial embargo, and raiding. At the extreme of mortal competition with a challenger, relative gain is more important than absolute gain: an enemy's loss is more important than a mutual benefit. By contrast, in China's asymmetric situation even nomads would be less averse to China's absolute gain as long as they remained mobile enough to dodge China's military. Better to raid a fat village than a thin one, or to be bought off by a rich emperor than a poor one. In the case of the coexistence of the Southern Song and the Jin, revenues from the border trade between the two segments of China exceeded the Song's tribute payments.[53] The cumulative productive and demographic success of traditional China and of Pacific Asia in general might be attributed in part to the absence of the curse of relative power and the consequent smaller role of destructive state competition. But competitive risk breeds innovation and military toughness, while a powerful center can become complacent.

This is not to say that Western empires were blind to the perils of over-extension. Edward Gibbon gives Augustus credit for perceiving the wisdom of set boundaries for the Roman Empire:

Inclined to peace by his temper and situation, it was easy for him [Augustus] to discover that Rome, in her present exalted situation, had much less to hope than to fear from the chance of arms; and that, in the prosecution of remote wars, the undertaking became every day more difficult, the event more doubtful, and the possession more precarious, and less beneficial.

He bequeathed, as a valuable legacy to his successors, the advice of confining the empire within those limits which nature seemed to have placed as its permanent bulwarks and boundaries: on the west, the Atlantic Ocean; the Rhine and Danube on the north; the Euphrates on the east; and towards the south, the sandy deserts of Arabia and Africa.[54]

---

[53] Mote, *Imperial China 900–1800*, p. 392.
[54] Edward Gibbon, *History of the Decline and Fall of the Roman Empire* (London: Strahan and Cadell, 1776), ch. 1, Project Gutenberg, www.gutenberg.org/cache/epub/25717/pg25717-images.html#chap01.1.

It should be noted, however, that in contrast to Ming Taizu's admonition to his posterity, quoted earlier, to leave the neighbors alone, Rome's limits set by Augustus were in terms of geography. And they were exceeded fifty years later by Trajan.

The Western fascination with the rise and fall of hegemonic states can be contrasted with the Asian interest in the fates of dynasties. From the *Iliad*, and most classically in Thucydides' *Peloponnesian Wars*, the displacement of one hegemonic nation by another has been a principal object of attention in the West. The exception is pharaonic Egypt; the exception that proves the rule is that of Israel in the Bible, whose centrality was as a people chosen by God and whose sufferings and wanderings confirmed worldly disequilibria. By contrast, not only China, but also Korea and Vietnam kept "veritable records" for the purpose of composing dynastic histories and thereby edifying their successors.[55] There was implicit confidence in the located stability of states in Pacific Asia. Explaining change in fortune fascinates all observers of history, and Asia and the West would agree that "the empire, long united, must divide." The difference is that in the Sinosphere it is the same place that "long divided, must unite."

Zheng He and Afonso de Albuquerque Compared

The difference between traditional Pacific Asia and the modernizing West can be illustrated by contrasting Zheng He's seven voyages to the Indian Ocean in the fifteenth century with Portugal's voyages of exploration somewhat later. Both were major attempts by their respective governments to expand influence, but they differed in context, process, and outcome. The Ming voyages were the maritime arm of Emperor Yongle's push to the south. Zheng led on each voyage approximately 50 major ships with 200 supporting vessels and 27,000 personnel. While the ships were probably half the reported size, they would still be longer than eighteenth-century European ships of the line.[56] The voyages were a series of huge displays of power and magnificence, leaving with gifts for local rulers and bringing back oddities

---

[55] Alexander Woodside, *Lost Modernities* (Cambridge, MA: Harvard University Press, 2006), p. 25.
[56] Sally Church, "Zheng He: An Investigation into the Plausibility of 450-ft Treasure Ships," *Monumenta Serica* 53:1 (2005), pp. 1–43.

such as giraffes and tributary envoys in return. They engaged in some military activities, against a hostile reception in Sri Lanka and supporting invested rulers against opponents in Indonesia. Conquest was not their purpose, however, and they left no colonies or resident embassies. The context was the expansion of the Chinese realm of deference, the process was similar to modern port calls, and the result, as with the occupation of Vietnam, was discontinuation. The continuing Mongol threat in the north and domestic priorities made these southern efforts an expensive bridge too far.

The Portuguese admiral Afonso de Albuquerque (1453–1515), like Zheng He, had a military background. He led several expeditions to India, conquering Goa and Malacca and becoming the viceroy of Portuguese India. One of the early military ventures was an attempt, partially successful, to seize the ornamental doors of the pavilion of the ruler of Calicut and bring them back to the Portuguese king.[57] Albuquerque's expedition for the conquest of Goa in 1510, establishing the first European colony in India, consisted of 23 ships, 1600 Portuguese soldiers, and 3000 "fighting slaves" for logistical support – a tenth of Zheng's fleet and a fifth of his manpower.[58] The context of Albuquerque's conquests was Portugal's attempt to bypass the Mediterranean powers by developing routes to Eastern spices around Africa and eventually to Japan. His method was one of ruthless attacks on native populations, subjugation or removal of native rulers, and colonization. Portugal became the first global empire, but eventually it could not sustain itself in competition with larger European powers when they followed Portugal's example.

We can get a clearer idea of the policy of thin connectivity using Zheng He's voyages as a limit case. Thin connectivity was not, as the later restrictions on maritime trade by the Ming and Qing might suggest, an isolationist distrust of the non-Han world, or even of the world beyond Asia. Thus, it was not a "no connectivity" policy, or even a minimum connectivity policy. It was not even a restriction of contact or trade to a low level. While Zheng did not present a traveling version of the Canton Trade Fair, his voyages certainly opened up possibilities of trade and increased contact. When later restrictions

---

[57] Roger Crawley, *Conquerors: How Portugal Forged the First Global Empire* (New York: Random House, 2015), pp. 214–225.
[58] Ibid., p. 234.

were put in place, lower connectivity was a policy outcome rather than a purpose of policy. And Zheng demonstrated that thin connectivity was quite ductile by stretching it to the African coast. Thin connectivity was the management of international contact by ritualizing relationships of mutual but asymmetric respect with rulers who were assumed to be in control of their domestic affairs. The more threads of such diplomatic relationships the better. But the root purpose was security through the management of uncertainty.

Albuquerque's connectivity policy was quite different. While he might appear to be a maritime Mongol, unlike the nomads, he served a king who was very much involved with a different, European center. His successes and the contemporaneous successes of Spain and Portugal in the New World began to move the central space of Europe from the Mediterranean to the Atlantic, and at the same time to expand Europe from being a regional center to a global one. Meanwhile, Portugal became one of the poorest countries in Europe by the nineteenth century, despite its colonies.

Commentary
Wang Gungwu

This is a comprehensive account of the major features of Chinese history down to the present. Its schematic approach highlights the main features of what made China the kind of state-based civilization or central kingdom it was, multifaceted with many layers and dimensions. Pulling them together into a frame that can be easily understood is a remarkable achievement.

I am impressed by its emphasis upon continuities, both China's resilience and the patterns of dynastic rise and fall that led the emperor-state to believe that it would rise again after every fall. That confidence came from having a long period of history that both rulers and subjects had come to share. That was ensured by officials who recorded the patterns of reunification and resurgence through the centuries and paid special attention to the ups and downs of every dynasty as well as the reasons why some dynasties succeeded and others failed. The records were compiled with great care as to what lessons might be learned. The continuities noted were not arbitrary. They were determined by historians who drew on the wisdom of Confucian and Legalist thinkers that was accepted by all the people tasked to govern the state.

The emphasis upon continuities captures the varied responses to all challenges to political order, especially after the dynastic central kingdom of the Western Zhou (1046–771 BC) was set aside and warring feudal states defined a new reality for more than five centuries. In the struggle for mastery during an age of creativity and ambition, a larger idea of China as *tianxia* 天下 (all under heaven) was produced. At its core was the drive to recover an undivided unity under the *tianzi* 天子 (Son of Heaven). The oneness, "one sun in the sky," promised that whoever could bring the states together would be respected by all.

This concept of centrality was one that the rulers had defined for their people. The founders of the Shang and Zhou dynastic houses confirmed that they had developed the most appropriate governance structure for what was to become the largest agrarian civilization in the world. They had built their power and wealth along the Yellow River with intensive relations with the states of the Yangzi valley to its south and brought the two cultivated worlds together. By so doing, they supported the lives of numerous communities that came to share cultural values and support a single political order.

This strong awareness of past achievements supported by the records lies behind the idea of China's centrality. This chapter picks out the key concepts that marked the country's progress from its early past to the nineteenth and twentieth centuries when it faced the most dangerous moments in its history. That is clearly outlined and I have little to add. What I shall do here is to connect that centrality to a paradigm that Brantly has done more than anyone else to advance, the concept of asymmetry in interstate relations, especially the theoretical model he provided to help us understand that asymmetry.

I have noted that the Chinese have long seen themselves as central and defined that quality of centrality for themselves. They did not wait for others to concede that to them. Nor was it merely a matter of pride in proven success, but of asserting the obvious, the reality of an exceptional state-building process. Brantly's concept of presence is very helpful in giving us its geopolitical dimension. Every history of China refers to the fact that its two river systems, both among the largest in the world and, unlike anywhere else, flow from the same uplands source from west to east in the same direction and end up in the same ocean. Without being overly deterministic, I would argue that this provided the foundation of China's continuous presence.

Added to this was the dimension that produced its cultural power: the Chinese script that still survives today. No other language has been so exclusive, and yet it impacted hugely on the region that included countries like Korea, Vietnam, and Japan. Allowing these neighbors access to key Chinese texts and records helped to project the sense of superiority that still remains in the minds of most Chinese.

Taking the vast agrarian base together with a distinctive literate system points to another kind of centrality, that arising out of the relationship between a strong centralized state and those nomadic organizations that did not need to learn from China but eyed its concentration of wealth with longing. Throughout history, most of China's rulers had to confront that mobile power with the utmost care.

Chinese records show that the nomadic forces of Central Asia occupied more attention than other outsiders. That suggests that any description of China's centrality with reference to peoples to the east and south must take account of the overland threats of wars and invasions. This was a centrality that had inbuilt imbalances. The threats did much to shape the very nature of China's first imperial power of the Qin and Han dynasties.

Having held off numerous attacks and even pushed Chinese rule into nomad terrains, this Han centrality was so entrenched that, four centuries later, its northern half could survive centuries of foreign rule and still be identified as Chinese. As for the Han people who moved south to establish separate kingdoms, they dominated the indigenous peoples there and assimilated them into the larger agrarian economy. In that way, after surrendering the northern provinces to the Toba Turks, Han Chinese civilization expanded to the southern provinces, including the lands of the Yue 越 peoples of modern Vietnam.

The Confucian-Legalist state encouraged its subjects to become Chinese; if they accepted key ideas and institutions, they joined those who had enriched China's civilization before them. Thus many descendants of the Xiongnu, Turkic, Tibetan, Mongolic, and Tungusic peoples started on the road to Chineseness and came to change the Chinese center itself. By the Tang dynasty, China had acquired a centrality encompassing a large part of the Eurasian continent. This did not mean that China was central to the known world, but its strategic centrality was recognized and defined by its precarious relationship with mobile non-agrarian enemies. In short, the concept of centrality was also shaped by the seriousness of the threats on China's land borders.

To return to the question of asymmetry, it is not only the asymmetry of kingdoms in eastern Asia or of the smaller political units of the southwest but also that of a host of nomadic polities overland. The asymmetry between them and China forced them to form confederations strong enough to push into Chinese territory. I mentioned the Turkic and Tibetan armies that played their part in shaping the great Tang empire. Later leaders also learnt how they might be able to govern China. By the end of Tang, fragmentation in the empire forced its lesser kingdoms to accept a reversed asymmetry. As a result, for the next three centuries, the Song emperors acknowledged the power of the Khitan Liao, lost half their lands to the Jurchen Jin and the Tangut Xixia, and finally lost everything when all of China came under Mongol rule.

This procession of territorial losses marked the asymmetry of a great agrarian state conceding the military superiority of nomadic power. It was no accident that it was only after the Mongol interregnum that the Ming rulers and mandarins redesigned the tribute system to manage the borders. They adapted the tribute system to the new asymmetry and evolved a brilliant way of re-centering themselves into an older framework. It devised specific links with each nomadic group and, as much as possible, kept the groups separate and divided. This also meant that the less predictable nomadic forces could focus on wealth and power and expect treatment that was adjusted to meet their different needs. In contrast, China's well-established relations with other agrarian states could remain tied to finer points of rituals and cultural exchange.

This might be seen as a cautious superiority, one that recognized an asymmetric reality in the agrarian society's efforts to keep out a highly mobile enemy. When the Great Wall built across the whole length of the northern borderlands failed to stop the invaders, it was not surprising that the kingdoms of Korea, Vietnam, and Japan should become skeptical of what China's centrality really meant. If that centrality was relative and changeable, at least the asymmetry remained a constant.

I shall be brief about how this condition might be compared to China's experience with the West since the middle of the nineteenth century. This chapter rightly points out that China was always land-oriented and paid far less attention to maritime affairs. When it had the capacity to build a great navy and found that there were no enemies at sea, the mandarins stopped the navigations and destroyed the fleets. Their concentration on the Great Wall symbolized the nomadic dimension of asymmetry, and it suggests that the Mongol conquest was more than a passing nightmare. It gave the Chinese an early taste of what total defeat could mean. To be conquered again by the Manchu Qing represented for China a deepening of that experience and demonstrated the diminution of Han civilization in the eyes of its eastern neighbors.

At the same time, it could also be said that surviving two such conquests provided China with a faith in the centrality of what was later called "Chinese characteristics." I am not suggesting that its elites were always confident of the outcome after each disaster. But if we look at the cultural residue of the two conquests on China's history since the early nineteenth century, we can identify a resilience that emerged from two kinds of asymmetric resistance. One saw the possibility of total collapse and the necessity for China to be modernized with Euro-America as its model future. The other emerged with its new rulers confident that the radical changes needed can be controlled and the governance structure can remain recognizably Chinese.

The first resistance was the feeble response to the military challenge at sea that was made possible by the massive economic assets coming from Western Europe's industrial capitalism. These incursions were further supported by a set of political institutions also never encountered before, the nation-state consciousness that shaped Western imperialism and went on to produce a new world order. China's loss of centrality here was not merely because the maritime powers dominated the China coasts. Throughout the nineteenth century, Qing China never lost sight of the Turko-Mongol challenge to its continental west and retained huge defence forces to guard against Russian and British advances into Central Asia.

This continued to be significant when the dynastic state gave way to the Western-inspired Republic in 1912. After the Russian revolution and the self-defeating consequences to the European empires in two World Wars, many Chinese were inspired by the overland alternative to imperial capitalism and organized to oppose the modernity that the latter had offered as a model. For a while, after the Maoist victory in 1949, the asymmetry shifted from seaward to a westward outreach into the heart of the Eurasian continent. In the end, the Chinese communists found that there was no safety in that orientation and turned back to seek the progress that only the market economy could offer.

These costly reversals led to the second resistance. The adaptability and resilience demonstrated during the next five decades have enabled China to overcome another kind of asymmetry. Here I think Brantly's concepts of presence, population, and production help to explain the relevance today of the multiple rise and fall experiences in China's heritage. Put simply, when presence cannot be fragmented and entrepreneurial peoples are allowed room and motivation to learn, the production factor can take off afresh. Together that can make a tremendous difference to any status quo.

The situation today after the end of the Cold War and the emergence of the United States as the sole superpower created an exceptional asymmetry that China has risen to question. I agree that China's partial centrality can be seen to have extended towards Pacific Asia because it is now awake to the dangers of neglecting maritime security. However, China has always had to deal with other kinds of asymmetry. It cannot afford to neglect the necessary balance to be safe and prosperous. In the new global order, it will still have to face the exceptional landlocked centrality of the Eurasian core that gave shape to the three ancient civilizations – the Sinic, the Indic, and the Mediterranean – that have survived to the present day.

3 | Sharp Connectivity
Western Modernization and De-centered Pacific Asia

Imagine Angus Maddison (1926–2010), the famous British economist who compiled historical statistics on global productivity, visiting the Emperor of China in 1820. After the customary kowtows, Emperor Jiaqing asks Maddison why he has come, and Maddison replies that he has come to bring good news and a warning. He says, "China is one of the most successful states in the world. It produces one-third of the global output and has one-third of the global population. Your production surpasses that of all of Western Europe!" Jiaqing is happy to hear this, but he is puzzled. "What is a globe?" he asks. Maddison skips that question, but warns, "Europe and the United States are only 28 percent of global production, but they are hungry and well-armed. China is therefore vulnerable." Jiaqing smiles and replies, "I know of these far-away places that send merchants and emissaries by sea. But our external threats have always come overland from the north. The seas have only pesky pirates." Maddison gets excited and prophesizes, "Beware the future! In 1950 China will have only 5% of global production and one-fifth of Europe's, and your per capita income will be lower than it is today!" Jiaqing turns away, and the audience is over.

Over the course of the nineteenth century, Western imperialism splintered most of Pacific Asia into colonies. Each conquered part of Pacific Asia now served a distant power, and even the non-colonies, Japan, China, Siam, Korea, were no less oriented – or dis-Oriented – toward the Western powers. A global centrality structured toward Europe replaced the regional, China-centered centrality. China's centrality came to a double end. It lost its importance to its neighbors, and its neighborhood lost its coherence. Meanwhile China fell apart internally, re-establishing an effective and unchallenged government only in 1949. Europe was not a conquest dynasty overthrowing the Qing and establishing its own. It couldn't care less about China's dynasty – in fact it supported the Qing against the rebellious Taipings.¹ It was instead a forcible reframer of regional horizons, making each part of what had been China's neighborhood into a small, separate, and subordinate part of a much larger global picture.

European imperialism claimed the high-minded motivation of a civilizing mission, the "white man's burden" sung by Rudyard Kipling² to Theodore Roosevelt at the time of the Spanish American War, or the tutelary authoritarianism justified by John Stuart Mill for uncivilized colonies.³ It is clear, however, that colonial rule and influence, and in consequence the creation of Europe as a center with global reach, was based on a preponderance of power. As the exploits of the Portuguese admiral Afonso de Albuquerque related in the last chapter suggest, the impulse of imperialism was to take what it could. Within its colonies and beyond, the soft power of Europe was first the gleam on its sword rather than the attractiveness of its system. The attempts of Pacific Asian countries to copy Europe were in the initial attempts at defense against imperialism, well-articulated by Zhang Zhidong (1837–1909) in his call for "Chinese learning as substance, Western learning for application" (中学为体西学为用). The failure of piecemeal copying led to more comprehensive and more radical efforts of self-strengthening, with Meiji Japan as the most impressive early success. However, regardless of success in fending off foreign power and preserving or acquiring independence, there was no backtracking on either modernization or on globalization.

As Wu Yu-Shan emphasizes in his commentary on this chapter, the power of the West presupposed organization. The new centrality of Europe could not be explained by its distant presence, its relatively low population, or even its productivity in the sense of tradable goods. Europe did not have the 3 Ps. The West established its power by means of determined organization – commercial institutions such as the British East India Company, the pursuit of converts

---

¹ Stephen Platt, *Autumn in the Heavenly Kingdom: China, the West, and the Epic Story of the Taiping Civil War* (New York: Random House, 2012).
² Rudyard Kipling, "The White Man's Burden: The United States and the Philippine Islands," *McClure's Magazine*, February 1899.
³ John Stuart Mill, *Considerations on Representative Government*, chapter 18, "Of the Government of Dependencies by a Free State" (1861, two years after *On Liberty*). www.gutenberg.org/files/5669/5669-h/5669-h.htm#link2HCH0018

by religions, disciplined navies and militaries, adventurous citizens, and willing governments. Behind these muscles sustaining imperial power was the growing national institutionalization of Europe itself as it modernized.

Europe accomplished its globalizing mission by what I am calling *sharp connectivity*, in contrast to the thin connectivity of the earlier era. Both were policy strategies as well as outcomes. Traditional China was more interested in controlling connectivity than in expanding it. Western powers were interested in profit and in competitive advantage among themselves, and therefore they wanted to develop connectivity, but only to their own national advantage. By the nineteenth century they had moved from monopolizing the trade in existing Pacific Asian products such as spices to transforming the domestic economies of their colonies to serve global markets, and also to serve as markets for their industrial consumer products.

The root factors of China's premodern centrality lost their salience. Its premodern situational advantages of presence, population, and production were turned on their heads. China became a non-presence, its large population came to be seen as an inertial drag, and its artisanal production was displaced by industrialization. Without its premodern situational advantages, China's former asymmetric relationship to Pacific Asia wilted, and its connectivity went from being a carefully managed thin connectivity to being insignificant.

This chapter begins with a discussion of Pacific Asia's connectivity to the West, not to China, which begins as a sharp, enforced connectivity serving specific step-mother countries, broadened after the Second World War into a less pointed but more intense global connectivity under the aegis of the United States. Similarly, Pacific Asia's modern perceptual asymmetry was between the superiority of the powerful, modern West and its own threatened identity and autonomy. The end of colonialism enabled the emergence of national sovereignties, but they were still fragmented into unrelated former colonies and constrained by a US-led global order that was beyond their influence.

We will discuss East Asia connectivity and asymmetry with the West in two phases: colonialism, 1840–late 1940s; and the American imperium, 1950–2008. Then we will analyze what happened to China's apparently solid situational advantages of presence, population, and production.

Colonial Sharp Connectivity in Pacific Asia

Western presence in Pacific Asia began first as the distant final purchaser of silk, ceramics and spices from chains of overland and maritime merchants. Marco Polo's account of his travels, first published around 1300, gives an idea of the difficulty of access and of the riches that might await European adventurers.[4] For Europeans, China was enticing because it was beyond the horizon. For China, Europe was uninteresting because it was beyond the horizon. But from the sixteenth century the West became a "significant other" to the region – not yet a presence – using military advantages and surprise arrival by sea. The philosopher Immanuel Kant (1724–1804) had this to say about the experience:

> Let us look now…at the inhospitable behavior of the civilized nations, especially the commercial states of our continent. The injustice which they exhibit on visiting foreign lands and races—this being equivalent in their eyes to conquest—is such as to fill us with horror. America, the negro countries, the Spice Islands, the Cape etc. were, on being discovered, looked upon as countries which belonged to nobody; for the native inhabitants were reckoned as nothing. In Hindustan, under the pretext of intending to establish merely commercial depots, the Europeans introduced foreign troops; and, as a result, the different states of Hindustan were stirred up to far-spreading wars. Oppression of the natives followed, famine, insurrection, perfidy and all the rest of the litany of evils which can afflict mankind.[5]

Kant goes on to praise China and Japan for limiting the presence of Europeans:

> China and Japan which had made an attempt at receiving guests of this kind, have now taken a prudent step. Only to a single European people, the Dutch, has China given the right of access to her shores (but not of entrance into the country), while Japan has granted both these concessions; but at the same time they exclude the Dutch who enter, as if they were prisoners, from social intercourse with the inhabitants.[6]

In the nineteenth century, Europe's presence in Pacific Asia grew from being a significant other into being the central presence of a

---

[4] Marco Polo, *The Travels*, Nigel Cliff, trans. (New York: Penguin, 2016).
[5] Immanuel Kant, *Perpetual Peace, A Philosophical Essay*, M. Campbell Smith, trans. (London: George Allen and Unwin, 1903), pp. 139–140.
[6] Ibid., p. 141.

global system. China's control over incoming foreign commerce was broken by the Opium War in 1840, and Japan's 1639 policy of *sakoku* (鎖国 locked country) was ended by the visit of Commodore Matthew Perry's "black ships" in 1853. Korea lost its "hermit kingdom" status as the Japanese strengthened their influence after defeating China in 1895. Meanwhile all of Southeast Asia except Siam (Thailand) was colonized.

The Splintering of Pacific Asia

Although Pacific Asia did not experience the total subjugation and massive population transfers that afflicted the Americas and sub-Saharan Africa, its local identities, previous regional relationships, and economies were transformed by European imperialism in the nineteenth century. Pacific Asia, and especially Southeast Asia, were repackaged. The British controlled Malaysia, Myanmar, and Singapore, the Dutch controlled Indonesia, the French controlled Vietnam, Laos, and Cambodia, and the Spanish controlled the Philippines until the United States took over in 1898 after the Spanish-American War. Thailand was the only part of Southeast Asia to remain independent, but only by adroit and deferential diplomacy with its new neighbors France and Britain and by territorial concessions. Its independence was preserved in 1896 by an agreement between London and Paris.[7] While Japan and China remained free of direct European rule, Japan responded to the imperial challenge by attempting its own modernization, using the Western model, while China made a growing number of concessions regarding treaty ports. Korea's fate, and Taiwan's, was to be colonized by Japan. Thus, all of Pacific Asia except Korea and Taiwan faced Europe as its source of greatest risk and opportunity, but it did so as individual polities, not as a region. Moreover, for colonies the European focus was sharp on both ends: one step-mother country with pointed interests in its own colony heightened by European competition at home with the other imperial powers.

Besides reorientation toward Europe, the splintering of Pacific Asia created sharper edges for its pieces. As their footholds became firmer, colonial powers used the traditional ambiguities of borderlands to push their territorial claims to the limit. What had been frontiers before

---

[7] *Declaration between Great Britain and France with Regard to the Kingdom of Siam and Other Matters* (signed in London, January 15, 1896).

colonization now became lines defining colonial reach. When colonies abutted colonies, then the colonial powers fought over ownership and eventually settled claims by treaty. The British and the Dutch settled their differences over colonial possessions and rights in the area of the Malacca Strait by treaty in 1824. But when colonial powers abutted not-yet-colonial powers they gnawed like industrious silkworms on their neighbors. For example, the British Straits Settlement at Penang began as an island in 1786, started its mainland holdings in 1800, and increased them several times, at the expense of Malay sultanates and Siam.[8] Ironically the creation of French Indochina in 1887 can be credited with preserving the states of Cambodia and Laos from being divided between Vietnam and Siam, but it did so only because they became French colonies. French Indochina itself was a prime example of governance by rearrangement.[9] Vietnam was divided into three parts, Tonkin in the north, Annam in central Vietnam, and Cochinchina in the south, and all three merged with Cambodia and Laos into one colonial unit which had no precedent.

Colonial Transformations

The initial European interest in Pacific Asia was to facilitate and control access to the luxury products to which they had become accustomed: spices, silks, ceramics, and, somewhat later, tea. During the eighteenth century spices dropped from three-quarters of Dutch imports from Asia to one-third, replaced by textiles, coffee, and tea.[10] By the nineteenth and twentieth centuries advances in military, transportation, and communication enabled a more direct transformation of colonial economies. Economic modernization served the various empires. In the Dutch East Indies (now Indonesia), Governor-General Van den Bosch, known for charitable projects at home, introduced the "cultivation system" (*cultuurstelsel*) in 1830, whereby 20 percent of the arable land

---

[8] Frank Swettenham, *British Malaya: An Account of the Origin and Progress of British Influence in Malaya* (London: Lane, 1907).
[9] John Whitmore, "The Thai-Vietnamese Struggle for Laos in the Nineteenth Century," in Nina Adams and Alfred McCoy, eds, *Laos: War and Revolution* (New York: Harper, 1970), pp. 53–66.
[10] Angus Maddison, *The World Economy: A Millennial Perspective* (Paris: OECD, 2001), p. 86. www.oecd-ilibrary.org/economics/the-world-economy_9789264189980-en

would be reserved for commercial crops such as indigo, sugar, and coffee. These would be worked by the farmers as a service tax and delivered to the government. By the 1850s half of all Dutch national revenue came from these colonial deliveries.[11] In French Indochina, rice became the principal export, at 65 percent of total exports. The French squeezed rice out of the countryside by eliminating the rotation of land within the village and encouraging large-scale landlordism. As rice exports went up, consumption of rice per capita in Vietnam went down. Meanwhile conditions in the mines and rubber plantations were kept at bare survival. At one Michelin rubber plantation one-quarter of the workforce died over a seventeen-year period.[12] Of course, the commercialization of the colonial economies brought in European imports, but typically they were luxury and mass consumption goods rather than infrastructure improvements. In Vietnam only 9 percent of imports were not for consumption, and this included military imports.[13]

Sharp connectivity reached to the bottom of society, far beyond the reach of traditional thin connectivity. Economies were connected, tightened, and redirected. Subsistence villages were now producing commodities rather than their own food. The intimacy of hand-to-mouth existence under a village elder was replaced by the more contingent relationship of hand-to-money-and-then-remainder-to-mouth, now under the watchful eye of the lowest level of colonial official. Landlords needed maximum extraction in order to fund their newly discovered needs of privilege, and increased taxes were necessary to fund a more active and intrusive government. Port cities were built, with Singapore as the lead example. Singapore was virtually uninhabited before Stamford Raffles arranged its transfer to the East India Company in 1819–24, and it became the most prized British port in Southeast Asia within a few decades.

From a distance, however, the transformation of colonial economies does not seem a disaster. Angus Maddison addressed the hypothetical question of whether British rule had been good for India. He considers three possibilities: one, no colonialism but some enclaves (like

---

[11] James C. Kennedy, *A Concise History of the Netherlands* (Cambridge: Cambridge University Press, 2017), pp. 290, 297.
[12] Ngo Vinh Long, *Before the Revolution: The Vietnamese Peasants under the French* (New York: Columbia University Press, 1991).
[13] Ibid., p. 105.

China); two, colonialism but by a different country; and three, British colonialism but earlier independence. With the first, a situation like China's, he estimates that India would have fallen apart into internal strife without the likelihood of eventual unification. Colonialism by a different country, Netherlands or France, would probably have produced results similar to the British. However, Maddison thinks that with Indian self-government in, say, 1880, after more than a century of British rule but sixty-seven years earlier than actual independence in 1947, the economy and population would have grown faster. He imagines less of a drain of external profits, more domestic protection and production, and greater attention to technical training. The changes that were delayed until after 1947 would have been even more effective earlier on.[14] After the fact, then, the modernization brought about by European imperialism, especially if taken in moderation, can be seen as a net benefit, at least by an economist, and by the standard of maximum GDP growth. In any case, imperialism could not be taken in moderation, and it did not depart willingly.

Chaos in China

The best evidence for Maddison's view of the perils of independence is provided by China. The various rebellions, of which the Taiping Heavenly Kingdom was the largest and most threatening, were not unrelated to the aftereffects of the Opium War and China's successive confrontations with Europeans, but internal causes were important to both the spread of unrest and the difficulty of controlling it.[15] After some initial Schadenfreude over the emperor's distress, the British decided that they would rather deal with a weakened dynasty than with victorious rebels. The "Ever Victorious Army," led at one point by Charles "Chinese" Gordon, helped to defend Shanghai from the Taipings.[16] But the imperialists still took what they could. A Pekinese dog taken from the Old Summer Palace (圓明園 Yuanming Yuan) which was destroyed in 1860 was presented to Queen Victoria and

---

[14] Angus Maddison, "The Economic and Social Impact of Colonial Rule in India," chapter 3 of Maddison, *Class Structure and Economic Growth: India and Pakistan since the Moghuls* (New York: Norton, 1971).
[15] Platt, *Autumn in the Heavenly Kingdom*.
[16] Richard J. Smith, *Mercenaries and Mandarins: The Ever-Victorious Army in Nineteenth Century China* (Millwood, NY: KTO Press, 1978).

given the appropriate name of "Looty."[17] China's series of defeats reached its official military climax in the naval defeat by Japan in 1894–5 and its diplomatic nadir in the Empress Dowager's surreptitious support of the Boxer Rebellion in 1900. Thereafter the dynasty attempted to change course, but was overthrown in 1911. The Republic of China then attempted to get off the ground, but by 1915 the devolution of power to local military leaders led to the warlord era. Chiang Kai-shek's Northern Expedition in 1927 officially ended the warlord era, but he did so by amalgamating many of the warlords into his coalition. In any case, the growing resistance of the Communists and Japan's invasion and segmentation of Manchuria in 1931 continued the chaos. Only in 1949 was China effectively reunified by Mao Zedong and the Communist Party of China. Political chaos resulted in a failure to thrive economically. China produced less than two ounces of steel per person in 1929, compared to the American 700 pounds.[18]

In 1820 the Chinese economy was 110 percent of that of Western Europe. By 1870 the proportion dropped in half, to 55 percent – still significant, but declining and increasingly preoccupied with dynastic survival.[19] While China remained too big to become anyone's sole possession, all imperial powers took bits and pieces. The British colony of Hong Kong went through a series of expansions similar to those of Penang described earlier: Hong Kong Island in 1840, Kowloon in 1860, and finally the ninety-nine-year lease of the New Territories in 1898. Similar lease arrangements were made in the same year of 1898 by France in Guangzhou Bay (Kouang-Tchéou-Wan – Fort Bayard) and by Germany in Jiaozhou Bay (Kiautschou Bucht), centered on Qingdao. Meanwhile there were ninety-two treaty ports established between 1861 and 1917, many with judicial authority over their inhabitants. In 1926 there were thirty-two British courts in China.[20] There

---

[17] I owe this delightful detail to Ian Morris, *Why the West Rules – For Now* (New York: Farrar, Strauss, and Giroux, 2010).

[18] J. Bradford DeLong, Allan Aquino et al., *Slouching towards Utopia: An Economic History of the Twentieth Century* (New York: Basic Books, 2022), p. 124.

[19] Calculated from *Maddison Project Database 2020*. www.rug.nl/ggdc/historicaldevelopment/maddison/releases/maddison-project-database-2020?lang=en

[20] Catherine Ladds, "China and Treaty-Port Imperialism," in *The Encyclopedia of Empire* (New York: Wiley-Blackwell, 2016). https://doi.org/10.1002/9781118455074.wbeoe079

were also pressures at the borders. The Russians and the Japanese were in competition in the northeast, while Lord Curzon tried unsuccessfully to obtain approval from the British Foreign Office to make Tibet a protectorate after Francis Younghusband slaughtered the Tibetan army and occupied Lhasa in 1903–4.[21] Xinjiang was one of the venues for the "Great Game" between Britain and Russia, as both maneuvered in Central Asia.

An important aspect of China's forced openness was the export of Chinese as laborers as well as their increased migration into Southeast Asia. Britain and France forced the government to authorize the export of mass labor after the second Opium War[22] for unskilled labor projects throughout the world. Chinese were involved in the 1848 California gold rush and then employed in the construction of the transcontinental railroad. Domestically, however, the ironic effect of China's cheap labor was to reduce the need for labor-saving machinery. As Ian Morris points out, "As late as 1880 the up-front costs to open a mine with six hundred Chinese laborers were estimated as $4,272 – roughly the cost of a single steam pump."[23]

In the twentieth century, China's decline and the development of the Southeast Asian economies led to massive emigration into the urban areas of Southeast Asia and into domestic and regional commerce. The new urban Chinese became an identifiable and comparatively well-off intermediate class between the Europeans and the mostly rural indigenous populations. In Indonesia, the Chinese population grew as fast as the European population from 1870 to 1929, and while its income per capita was only 8 percent of the Dutch colonials, it was almost four times that of the Indonesians.[24] Chinese separateness from the indigenous population in Indonesia as well as from the Dutch was enforced by apartheid.[25] There were strong ties between the overseas

---

[21] Patrick French, *Younghusband: The Last Great Imperial Adventurer* (London: Harper, 1994), especially p. 224.
[22] Zhuang Guotu, "The Overseas Chinese: A Long History," *Unesco Courier* (April 2021). https://en.unesco.org/courier/2021-4/overseas-chinese-long-history
[23] Morris, *Why the West Rules – For Now*, p. 622.
[24] Calculated from Maddison, *World Economy*, p. 89.
[25] Deborah James and Albert Schrauwers, "An Apartheid of Souls: Dutch and Afrikaner Colonialism and its Aftermath in Indonesia and South Africa," *Itinerario* 27:3–4 (2003), pp. 49–80.

Chinese and their hometowns, and more generally to Chinese culture, and there was active support for Sun Yat Sen's efforts against the Qing dynasty and later for his KMT (GMD, Guomindang) party.

The Japanese Exception

Among the Pacific Asian countries Japan was the only one that excelled at distance learning from the West. The alert and self-assured autonomy that Japan had developed in its relations with China was redirected toward a new threat and opportunity. Japan's initial policy of tightly controlled access to the Dutch trading mission confined to Nagasaki from 1641 to 1853 allowed it to adopt some innovations and also to require the manner of its interactions to be on its own terms. Considering Dutch predatory behavior in its colonies, this was a crucial control. Japan's *rangaku* (Dutch learning 蘭学) kept it informed of practices and innovations in the West. After the visit by Commodore Perry in 1853, it was clear that more systemic adjustment was necessary, and the Meiji Restoration made possible a determined national effort. The redirection toward Western-style modernization was confirmed by the Iwakura Mission (岩倉使節団) of 1871–1873, a major visit by top statesmen and scholars to the United States and Europe.[26] They went dressed as Europeans, were received hospitably, and had the opportunity to visit factories and schools as well as meeting heads of state.

Part of the lessons learned from the West by Japan was the importance of international assertiveness. The Iwakura Mission was unsuccessful in its attempts to redress Japan's unequal treaties with the United States. However, Japan was more successful in influencing Korea, both as a model and as an alternative patron to China. Friction over Korea led to war with China in 1894–5, in which the modern ships and training of the Japanese navy were triumphant. The defeat was a great shock to China, but even more impressive to the Pacific Asian region was Japan's defeat of Russia in 1905. Reform leaders from around the region came to study the Japanese model of success, and Japan was especially proactive in reform assistance to China.[27]

---

[26] Ezra Vogel, *China and Japan: Facing History* (Cambridge, MA: Harvard University Press, 2019), pp. 73–76.
[27] Ibid., pp. 132–174.

Much of China's new vocabulary for reform, beginning with the rebranding of "change of mandate" (*geming* 革命) as "revolution," came from the Japanese.[28]

The militarization of Japanese politics after the First World War also followed a Western model, one sharpened by the simultaneous rise of fascism in Europe. Japan's initial concentration was on East Asia – Korea, Taiwan, and Manchuria – but with the announcement of the Greater East Asia Co-Prosperity Sphere in 1940 Japan attempted to subject all of Pacific Asia to its rule. The claim that it was rescuing Pacific Asia from the West was belied by the brutality and racism of Japanese control. Of course, these too had Western precedents, as well as simultaneous models in Mussolini's conquests of Libya and Ethiopia and the racist arrogance of Hitler's advances on the eastern front. Japan did briefly re-center Pacific Asia by becoming the common focus of attention, but its overextension and its antiphonal relationship to Western global modernization marked its centrality as an aberration. Japan's defeat in 1945 inaugurated a new era of increased globalization, but now centered on the United States rather than on the European imperialists.

Integrated Globalism and the American Imperium

The long half-century of American hegemony, from 1945 to 2008, was preceded by a long run-up of American strengthening capacities and increasing turbulence in Europe. In all likelihood, American hegemony will be succeeded by an even longer denouement in which the United States will remain the most important and best-armed wealthy state in an increasingly multinodal global system. Both before 1945 and after 2008 the United States was the most powerful country in the world, but nineteenth-century colonial splintering and European wars persisted until 1945, while after 2008 the uncertainties of American economic and political leadership, as well as the diversification of necessary points of attention in the global system, stimulated a general economic outlook that was still global but not univocally focused on the United States. In between 1945 and 2008 there were sixty-three years in which European splintering was replaced by an integrated

---

[28] Wang Gungwu, *China Reconnects: Joining a Deep-Rooted Past to a New World Order* (Singapore: World Scientific, 2019), pp. 69–72.

hub-and-spoke order with the US in the middle. This was true even for Pacific Asia, despite the emergence of communist regimes in China, Vietnam, Cambodia, Laos, and North Korea.

As the above Pacific Asian exceptions suggest, the American global wheel was neither totally inclusive nor perfectly round. There was, after all, a Cold War, with the Soviet Union and Eastern Europe on the other side, and a number of other states leaning in that direction at various times and to various degrees. There were also states, led by India, that professed non-alignment and that insulated their economies from global markets. But the American and Soviet sides were different in their attitudes toward globalization. The United States was inclusive and market-oriented; the Soviet Union's approach was that of a state command economy aimed at self-sufficiency. To others, the Soviet Union did not offer an alternative globalization, but rather membership in an exclusive alternative to globalization under its leadership. Market-based globalization won the Cold War.

Even if we ignore its missing spokes, the American global wheel did not run as smoothly as it imagined. As Amitav Acharya[29] has argued, the complacent view of the liberal world order formalized by hegemonic stability theory[30] overlooked its blind spots. Acharya notes that the liberal world order was neither as universal, nor as consensual, nor as benevolent, nor as exclusively American as it assumed, and it ignored the political disruptions that democracy could produce. It is particularly important to recall these flaws as nostalgia grows about the passing of American globalism. The system's flaws do not prove that the system did not exist, but a more realistic picture of its processes is a better guide to future possibilities.

New Leadership, New Institutions, and New Sovereignties

The modernization experience of the United States has been the opposite of China's. Although producing only 7 percent of Western Europe's GDP in 1870, the US enjoyed vast frontiers of opportunity, achieving 56 percent of Western Europe's GDP by 1900. America's

---

[29] Amitav Acharya, *The End of American World Order* (New York: Polity, 2014), especially chapter 3, "The Myth of Liberal Hegemony," pp. 33–58.
[30] See for example John Ikenberry, *Liberal Leviathan: The Origins, Crisis, and Transformation of the American World Order* (Princeton: Princeton University Press, 2011).

insulation from Europe's wars enabled it to attain 87 percent by 1920 and finally to surpass Europe in 1950. With its wartime growth and Europe's devastation, the United States reached 28 percent of global GDP. In 2010 the United States was still ahead of Europe, but it had dropped to 17 percent of global GDP.[31]

The defeat of Germany and Japan and the weakening of European colonial controls presented the United States with a situation of default global leadership, and it adapted to the new challenges creatively and successfully.[32] The formation of the United Nations, the World Bank, the International Bank for Reconstruction and Development, the International Monetary Fund, the General Agreement on Tariffs and Trade (GATT), and the Marshall Plan provided elements of a much stronger central structure to the world political economy and at the same time embedded the American position of central and coordinated leadership. With the success of independence movements against European colonialism, these international institutions stimulated a situation of integrated globalization centered on the United States.

Security leadership was more problematic. On the one hand, the creation of the North Atlantic Treaty Organization (NATO) in 1949 was an effective response to European concerns about Stalin's suppression of Eastern Europe and the need for collective security. On the other hand, American security policy tended toward a simplistic view that good and evil were locked in a mortal struggle. Deliberations on specific global situations were reduced to how they affected the global balance with the Soviet Union. Compromise was impossible, and any measure that might advance the cause of the righteous, however interventionist, was justified. As a result, the "hot wars" – Korea and Vietnam – and other military interventions by the United States were attempted, and alliances became structures of compliance to American policy rather than consultative security arrangements.

The three unquestioned pillars of the ideology of American intervention were the belief in the benevolent superiority of the United States, the conviction that market-led development would produce cooperative democracies, and that resistance was either the symptom

---

[31] All data is in terms of "real GDP," estimated purchasing power parity (PPP). Calculated from *Maddison Project Database 2020*.

[32] John Ikenberry, *After Victory: Institutions, Strategic Restraint, and the Rebuilding of Order after Major Wars* (Princeton: Princeton University Press, 2001).

of an irrational fear of modernization or the duping of ignorant people by the communist agents. Development assistance went hand in hand with fighting communism. Communism was seen as a disease of underdevelopment, to be fought mercilessly but whose ultimate cure would lie in the prosperity and democracy that were the inevitable results of market development. American joy at seeing Deng Xiaoping's reforms in the 1980s was the final expression of these assumptions.

Independence and Re-association in Pacific Asia

The first decade after World War Two saw the creation and strengthening of sovereign nations throughout Pacific Asia. However, for the first time these states were looking directly at one another rather than through the fingers of colonial (including Japanese) masters. In Northeast Asia, the subordination of Japanese and Korean security concerns to the United States left a dimension of external control that buffered regional interactions, but in Southeast Asia, new nationalisms speaking different colonial languages faced one another across boundaries that could be disputed. There was little regional connectivity. Moreover, Thailand, Philippines, and Taiwan hosted American troops during the American war in Vietnam. Korean, Thai, and Philippine troops fought with the Americans, while China and the Soviet Union supported North Vietnam. Meanwhile there were riots and government actions against ethnic Chinese as well as various regional resistance movements against the post-colonial governments. In the 1960s, Southeast Asia was a cockpit, not a region.

In 1967 the leaders of Indonesia, Thailand, Malaysia, Singapore, and the Philippines formed the Association of Southeast Asian Nations (ASEAN) in order to cope with the shared problems of interventions in the region, intraregional disputes, and domestic unrest.[33] ASEAN could have become an anti-communist alliance, especially since all five of its original members were collaborating with the US military in various ways. Instead, ASEAN did not invite either the Hanoi or the Saigon governments to its founding meeting. Though it was unsuccessful in persuading neutral Burma and Cambodia to join, from the beginning ASEAN's mission was to become an inclusive, region-wide

---

[33] Alice Ba, *(Re)Negotiating East and Southeast Asia* (Stanford, CA: Stanford University Press, 2009).

association of sovereign members willing to work with their neighbors. But Southeast Asia was a region cleft by the American war in Vietnam, followed by Vietnam's alliance with the Soviet Union, and China's emergence as an active neighbor. It was three decades before ASEAN completed its regional membership.[34]

Despite its regional ambitions, ASEAN was no NATO. Its central institutions were minimal, and there were few membership obligations other than expected participation in a plethora of meetings at all levels. Since ASEAN functioned on a consensus basis, its official statements were bland, and common plans moved slowly. With each major change in the regional context – the end of the Indochina war in 1975, the China-Vietnam war in 1979, the resolution of that war in 1991, the admission of the poorer countries in the 1990s – skeptical external observers expected it to fall apart. Instead, it grew and flourished, becoming the credible public face of Southeast Asia. While a succession of exceptionally gifted statesmen from various member states played crucial roles in ASEAN's survival, the consensual and communicative process embedded in ASEAN was the institutional key to success.

Ironically, the "ASEAN way" of inclusive consensus enabled ASEAN to become a leader in international initiatives at the regional level and even beyond. ASEAN became the venue for broader efforts to involve other countries in peaceful cooperation. It initiated the ASEAN Regional Forum (ARF) in 1994 for the discussion of issues of peace and security, and ASEAN provides regular forums for Pacific Asia ministerial discussions and contacts through the ASEAN plus 3 initiative (including China, Korea, and Japan), begun in 1997, and the East Asian Summit inaugurated in 2005. The Regional Comprehensive Economic Partnership (RCEP), whose fifteen members account for one-third of the world's population and GDP and which went into effect on January 1, 2022, was an ASEAN initiative. ASEAN is successful in its international outreach precisely because it is not an intimidating or demanding organization.

Beyond ASEAN and its efforts, the Pacific Asian region was not successful in specifically regional activity, although by 1990 all countries except North Korea were increasingly active participants in the global

---

[34] Nguyen Vu Tung, *Flying Blind: Vietnam's Decision to Join ASEAN* (Singapore: ISEAS Publishing, 2021).

economy. There was an American attempt to form a NATO-like alliance, the Southeast Asia Treaty Organization (SEATO) in 1954, but it was essentially stillborn. The Asian allies of the United States – Japan, Korea, Philippines, and Thailand – actively supported the American war in Vietnam, but there was persistent hostility between Korea and Japan resulting from Japanese colonization. Japan became a major investor in the rest of Pacific Asia, but primarily in order to outsource the labor-intensive stages of its production for the global market. As a former American colony, the Philippines has a "special relationship" with the US, sometimes tense, as demonstrated by the removal of American bases in 1991, but with a strong and persisting people-to-people tie. ASEAN's efforts at soft inclusivity within an inclusive and global framework was the major contribution of the post-colonial era to regional configuration in Pacific Asia.

Asymmetric Perceptions of Western Centrality

The sharp connectivity of Western modernization produced modalities of asymmetric relationships quite different from those of the previous era. They were both more asymmetric and more intense. China's centrality to northern nomads was sometimes reduced to the basic regional configuration of wealth versus mobility, with the balance of power occasionally being on the side of the periphery. But the West's preponderance of power and active use of it to obtain its wishes was key to its relationships. Asymmetry was no longer an exchange of autonomy for deference. Autonomy was denied to colonies, and post-colonial governments (as well as the earlier non-colonial ones) remained unequal sovereignties vis-à-vis the United States. And deference was not enough for colonial powers. They wanted profit from their colonies, not just peaceful relations. The US in the post-colonial era was rather closer to requiring deference, but it was not a relationship of thin connectivity. Moreover, the US was the superpower underwriting the global system. Globalization was an enforced configuration, a hegemonic system.

With power playing the central role in Western centrality, an asymmetric relationship became one of superior and subordinate. This could be a continuing relationship as long as the power differential remained, and thus "normal" in that sense, but it is a very different normalcy from the ritualized acknowledgment of asymmetric agency in premodern Pacific Asia. The colonial superior had more to gain from domination, but it was at risk from the rise of relative power in the colony, not simply from direct challenge. It is a double risk, because what it drew from the colony formed part of its relative strength in the European theater of great power rivalry. So England, for example, was not at mortal threat from India, but its loss of India might put it at mortal threat vis-à-vis Germany. Meanwhile the colony did not have autonomy to defend, but the modernizing transformations of becoming globally centered provided a variety of opportunities as well as risks to its inhabitants.

Meanwhile the development of the era of Western modernization shows two broad trends that are initially complementary but ultimately in tension. The first trend is the divergence in life chances – health, education, and productivity – between "the West and the Rest." The divergence is due in large part to the endogenous dynamics of modernization, but it is also a result of what the West took from the Rest. The other trend is that productivity of the new globalized periphery also increases. Life chances dip for many, because health and education lag far behind, but the imperial powers profited from colonial production and so they vigorously encouraged it. Ultimately, however, increased production affected the power realities in the colonies, and the distraction of European wars afforded the opportunity for autonomy. Still, the economic divergence between developed and developing countries expanded – until the twenty-first century. As we shall see in Chapter 5, the rise of demographic power is now posing challenges to the primacy of power based on wealth.

From Above

From the standpoint of the West, victory by the preponderance of power justified the right to rule and demonstrated cultural superiority. While there were always critical voices at home, they modified the edges of governance rather than its general direction.[35] The basic driver behind decolonization was not the conscience of the West but the growing resistance of the Rest.[36] Similarly, the corollary of the

---

[35] See Platt, *Autumn in the Heavenly Kingdom*, for the variety of domestic opinion.
[36] Caroline Elkins, *Legacy of Violence: A History of the British Empire* (New York: Knopf, 2022).

claim that the United States was "the indispensable nation" was its willingness to correct threats to its view of the proper world order by means of aid, "small wars," covert action, and sanctions. The consciously sharp connectivity of European imperialism was replaced by the benevolent parochial universalism of the "city on the hill." For most countries most of the time, participation in a relatively predictable world order was satisfactory, even if its design and control were not a matter of either individual or collective choice.

Traditional China and the modern West were equally complacent about their superiority. China's basic attitude was usually to induce civilization on the periphery by its claims of good behavior, but the West was actively engaged in bringing progress and prosperity to backward, and later, underdeveloped, and still later, developing lands. While tribute missions to Beijing were a core symbol of Beijing's centrality, the physical presence in the country of Western missionaries, merchants, officials, and armies asserted Western centrality. Part of the interest in transformation was the exploration for raw materials that could feed developed country industries and their profits. Raw materials declined in relative importance for the United States as advances in transportation made possible the outsourcing of labor-intensive production, and advances in communication made possible the shift to global financial services.

The European colonial powers and the United States both had great power distractions that affected their asymmetric relations with the "Rest." For the European powers, it was competition among themselves. For the United States it was the Cold War. For both, the question of a relative advantage or disadvantage in their great power rivalry was decisive in managing relations with the periphery. In general, then, the "from above" side of asymmetric relationships in this era was characterized by superiority, the presumed right of intrusiveness, and distraction by more important symmetric rivalries.

The View from Below

The enforced and exploited subordination that was explicit in the colonies created communities of national outrage. There was a basic urge to defend national identity, even though to some extent the contours of that identity had been shaped by the intruders. Nevertheless, the wealth and power demonstrated by the West were deeply impressive.

Thus, besides radical critique and resistance, there was also collaboration and the transformation of world views.[37] Despite elegiac nostalgia for the past and searching through collective memory for authentic identity, national liberation movements borrowed the goal of future transformative progress from their experience of imposed modernization. The appeal of the Russian revolution and the Communist International combined these contrary reactions of resistance and forward transformation. Communism was radically critical of imperialism, but claimed to be the next stage of history, not a step back, more modern than modernization. As Lenin put it, "Communism is Soviet [workers' councils] power plus electrification of the whole country."[38]

With the achievement of sovereignty, the defeat of Japan, and the securing of South Korea, most of Pacific Asia made a relatively peaceful transition from competitive imperialism to the hub-and-spoke centrality of American globalism. There were hot wars in Korea and Indochina, and China was isolated, but for most countries most of the time compliance with American Cold War strategy was the entry price for participation in more integrated globalism. Increasingly American centrality began to resemble a more intense version of the old Chinese *tianxia* (all under heaven). With globalization American soft power was everywhere, its consumer population became the final focus of global value chains, and it had a core financial role in the system of global production – a version of the 3 Ps. As with China, the normalization of American centrality did not produce grateful willingness and mutual understanding on the part of the periphery, but the periphery did depend on the system anchored by the United States for its global orientation.

China's 3 Ps Transformed

Strange as it might seem, traditional China's attributes of presence, population, and production that supported the resilience of its centrality in Pacific Asia for two millennia lost their salience in the modern era.

---

[37] Sarah Womack, *Colonialism and the Collaborationist Agenda: Pham Quynh, Print Culture, and the Politics of Persuasion in Colonial Vietnam* (PhD dissertation, University of Michigan, 2003). www.proquest.com/openview/28a0b6b265daaf4b63facb33200e7c8e/1?pq-origsite=gscholar&cbl=18750&diss=y

[38] V. I. Lenin, "All Power to the Soviets!" *Pravda* 99, July 18, 1917. www.marxists.org/archive/lenin/works/1917/jul/18.htm

This was due in part to China's decline, but even more importantly it was due to the dissolution of Pacific Asia as a region under the impact of European imperialism. In the case of colonies, the Western powers simply reached in and forcibly turned heads around to face them. But in general, the manifest wealth and power of Europe distracted attention from China. Siam, not a colony, decided to discontinue its tribute missions in 1855.[39] By 1880 China was not the most important concern of any of its neighbors. The configuration of attention had shifted to global. There was no regional configuration except for the Japanese empire of 1940–5. China had become a fellow sufferer in Pacific Asia, but not a center. China's 3 Ps had lost their salience.

With the founding of the People's Republic of China in 1949 China had put its own house in order, but it was both excluded from and cautious about the increasing American-led globalization of the rest of the region. Reciprocally, the neighbors were increasingly alienated by China's isolationist radicalism, and especially by the government's suspicious hostility during the Cultural Revolution toward Chinese with relatives abroad. The logic of American anti-communism was especially appealing to South Korea and Japan, in part because of their acute dependence on the American security umbrella, but also because the fear of a domino effect was especially vivid to them. Meanwhile, China's radicalism stimulated activities against ethnic Chinese throughout Southeast Asia. Relations began to normalize in the 1970s, but connectivity did not become significant until Deng Xiaoping's policies of reform and openness in the 1980s. By the 1990s China was increasingly becoming a "significant other" to its neighbors, but the global order remained more important than the Pacific Asian neighborhood.

Presence

China's presence in the Pacific Asia region diminished with the increasing exposure of its parts to the West. The final tests were the desperate appeals of Vietnam for assistance against the French and of Korea for assistance against the newly Westernized Japanese. The

---

[39] Jack Wills, "Functional, Not Fossilized: Qing Tribute Relations with Đại Việt (Vietnam) and Siam (Thailand), 1700–1820," *T'oung Pao*, 2012, Second Series, 98:4/5 (2012), pp. 439–478, here p. 453.

former led to the loss of the Sino-French War in 1885, which certified the end of Chinese claims to suzerainty in the Treaty of Tientsin, and the latter culminated in the Sino-Japanese War ten years later. The Treaty of Shimonoseki in 1895 ended China's tributary relationship with Korea as well as ceding Taiwan to Japan. Ten years after that, Russia's attempt to add Korea to its sphere of influence led to the Russo-Japanese War. China became the backwater to a globalized Pacific Asia, not even a colony. The numerous treaty ports provided storefronts for 9,500 foreign firms, but no general or effective organization of national development.[40] With the Japanese invasion beginning in 1931, and especially with the Nanjing Massacre of 1937, China achieved global presence as a victim, but newsreel attention brought sympathy rather than respect.

The dialectics of history continued. H. B. Morse, Commissioner of the Chinese Customs Service, distinguished historian of China, and "adopted grandfather" of John King Fairbank, who himself had a vast academic progeny, was one of the most insightful participant-observers of the end stages of the Chinese imperial order.[41] He noted the following in the preface to his 1908 book, *The Trade and Administration of the Chinese Empire*:

No attempt is made [here] to forecast the future, or even to refer to the revolution which, under the name of reform, has been begun. The development of many centuries is to be recast, and in a year or a generation, according as the pace is forced or not, it will assume an unaccustomed garb.[42]

The fall of the Qing better fit Morse's expectations than the eventual victory of Mao Zedong's rural revolution, but Mao's success was premised on China's status as a global orphan, its inert rural population without effective governance, and its inconsequential production. The absence of the traditional 3 Ps was a prerequisite for the incubation of a modern but village-level revolution. If China had continued to be the regional center the neighbors would have taken advantage of

---

[40] Ladds, "China and Treaty-Port Imperialism," p. 5.
[41] John King Fairbank, Martha Henderson Coolidge, and Richard J. Smith, *H. B. Morse: Customs Commissioner and Historian of China* (Lexington: University Press of Kentucky, 1995).
[42] H. B. Morse, *The Trade and Administration of the Chinese Empire* (London: Longmans, Green and Co., 1908), p. 13.

its distress. While the mobilization of the villages was analogous to earlier peasant uprisings, this was a *geming* in the new sense of revolution rather than a righteous uprising demanding a change of mandate. If China's production had been significant on a global scale it is easy to imagine that there would have been more international involvement. Imagine if China in the 1930s had been a major source of the world's oil. Then the Middle Kingdom would have been treated like the Middle (Eastern) Kingdom. But even without the 3 Ps, a successful rural revolution was not inevitable. Indeed, it might be considered the least likely major event of the twentieth century.

The establishment of the PRC impressed the overseas Chinese in Southeast Asia, but its membership in the Communist bloc alienated the non-communist regional majority. While Zhou Enlai's diplomacy at the Bandung Conference in 1955 led to cautious handshakes with non-aligned third world leaders,[43] the radicalization of Chinese politics from 1957 onwards increasingly alienated the region. In any case, the American hot war in Vietnam and increasing globalization tightened the region's hub-and-spoke relationships. The region's concerns relaxed somewhat with Nixon's 1972 Shanghai visit. With Deng Xiaoping's policies the region began to pursue opportunities, and after the Tiananmen incident of 1989 Deng's resolution of the conflict with Vietnam and new emphasis on regional relations were welcomed.[44] China's support of the value of its currency and of the Hong Kong dollar during the Asian Financial Crisis of 1997 deeply impressed the neighbors. China's economic strength was in stark contrast to the vulnerability of the other Pacific Asian economies, and China's support contrasted with the cold opportunism displayed by the World Bank's "Washington Consensus" and by the Japanese.[45] From this point China became a significant other to its neighbors, and to some extent it buffered their exposure to the fluctuations of the global market and of American policy, but Pacific Asia was not yet a region and China was not its center.

---

[43] Amitav Acharya and See Seng Tan, eds, *Bandung Revisited: The Legacy of the 1955 Asian-African Conference for International Order* (Singapore: NUS Press, 2008).

[44] Brantly Womack, "China and Southeast Asia: Asymmetry, Leadership and Normalcy," *Pacific Affairs* 76:3 (2003–4), pp. 529–548.

[45] Wimonkan Kosumas, *Half a Hegemon: Japan's Leadership in Southeast Asia* (PhD dissertation, University of Virginia, 2000).

Population

It is important to recall why population was a basic factor in China's traditional regional centrality. It could be mobilized into large armies and could complete large construction projects like the Great Wall and the Grand Canal. Its intensive agriculture could support urbanization and commerce. But it was difficult to govern, either by domestic or by conquest dynasties. In the modern era China's population dropped from one-third of global population in 1820 to one-quarter in 1900. The contrast with Western Europe was even greater. In 1820 China's population was 165 percent of Europe's, but by 1900 it had dropped to 36 percent.[46] These were the dramatic effects of war and crowded agricultural resources in China versus the improved life chances in Europe.

Nevertheless, the major changes in the salience of China's population in the imperial era were that the armies that it might mobilize were not effective in modern warfare, and in any case were mostly employed within China to fight first against rebels, and then in the warlord era against other warlords. Non-military mobilization was also a problem. There was insufficient coordination and capital for infrastructure projects. As Sun Yat Sen described it, China was "a sheet of loose sand."[47] China's population was seen as inert, and too poor to be a major market except for basic consumer goods. As the British historian R. H. Tawney famously put it in 1932, "the position of the rural population is that of a man standing up to his neck in water, so that even a ripple is sufficient to drown him."[48] In this situation, a greater population only produces a greater calamity, and makes progress more difficult.

Since the rural revolution that made the PRC possible was based on the mobilization of the peasantry, Mao had a more optimistic view of population increase, claiming that "More people mean a greater ferment of ideas, more enthusiasm and more energy. Never before have the masses of the people been so inspired, so militant and so daring

---

[46] Calculated from the *Maddison Project Database*.
[47] Sun Yat-Sen, *San Min Chu I: The Three Principles of the People*, trans. Frank W. Price, ed., L. T. Chen (Shanghai: China Committee, Institute of Pacific Relations, 1927), p. 189.
[48] R. H. Tawney, *Land and Labour in China* (New York: Harcourt Brace, 1932).

as at present."[49] He said this in 1958 on the eve of the Great Leap Forward, the greatest man-made famine in history, but despite those losses China entered a population boom. While it took China over a hundred years to go from 400 million to 500 million, its population doubled between 1950 and 1988.[50] From the early 1970s demographic policy changed to discouraging population growth, culminating in the one-child policy initiated in 1980. The boom years of Deng's reforms were famous for their "demographic dividend," the high proportion of working-age population to total population because of birth restrictions, but the high birth rate of the pre-reform years produced a demographic deficit of the same magnitude as the subsequent dividend.[51]

Clearly China was no longer a sheet of loose sand. In 1980 the People's Liberation Army (PLA) reached four million personnel, though its size has been continually reduced since then and in 2019 stood at two million. Non-military mobilization for major projects tragically overreached itself in the Great Leap Forward, but the habit of reaching for the megaphone and concentrating attention on an urgent project continues, as China's zero-Covid policy demonstrates.[52] The challenge of governance remains immense, though the major problems of social chaos faced by the PRC have been caused by its own policies rather than by the breakdown of its control.

While 1949 was a watershed for China's population, it did not have much impact on regional configuration. The PLA was structured for defense, and its brief forays into India in 1962 and into Vietnam in 1979 were brief and localized. Its weaknesses for modern warfare were demonstrated in Vietnam and more decisively, though at a distance, by the collapse of Iraq in the Persian Gulf War. From the 1990s the PLA budget was increased while its size was reduced. The major industrial projects started by the Russians strengthened the core of China's capacity but were not for export. The vast increase in life expectancy and basic education that occurred before the reform era were also prerequisites for China's takeoff but did not attract external attention.

---

[49] Mao Zedong, "Introducing a Co-operative" (April 15, 1958), in *Selected Works of Mao Zedong*, vol. 8. www.marxists.org/reference/archive/mao/selected-works/volume-8/index.htm
[50] Calculated from the *Maddison Project Database*.
[51] Arthur Kroeber, *China's Economy* (Oxford: Oxford University Press, 2016), pp. 163–179.
[52] Peter Hessler, "Life on Lockdown in China," *New Yorker*, March 23, 2020.

Production

The collapse of China's production during the era of Western modernization is best illustrated by two facts. In 1965 China finally achieved the level of per capita production that it had in the year 1000, a millennium before.[53] The second fact is less dramatic but telling. In the early 1900s Mongolia began to import its tea from Russian Georgia.[54] The northern tea trade had begun with the exchange of Chinese tea for Mongolian horses at Kalgan (now Zhangjiakou, Hebei) in 1572, and the trade had been extended to Russia after the Treaty of Nerchinsk in 1689, and was formalized as a trade route by the Treaty of Kiakhta in 1727. In order to save its silver, Russia traded wheat and industrial textiles for tea, and the border town of Kiakhta reached its apogee in 1824. But then the price of overland tea was undercut by seaborne tea carried by Britain, and later tea began to be produced in Georgia.[55] To make a long fact short, even on an inland border, even with an established traditional export and an established trade route, China had lost its market. If even Mongolians were looking elsewhere for their basic beverage, then China had truly lost its regional centrality.

From the Opium War in 1840 onwards, China began losing control of its foreign trade, and of its foreign relations more generally. The bulk of China's production was necessarily the subsistence agriculture of its large population, and it was not in a position to export basic crops. Its commercial forte had been sophisticated artisanal products, especially tea, silk, and porcelain. As H. B. Morse's 1908 study of Chinese trade showed, from 1864 to 1904 Chinese silk exports were roughly comparable to its opium imports, and by 1903 China had gone from being virtually the only silk exporter to only one-fourth of the global market, comparable to Japan and Italy. Tea exports did not increase, and British tea consumption shifted from almost all Chinese in 1864 to almost all Indian in 1905. Ceramics had disappeared from the enumeration of exports. China exported raw cotton and imported cotton goods, 40 percent of its total imports in 1905.[56] As Morse notes, "From 1860...the foreign powers have been masters

---

[53] *Maddison Project Database.*
[54] Martha Avery, *The Tea Road: China and Russia Meet across the Steppe* (Beijing: China Intercontinental Press, 2004), p. 15.
[55] Ibid.
[56] Morse, *The Trade and Administration of the Chinese Empire*, pp. 270, 295, 296.

of the situation, and foreign trade has been conducted on conditions laid down by them and not by China."⁵⁷ China's deficit in exports was met to a great extent by remittances by overseas Chinese to their kin in coastal cities and villages, but such private efforts were not enough to prevent stagnation.

From 1949 the domestic picture of Chinese production changed rapidly, but it had little effect on the region or beyond. With the staggering exception of the Great Leap Forward years, agricultural production went up, but it was within a cellular economy aimed at self-sufficiency, not commerce. Fujian Province sacrificed its famous mountainside tea fields to grow more rice. Initially the Russians helped in developing core industries, but after 1960 China was on its own, and it tried to develop a "third front" of industry in interior provinces.⁵⁸ Greater pragmatism in the 1970s led to some improvements, but the marketization of China – domestic and external – began with Deng Xiaoping's reforms in the 1980s. Although rates of growth were impressive, both in terms of GDP and trade, the starting points were quite low. China's per capita income did not surpass that of the lowest four Southeast Asian states until 1988, and despite its population advantage, its GDP did not equal ASEAN's until 1992.⁵⁹ In any case, both China and ASEAN had their trading eyes set on the American consumer market, not on one another.

The 1997 Asian Financial Crisis began a golden decade in relations between China and Southeast Asia. Despite also suffering losses in the crisis, China had displayed the solidity of its economy. China's economy reached the size of Japan's in 2000 in purchasing power parity terms, and by 2008 it was already twice Japan's size.⁶⁰ More important than the size comparisons, China's global and regional trade has exploded since joining the World Trade Organization (WTO) in December 2001. From 2000 to 2008 China's goods exports grew at an average annual rate of 22 percent, while the US averaged 5 percent. China was becoming a major global player in a globalized region. It

---

⁵⁷ Ibid., p. 282.
⁵⁸ Barry Naughton, "The Third Front," *China Quarterly* 155 (1988), pp. 351–386.
⁵⁹ Both in PPP terms. Calculated from International Monetary Fund (IMF), *World Economic Outlook*. www.imf.org/en/Publications/SPROLLs/world-economic-outlook-databases#sort=%40imfdate%20descending
⁶⁰ Calculated from ibid.

stood shoulder to shoulder with its neighbors in supplying global markets, and its shoulders were getting very big indeed.

Conclusion: Westernization, Modernization, and the Pacific Asia Region

In Chinese discourse in the 1920s, the terms "Westernization" (西方化) and "modernization" (现代化) were used interchangeably.[61] This is hardly surprising since it was a complex experience that came from the outside and was transformative. But we can distinguish between Westernization as the configuration of globalization, and modernization as its transformative content. Both are facing a watershed of qualitative change in the present era. While Pacific Asia is not the only region affected by both, the effects were profound and the prospective changes equally challenging.

While China treated its periphery as outsiders, the West treated the Rest as subjects, first literally in the colonial era and afterwards as lesser polities with no proper path other than following the leader. Traditional China did not treat its periphery as equals, but it was aware of the agency of the periphery and of the limits of its own agency within their internal affairs. Hence the policies of thin connectivity. Colonization was premised on the denial of agency. The American imperium encouraged agency as long as it moved toward compliance with US foreign policy and more generally with the American model, but agency in any other direction was suspect and sanctioned.

Westernization was a forced configuration of a global order. It did not add a new global layer to the previous regional configuration of Pacific Asia. Rather, like an axe hitting ice, its sharp connectivity splintered the region's existing thin connectivity. Suddenly Sino-centric Pacific Asia became history, both as Sino-centric, and as a region. Except for the large increase of overseas Chinese in Southeast Asia and the Japanese presence in Korea and Taiwan, there was little intraregional connectivity before the Japanese empire in 1940–5. Westernization was a common experience, but it was not a specifically regional one. After decolonization, ASEAN began building a sense of

---

[61] Yu Keping, "Culture and Modernity in Chinese Intellectual Discourse," in *Democracy is a Good Thing* (Washington: Brookings, 2009), pp. 93–113, here p. 96.

regional community in six countries of Southeast Asia, and then Japan and later Korea and finally China developed regional trade and investment networks, but the focus remained on the global configuration centered on the United States.

The basic problem with forced connectivity is that coercion implies a lack of common interests. Hence globalization on these terms is not a global community of interests but rather global hegemony. The postcolonial centrality of the United States is different in that there is the presumption that the predictability of the system is in the interest of all, but its stability is still underwritten by hegemony. The assumption that a preponderance of power is necessary for stable asymmetric relationships implies that ultimately the agency of the periphery must be constrained, if not denied.

The experience of the twentieth century provides lessons about the instability of hegemony. The colonies became powerful enough to frustrate their step-mother countries, and the frightening and exhausting experience of the Second World War was as important as American sagacity in inspiring the design of a softer and more inclusive hegemonic system. Within that system the periphery has now become stronger and more interconnected. It is no longer one of a big hub and isolated spokes, but rather a global pattern of actors with varieties of connectivity choices and capacities. Trying to preserve supreme American power and control now is as fatuous as the Chinese emperor trying to preserve Chinese centrality in the nineteenth century, and it is considerably more dangerous.

Despite Western intrusion and domination, the transformational changes brought on by modernity were and are generally accepted. Resistance tended to be against force and inequality rather than a rejection of modernity itself.[62] Moreover, there was a growing awareness of interacting in a global community, a fundamental transformation of traditional horizons and to some extent of traditional identities. No one in any Asian village would ask in 2008, as Jiaqing might have in 1820, "what is a globe?"

Since developed countries provide examples of best practices for developing countries as well as external markets and capital, it should

---

[62] The existential complexities of colonial hybridization of cultures are classically detailed in Nirad Chaudhury, *The Autobiography of an Unknown Indian* (London: Macmillan, 1951), and Pramoedya Ananta Toer, *The Buru Quartet* (1980–88).

not be surprising that the 500 years of increasing divergence in life chances between the West and the Rest has reached a watershed in this century. As Chapter 5 will argue, China may be the leading example of the growth of demographic power, but it is a more general trend. But the state-led governance that is appropriate for catch-up development becomes more problematic as the gap is reduced. Moreover, it is increasingly the case that global challenges face all countries regardless of level of development, both strategic problems like environmental change and global warming, and immediate problems such as the management of Covid. These raise questions of appropriate global governance that challenge the assumptions of hegemonic sharp connectivity, but they are issues at the regional level as well.

Commentary
Wu Yu-Shan

Professor Brantly Womack encapsulates Pacific Asia's long history by dividing it into three periods: continuous centering, decentering, and recentering. For each historical period, he talks about China's presence, population, and production (3 Ps), the asymmetric relation between the center and the periphery, and different modes of relational connectivity (thin, sharp, and thick). With these important dimensions, Womack captures the essence of the three historical periods. In the following discussion, I will apply his analytical framework and probe deeper into the dynamics of evolution of the Pacific Asian international system.

The centering, decentering, and recentering of Pacific Asia actually reflects China's power. China's relation with its neighbors and with nations outside Pacific Asia are all based on China's power. The Chinese culture of course is important in influencing China's relation with other nations, and so it seems that we should not simply concentrate on power per se and limit ourselves to a realist perspective. However, the Chinese culture itself was formed during centuries of China's hegemony in Pacific Asia. It is thus impossible to separate power and culture. Of the two, power is the base and culture grows out of it.

How China perceives itself and how China is perceived by its neighbors, and by countries outside Asia, are also determined by China's power. Today, the rising tension between the West and China has more to do with China's rising power than with anything else, as the nature of China's political system and ideology have not changed much since the reform and open-door policies were adopted in the 1980s, and yet Sino-Western relationships are witnessing a sea change as China is rapidly rising to challenge the US hegemony. The tension between China and the West is the direct result of "power transition," or the Thucydides Trap, a process in which an existing hegemon is challenged by a rising power. Hence power is the essence of international relations in Pacific Asia.

How is China's power constituted? Among the 3 Ps, China's population is more or less a constant. Although it fluctuated over time, both in absolute terms and in relation to other population centers in the world (it dropped from one-third of global population in 1820 to one-quarter in 1900), China's population size has remained the largest among nations, and has dwarfed its Asian neighbors. Hence the variation of the Chinese power is to be found elsewhere. Presence is important, but it may reflect the Chinese power more than determine that power, and thus constitute a dependent variable, not a determinant. Among the 3 Ps, productivity is indeed the core of power. Then the question boils down to what determines productivity. Institutions are arguably the most important factor in raising productivity, and through that, augmenting national power. In this sense, the centering, decentering, and recentering of Pacific Asia are basically determined by whether China can adopt a system that raises its productivity, a set of politico-economic institutions that can rapidly modernize the country's economic base.

Four Modernization Routes

Now let's take a closer look at the period of modernization and decentering of Pacific Asia covered in this chapter. When the multipolar competitive Westphalian system of the West met the hierarchical China-centered system of the East, initially there were only some minor encroachments on the Chinese system by the Portuguese, the Spaniards, and the Dutch in the sixteenth through the mid-nineteenth century. Industrialization in Europe then made a huge difference. From the mid-nineteenth century on, the West led by the British came not as merchants, missionaries, arms dealers, but as conquerors. As the history of the encounters of the two worlds clearly shows, from the very beginning it was the size of their technology and thus the productivity gap that determined the relation between the West and the East, Europe and Asia, Westphalian system and Sinic order. The great Chinese empire was brought to its knees after several humiliating defeats in the latter half of the nineteenth century, and it was lucky for China that it was not directly partitioned into colonies, but only spheres of influence dominated by different Western powers. Before the Chinese learned how to modernize itself, to raise its technological level, to increase its productivity to near the West, and with all that of course to build a modern army, China could not expect to reverse its relation with the West and regain its dominant position in Pacific Asia.

The balance of power between China and the West hinged on institutions. There are four modernization routes in Pacific Asia, each with its ideal and institution. The first one is renovation of the old system, of which Japan's Meiji Restoration was a success, while Wuxu Reform of 1895 in China, the "Hundred Days Reform," was a failure. The second route is liberal democratic republic, an ideal that inspired Sun Yat Sen and the revolutionaries to found the Republic of China, but rendered unrealizable in the following years of warlordism. The third is modernizing authoritarianism, as represented by the post-1924 Kuomintang (KMT). The fourth route is state socialism, or communism that was championed by the Chinese Communist Party (CCP).

By ending the Qing dynasty, the Xinhai Revolution of 1911 spelled the end of the renovation approach, and the ineffective May Fourth Movement of 1919 was the last gasp of liberalism. After May Fourth, liberals flocked to modernizing authoritarianism and communism. The duel between these two routes of modernization occupied the center stage of modern Chinese history in the following decades. Although the KMT's modernizing authoritarianism held sway after the completion of Chiang Kai-shek's successful Northern Expedition that ended warlordism, and during the "Golden Decade" (1928–37), the CCP's state socialism resurged during the anti-Japanese War (1937–45). The Chinese Civil War ended in 1949 with the KMT retreating to the island of Taiwan, and the CCP launching its program to reconstruct the nation on the Chinese mainland. The duel persisted between the two from the 1950s through the 1980s.

Towards the end of the Cold War, the cross-Strait stalemate took a new form. The painful experience with Mao Zedong's ultra-leftism led the CCP elite to a soul search, and a reversal. In the 1980s, with the launch of economic reform and open-door policy, mainland China embraced modernizing authoritarianism by gradually dropping the socialist utopia and implementing state capitalism. In 1987–92 Taiwan transitioned to a liberal democracy by lifting martial law and instituting regular multi-party elections. Although both transitioned into a new set of institutions, their conflict persisted, as the institutional gap between the two new systems remained large, and an identity shift in Taiwan pulled the island further away from the mainland.

Confused Modernization

During the period of China's decline, Europe surged. As Womack points out, a global centrality structured toward Europe replaced the regional, China-centered centrality. In the eyes of its neighbors, China became a fellow victim in the hands of the Europeans, not a center of attention and reverence. The West was seen as having a higher culture, and Chinese identity was transformed. Pacific Asia was oriented toward the West, not toward China. The region was also fragmented, as different colonies were beholden to their respective colonial masters. The end of European colonialism in Asia and the rise of American imperium did not alter this basic picture, as China remained weak and turned inward in its ideological fervor and Pacific Asia shifted its dependence to the US. At the bottom of this radical reorientation from China to the West, from thin connectivity to sharp connectivity, was China's waning power, caused by its lack of economic growth and widening technological gap with the West.

For China to again constitute itself as center of Pacific Asia, it needed to adopt a set of competitive institutions, to determine its route of modernization. It could not resurge when it was bogged down in conflicts among forces representing different modernization alternatives. And then the route chosen needed to be effective in raising the technological level and productivity. When China suffered in the strife of choosing the route, fought invasion by Japan, a successful modernizer, and then suffered again from experimenting with the chosen route, namely Mao's utopian state socialism, it could not surge. This was the period of "confused modernization."

The "right" institutional mix had to be found in order for China to grow rapidly. That institutional mix turned out to be authoritarian (not totalitarian) politics plus state capitalism. This formula proved its effectiveness for Taiwan when it was under the authoritarian rule of the KMT. It also worked for South Korea (and to a less extent Hong Kong and Singapore). A version of this formula, the "post-totalitarian developmental state," has been serving China since it adopted its open-door policy and economic reform. Of course, there are differences between the modernizing authoritarianism of the KMT under the martial law in

Taiwan, and the post-totalitarian developmental state practiced by the CCP in today's China, but there are striking similarities, including their ability to achieve sustainable high growth for long periods of time. The economies of Taiwan and South Korea are small, and so their decades of high growth could not alter the basic structure of the international system in Pacific Asia. Countries in this region were oriented first toward Europe, and then the US. China, however, is a different story. Prior to the adoption of the new modernization route, when China was still confused as to the optimal strategy to develop its economy, there were Western colonization, de-centering of Asia, and American imperium, so vividly narrated by Womack. When the right institutional formula was chosen, China with its huge population and resources then rapidly rose to challenge the US hegemony. Titanic changes of the international system in Pacific Asia and the world ensued.

Conclusion

The decentering of Pacific Asia from China coincided with the dominance of the West and China's confused modernization. As China failed to settle on an effective modernization route, its power waned, Pacific Asia turned away from its traditional center, connectivity was reoriented toward the West, and the region was fragmented. During the Cold War and under American imperium, some Asian countries demonstrated the effectiveness of the institutions of authoritarian modernization. However, before China embraced its version of this strategy, Pacific Asia continued to be beholden to the US, to the West. The death of Mao and the ascendancy of Deng Xiaoping provided a unique opportunity for China's historic shift in its modernization strategy. The embrace of the pro-growth modernizing authoritarianism, with its effect so successfully demonstrated in Taiwan and South Korea, led to an epochal rise of China's productivity and growth of the economy. Given the huge population base and rich resources of the country, China rapidly raised its profile, threw into sharp relief its presence in the region, redefined its relations with neighboring countries, reconnected with nations near and far, challenged the US hegemony, and remolded the international system in Pacific Asia and the world.

The Chinese responses to the challenge by the West, be it liberal democratic (Anglo-Saxon model), modernizing authoritarian (German model), or communist (Soviet or Russian model), all stemmed from the West. But as China regained its strength and confidence, it increasingly harks back to its own history and culture. It is amazing to note that the Cultural Revolution under Mao has increasingly yielded to cultural renaissance. The base of the renaissance is the country's rising power. This may bring about a new version of modernizing authoritarianism, instead of a distinctively new formula. Together with that, we are going to see Pacific Asia recentered, albeit in the context of global competition between the United States and China. The new centrality mode may be bifurcated, with the US and China acting as two poles, pulling countries in the region to their direction in a hegemonic competition. To sum it up, the centering, decentering, and recentering of Pacific Asia are determined by China's power, which in turn is determined by whether China can choose an institutional path that leads to rapid rise in productivity and growth of the economy. In sum, institutions are the core that drives international relations. History in Pacific Asia bears that out.

4 | *Thick Connectivity*
The Re-centering of Pacific Asia

Specifying the date of the end of one era and the beginning of another is always frustrating, since the new era must have had a substantial gestation period and the old era does not leave without a trace. The date rarely marks a cataclysmic event that ends the old and establishes the new, but rather a watershed, like a continental divide, where one drop of water eventually ends in one ocean while its neighboring drop ends in another.

Nevertheless, the year 2008, and indeed its middle six months, marked a more dramatic breakpoint between eras than does the average mountain stream. There were uprisings in China's ethnic Tibetan areas in March that amplified long-standing global sympathy for the Dalai Lama. This was followed by the Sichuan earthquake in May that killed around 70,000 residents and stimulated an unprecedented upsurge of spontaneous Chinese relief efforts.[1] Then came the 2008 Summer Olympics in August with its stupendous opening ceremony and spectacular public architecture. Last and certainly not least, the collapse of Lehman Brothers Investment Bank in September turned an increasingly unsettled global financial system into a rout.

These four events of 2008 did more than signal a change in China's relationship to the Pacific Asia region. Each of them portends an aspect of the new regional and global perception of China. The most negative aspect of China's image abroad are the instances of its intolerance and brutality. In the case of Tibetans in 2008, the extent of the widespread local uprisings was the best evidence of suppression, but the later mass internment of Uighurs in Xinjiang Province showed an even more determined attempt to enforce uniformity. By contrast and in implicit tension with the image of top-down uniformity, the

---

[1] Shawn Shieh and Guosheng Deng, "An Emerging Civil Society: The Impact of the 2008 Sichuan Earthquake on Grass-Roots Associations in China," *The China Journal* 65 (January 2011), pp. 181–194.

113

volunteers who donated to help the earthquake victims and who drove their SUVs to Sichuan were evidence of a vibrancy in Chinese society, though one that supplemented government efforts rather than challenging them. Shortly after the earthquake, the pageantry and efficiency of the Olympics was a credible demonstration of Chinese culture and of what contemporary China could do. Finally, the Global Financial Crisis (GFC) increased everyone's anxieties about the global system centered on the United States. The contrast between financial turmoil and China's steady growth raised China's stature from being important to Pacific Asia as part of regional participation in the global economy to becoming more central to the region's prospects and fears. The year itself was a foreboding of the complexities of adjusting to China's increasing presence.

From 2008 China became central to its neighbors and a significant other to the world. By that time, it had already become the main cheap labor cog of the global economy, making labor-intensive but fairly simple products to be branded, marketed, and sold to developed countries. Beyond its own products, China did the final assembly of electronics such as iPhones from imported components in foreign-owned factories. To its neighbors, China's size and rapid development was impressive, and its cooperative support for the Association of Southeast Asian Nations (ASEAN) was reassuring. The Special Economic Zone of Shenzhen was the living symbol of China's transformation. Shenzhen became a city only in 1979, but its economy grew at an annual average of 23 percent from 1979 to 2015, growing to 172 times its original size.[2] In 2019 its production surpassed next door Hong Kong. But before 2008 China was viewed not as a new center, but rather as a new and growing part of a much larger picture of global prospects. Until the GFC there appeared to be a solid, strong, and powerful global center – the United States – and the US was confident of and committed to global leadership. Pacific Asia, including China, was globally integrated in 2008, but it was not regionally centered.

Despite its spectacular events, 2008 did not mark an instant transition to a different regional situation. However, China's continued rapid growth and low inflation contrasted sharply with its neighbors and with the rest of the world, and Chinese trade and investment provided

---

[2] Calculated from *Shenzhen Statistical Yearbook 2016* (Shenzhen: Shenzhen Statistics Bureau, 2016).

needed help to distressed economies. China continued to thrive, though at lower growth rates. In 2016 the election of Donald Trump added a dimension of political uncertainty to American leadership of the global order, a shock modified but not reversed by President Biden's election. In 2020 the Covid-19 virus added a new global challenge. Although the pandemic originated in China, the country was impressive in containing its domestic spread in 2020 and 2021. However, in 2022 China's harsh quarantine measures became less effective, less popular, and more costly to the economy. Combined with downturns in the real-estate market, local government debt, and grim prospects for the global economy, further progress appears slower and more difficult. Not surprisingly, the title of the IMF's October 2022 Annual Report is *Crisis upon Crisis*.[3]

This chapter will focus on the significance of Chinese centrality in the Pacific Asian region, while the next will address the global implications, not only of China's rise, but of the growing global significance of Pacific Asia as well as that of the developing world more generally. Regional and global effects are interrelated, but it is easy for those outside the region to fixate on the direct global effects of China's rise and to ignore changes in the regional configuration. It is a basic premise of this book that China is first a regional center. China's global position is and will be founded on its relationship to Pacific Asia.

As Qin Yaqing argues in his commentary on this chapter, if centrality is understood as hegemonic control, then China cannot become a regional center. Given the belief in the primacy of power that dominated the previous era of sharp connectivity, it is a natural assumption that to be a regional center means to dominate the region, and to become more important globally means to challenge the United States. First the region, then the world! Unfortunately, there are many inside and outside of China who share the belief that power prevails and that power controls. There is much evidence against this assumption even in the twentieth century, and since 2008 it is particularly misleading. The hub-and-spoke political economy of the American era has evolved into a less-centered matrix in which every actor has more choices and no one is in hegemonic control. Of course, more choice for everyone also implies more uncertainty for all. And as Covid and cyber threats

---

[3] IMF Annual Report 2022: *Crisis upon Crisis* (October 6, 2022). www.imf.org/external/pubs/ft/ar/2022/english/

have demonstrated, even security is no longer a matter of who has the most powerful weapon. Power still matters, and the United States remains the most powerful global actor, but its lack of control was made evident in the GFC. Similar to traditional China losing its place as regional center because the region disappeared, the US has lost its global hegemony because the world that could be controlled by that hegemony now has more options. China cannot snatch hegemony from the hands of the US because the hegemonic option no longer exists. Similarly, China's regional centrality is not regional control, but rather the re-emergence of a regional configuration under conditions very different from those in the past, and under very different conditions than Japan imagined when it announced its Greater East Asia Co-Prosperity Sphere in 1940.

The 3 Ps

Regionality beyond Hegemony

In a world without a credible hegemonic center but that remains interactive and interconnected, each part must seek to reduce its own uncertainties. This is primarily a matter of "self-help," developing comprehensive internal resilience and strength. The sudden appearance of Covid, of Putin's war, and of supply chain shocks have underlined the importance of national resilience. But coping with uncertainty is also a matter of developing relationships of mutual reassurance. Although alliances against a common threat might be necessary, softer and more extensive assurances of reciprocity form the basic texture of international relationships. Since the most immediate and diverse points of contact are with neighbors, the post-hegemonic context encourages the re-emergence of regional configurations, although they are not inevitable.

Post-hegemonic regional configurations are not the result of a "power vacuum," but rather of a "certainty vacuum." Since there is not a credible proprietor and enforcer of a global order, each political community needs reassurance about its significant interactions and relationships. Relationships with some neighbors are more significant than with others. The region, like the world, is asymmetric. However, a relationship with a more powerful neighbor can be the source of uncertainty rather than its cure. Reassurance vis-à-vis a larger neighbor comes in part from the direct relationship, and in part from the hedging and buffering of that relationship by means of other relationships.[4] A healthy regional order is a texture of relationships produced by autonomous agents pursuing mutual reassurance.

Post-hegemonic regional configurations are not inevitably stable and unchallenged. In a globalized world, regions remain sub-systems.[5] Every state has global options as well as options beyond regional peripheries – vertical and horizontal options. Therefore, a state can reduce its uncertainties by establishing extra-regional reassurances as well as by regional arrangements. Indeed, the option of seeking extra-regional reassurances is important for increasing confidence within regional configurations. If a regional power seeks to corral its neighbors, the neighbors have reason to balance against that uncertainty by strengthening relationships outside. In any case, in a globalized era a healthy regional order presumes the availability of outside options.

Regional configurations are, therefore, not an alternative to globalization. Global uncertainties are more difficult to control than regional ones. When they are amicable, regional configurations can be seen as a form of collective self-help – softer than domestic policy because there is no enforcing authority, but increasing both resilience and relative strength. ASEAN is the perfect example of a regional configuration that increases the global confidence and relative strength of its members.

With these general considerations, it is hardly surprising that Pacific Asia is reconfiguring as a region, and that China is becoming its center. But a sustainable China-centered Pacific Asia is neither an isolationist nor a China-controlled region. To the extent that Pacific Asia would decouple from the global political economy, its internal relations would become more tense. To the extent that China would use its power to enforce its preferences on its neighbors, it would give them reason to preserve their autonomous interests by hedging or by realignment. And it is possible that regional political alienation could lead to economic de-regionalization rather than simply to global

---

[4] Cheng-Chwee Kuik, "Getting Hedging Right: A Small-State Perspective," *China International Strategy Review* 3 (2021), pp. 300–315; Cheng-Chwee Kuik, "Shades of Grey: Riskification and Hedging in the Indo-Pacific," *Pacific Review*, September 9, 2022. https://doi.org/10.1080/09512748.2022.2110608

[5] Brantly Womack, *Asymmetry and International Relationships* (New York: Cambridge University Press, 2016), pp. 125–146.

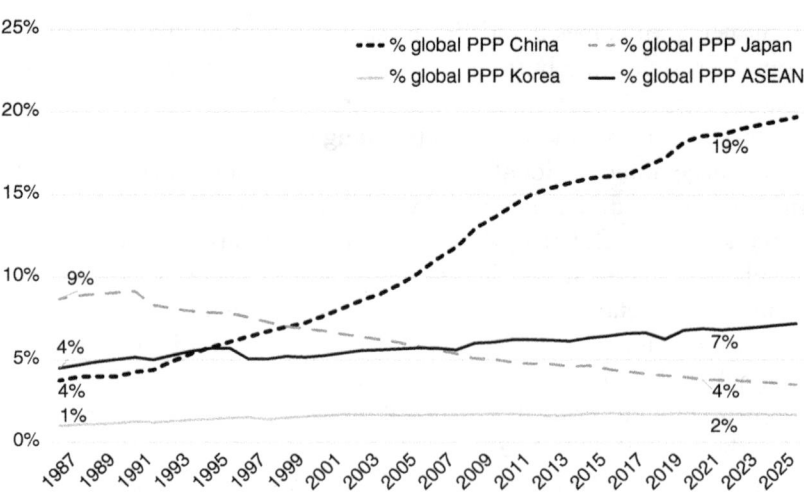

Figure 4.1 Pacific Asia's percentage of global GDP

integration. Nevertheless, China's old "3 Ps" – presence, population, and production – have reappeared in new forms in post-2008 Pacific Asia. But the premodern situation of China's thin connectivity, which could be viewed as China hedging against complications caused by its neighbors, is now reversed. With thick connectivity, China's neighbors want to preserve their side of the win-win, but also to insure against negative consequences of dependency.[6] Hedging requires an adroit and flexible mix of diversification, opportunism, and caution.[7]

Presence

China has definitely returned to center stage in Pacific Asia, but to a mixed reception. As Figure 4.1 illustrates, the change in relative mass between China and its neighbors has shifted dramatically.

By 1993 China's GDP in Purchasing Power Parity (PPP) terms surpassed ASEAN's total. It surpassed Japan's in 2000, and by

---

[6] Alfred Gerstl, *Hedging Strategies in Southeast Asia: ASEAN, Malaysia, Philippines, and Vietnam and their Relations with China* (London: Routledge, 2022).
[7] Wen Zha, "Leader Security and Hedging in the Era of Great Power Rivalry: Responses of the Philippines and Singapore," *China International Security Review* (2022). https://doi.org/10.1007/s42533-022-00111-4

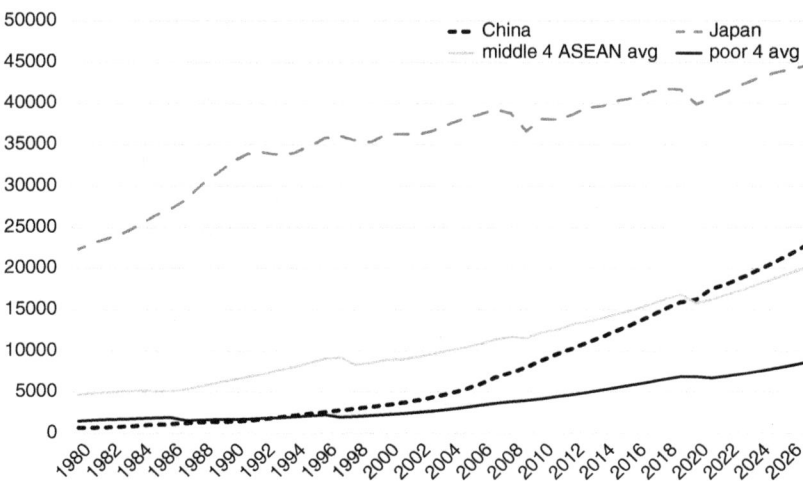

Figure 4.2 Pacific Asia's GDP per capita

2009 it equaled the combined totals of Japan, ASEAN, and Korea. If we include Taiwan, Hong Kong, and Macao, Mainland China exceeded the total for the rest of the region in 2011. If we bunch Taiwan, Hong Kong, and Macao with Mainland China, then Greater China surpassed the rest of the region in 2007. Clearly China in either form – Mainland only or Greater China – would attract regional attention.

While the previous figure addresses China's economic magnitude, Figure 4.2 concerns the more subtle question of developmental status.

This chart shows why other countries felt secure and superior in encouraging China as Deng Xiaoping began his reforms, and later became impressed by but also concerned about China's continued growth. In 1980 China was behind almost everyone in the region, and not just the developed countries. Its per capita GDP PPP was only 45 percent of the average of the four poorest Southeast Asian countries, Laos, Myanmar, Cambodia, and Vietnam, and it was 14 percent of the middle four, Malaysia, Indonesia, Philippines, and Thailand. It was only 3 percent of Japan's, its major source of development assistance. In 1993 China passed the four poorest, and by 2009 China had doubled their per capita GDP. The middle four watched China's steady approach to their level, passing 50 percent in 2005, and finally reaching 100 percent in 2020. China now stands at 44 percent of

Japan's GDP per capita, quite a change from 3 percent forty years ago, or 11 percent twenty years ago.

It is important to consider how China's development looks from the standpoint of its various neighbors. For poorer developing countries, China is impressive not only for the rapidity of its development but because it has far surpassed their own. This is not to say that the others were stagnant, and recently they have sometimes grown faster than China. But economically China is no longer in their league. For the mid-range countries China has become an overall peer competitor in developmental status. And for developed countries such as Japan, China is not likely to close the per capita gap, but the convergence is impressive. China is only a generation behind Japan in individual productivity. And these numbers only substantiate the impressions created by neighbors' visits to Chinese cities and news about China's technological advances.

China's changes in relative mass and in relative status are noted with some trepidation by its neighbors. Both Korea and Japan strongly prefer their economic ties with the US to their ties with China in 2021, even though in 2015 Korea had a slight preference for its China ties.[8] Of the developed countries surveyed by Pew in 2022, Japan had the least favorable view of China at 87 percent, and Korea's was not far behind at 80 percent.[9] For Korea the importance of the economic relationships with China and the US were similar, while Japan ranked the US relationship significantly higher.[10] For both, the military threat from China was second to that from North Korea.[11]

In Southeast Asia the overwhelming security concern has been the Covid pandemic for the past two years, according to a well-respected elite poll.[12] China's assistance in the pandemic is much appreciated,

---

[8] Pew Research Center, "How Global Public Opinion of China Has Shifted in the Xi Era" (2022). www.pewresearch.org/global/2022/09/28/how-global-public-opinion-of-china-has-shifted-in-the-xi-era/
[9] Ibid.
[10] East Asia Institute and Genron NPO, *The 9th Korea-Japan Joint Public Opinion Poll* (Seoul: East Asia Institute, 2021), p. 54. www.eai.or.kr/new/en/project/view.asp?code=54&intSeq=20810&board=eng_event&keyword_option=&keyword=&more=
[11] Ibid., p. 58.
[12] *The State of Southeast Asia Survey Report 2022* (Singapore: ASEAN Studies Centre at ISEAS Yusof Ishak Institute, 2022). www.iseas.edu.sg

earning a positive rating of more than twice that of the US, although American vaccines are preferred. Concern that China is a revisionist power has come down slowly from 45 percent in the first poll in 2018 to 42 percent in 2021. Similarly, those thinking that China is the most significant regional economic partner has grown from 73 percent to 77 percent, and China's ranking as the most significant strategic and political power has risen from 45 percent to 54 percent. But the US rates twice as high in championing a rules-based order, and China is outscored by ASEAN and the EU as well. In Indonesia, trust in China has fallen between 2011 and 2021, but trust in the United States and Australia has also declined.[13] Most in the region are anxious about the tightening global tensions in the area, and do not want to choose between the United States and China. If they did have to choose, 43 percent would choose China, with the strongest being Brunei, Cambodia, and Laos, and 57 percent choosing the US, with Myanmar, Philippines, Singapore, and Vietnam being the strongest. Despite most expecting their own relations with China to improve or remain the same in 2022, they are concerned about pressure from China. When asked what China could do to improve its image, "respect my country's sovereignty" clearly outscored the second-place, "resolve all territorial and maritime disputes."[14]

In sum, China has again become the center of regional attention, and in return it is attentive to the region.[15] But China's new presence does not imply cultural superiority or even attractiveness, and its new power causes anxiety. Unlike the premodern era, Pacific Asia has a web of regional and global alternatives, and if China's rise threatens these alternatives, then it is not respecting the autonomous agency of its partners. The region does not want a return to the previous era of sharp connectivity, this time with a regional hegemon who is closer, bigger, and more organized than Europe ever was. If China becomes a menacing regional presence, it will diminish its own capacities for coping with uncertainty and increase the likelihood of unwelcome surprises.

---

[13] Ben Bland, Evan Laksmana, and Natasha Kassam, *Indonesia Poll 2021: Charting their Own Course* (Sydney: Lowy Institute, 2022).
[14] Ibid., p. 43.
[15] Robert Sutter, "China's Growing Influence Overshadows U.S. Initiatives," *Comparative Connections* 23:3 (2022), pp. 71–78.

Population

As with presence, the population of China has changed markedly from the previous two eras. It has again become a "solid center" for the region, but the region is quite different from the earlier dispersed agricultural subsistence economy. Rural-urban migration, the internet, and high-speed rail have made China's population a more unified cooking pot, if not a melting pot. The material and intellectual life of a young Chinese is likely to be more similar to her counterparts in Seoul or Madrid than to her grandparents. The transformation of the world of China's reform generation has been virtually total.[16] Since similar changes have been occurring throughout Pacific Asia, some earlier than China, some slower, and all sharing much of the same popular culture, the regional immediacy and connectivity of people have been transformed.

The most obvious regional effect of China's population is that it has become a market. In the reform-era life in China became monetarized and marketized. The annual increment in per capita GDP in 2021 was equal to the entire per capita GDP in 1996, twenty-five years earlier. With one-fifth of the world's population, and over one-half of the region's, China is an irresistible market. According to Brookings, China is already the world's largest consumer market.[17]

There are other effects of demographic scale that affect China's regional centrality. China is a unified market, in fact, the world's largest common market. Products can be standardized and uniformly distributed, though there is also competition among firms and to some extent protectionism among localities. If a product succeeds in China, the domestic economies of scale are virtually endless. As a result, a Chinese consumer product is likely to be cheaper and better than what can be produced by many of its neighbors for their smaller markets. For example, a Vietnamese beer brewer, Bia Hanoi, during the Sino-Vietnamese hostility of 1979–91 had limited production, an insatiable market, and no external competition. Lines formed to buy its

---

[16] Peter Hessler, "China's Reform Generation Adapts to Life in the Middle Class," *New Yorker*, January 3, 2022.

[17] Homi Kharas and Wolfgang Fengler, "Which Will Be the Top 30 Consumer Markets of This Decade?" *Brookings*, August 31, 2021. www.brookings.edu/blog/future-development/2021/08/31/which-will-be-the-top-30-consumer-markets-of-this-decade-5-asian-markets-below-the-radar/

beer. When the border opened in the 1990s, Chinese beer started to flood in, and even a Chinese brewery that at the time was losing its competitive edge in its home market could do well in Vietnam. Bia Hanoi disappeared, and then later reappeared as a Heineken product. Generally Vietnamese go north to the Chinese border to buy, not to sell.[18] Vietnam balances its chronic trade deficit with China by running a trade surplus with the United States.

Last and certainly not least, China's population contributes to China's regional presence by going abroad as migrants, students, and tourists. By 2010 there were already two and a half million new migrants added to the twenty million ethnic Chinese in Southeast Asia.[19] The migrants are part of the general increase in connectivity with China, but not always a welcome part.[20] Similarly, Chinese tourists were not always smiled upon by their hosts, but the $260 billion they spent in 2019 was sorely missed when Covid rules have all but eliminated international travel.[21] There has been a significant but smaller downturn in the numbers of students abroad.[22] Although "decoupling" is usually discussed in terms of trade, the pandemic's disruption of people-to-people contact has been particularly severe. But both the tourists and the students are likely to return, and their absence has demonstrated their importance.

The regional importance of China's population will shift somewhat with rapid aging. China's population is expected to peak in 2022, and by 2080 the population over 65 might exceed the younger population.[23] However, the decline is part of a general global fertility decline that is equally acute and more advanced in many developed countries,

---

[18] Gu Xiaosong and Brantly Womack, "Border Cooperation between China and Vietnam in the 1990s," *Asian Survey* 40:6 (2000), pp. 1042–1058.

[19] Zhuang Guotu and Wang Wangbo, "Migration and Trade: The Role of Overseas Chinese in Economic Relations between China and Southeast Asia," *International Journal of China Studies* 1:1 (2010), pp. 174–193.

[20] Diana Wong, "Introduction: The New Chinese Migration to Southeast Asia," *Asian and Pacific Migration Journal* 22:1 (2013), pp. 1–6.

[21] Sui-Lee Wee et al., "When the Biggest Spenders Aren't Coming Back Any Time Soon," *New York Times*, December 5, 2021.

[22] Mandy Zuo, "China Plans to Put Children Off Studying Abroad as More Pupils Head Overseas at Younger Ages," *South China Morning Post*, February 17, 2021.

[23] Sujian Peng, "China's Population is Set to Shrink for the First Time in Sixty Years," *World Economic Forum* (July 26, 2022). www.weforum.org/agenda/2022/07/china-population-shrink-60-years-world/

including Japan. How rich China gets before it gets old will be the result of many factors, and in any case it will retain its population advantage in Pacific Asia.

Production

China's run of "super rapid growth" – above 6 percent annually – in the reform era has been a world record.[24] GDP growth in each of the thirty years between 1989 and 2019 was above 6 percent, and China's average growth rate from 1980 to 2019 was 9.4 percent. The IMF's projection of China's GDP from 2019 to 2025 averages 5.3 percent.[25] Although China's GDP started small, considering its population, these gains mount up. By 2020, China's GDP was fifty times its 1980 production, and its production increment in 2020 was equal to its entire production in 1992, or equal to the entire economy of Sweden. The only Southeast Asian country with a total GDP larger than China's annual increment that year was Indonesia, at double the increment.[26]

The transformation of China's production is the most striking difference from the previous two eras. As Barry Naughton puts it, "Since 1978 China has gone through multiple industrial revolutions."[27] Deng Xiaoping's primacy of maximum growth justified decollectivization of the countryside, market incentives, and special economic zones, and these led to mushrooming exports utilizing low-cost labor. In turn, the scale of the labor factor advantage led to further advantages of specialization and concentration. Especially in the Pearl River Delta between Guangzhou and Hong Kong, the mass of competing, foreign-invested firms developed an efficiency and agility of production unimaginable in a command economy, or even in a smaller market economy. Although rising wages and more humane working conditions have led to the migration elsewhere of some of the more basic industries, the

---

[24] Lant Pritchett and Lawrence Summers, "Asiaphoria Meets Regression to the Mean," *Mossavar-Rahmani Center Faculty Working Paper* No. 2014–04 (Cambridge, MA: National Bureau of Economic Research, 2014).
[25] Calculated from International Monetary Fund, *World Economic Outlook*, October 2021.
[26] Calculated from ibid.
[27] Barry Naughton, *The Chinese Economy: Adaptation and Growth*, 2nd ed. (Cambridge: MIT Press, 2018), p. 333.

momentum already established and capital reinvestment contribute to competitive upscaling of consumer products and components.

While China's fastest economic growth has occurred in the private and foreign-invested sectors, the state-owned enterprises have also been reorganized and are still responsible for 22 percent of GDP. More importantly, they are primarily responsible for remaking China's basic infrastructure. China's domestic transformations in rail, highway, and air connectivity, in electrical production and networks, in telecommunications and ports, and in tertiary education, are the major guarantee of its future as an economic center. They provide a tight and efficient domestic anatomy of production, and the skills acquired in the process of development undergirds confidence in the export of infrastructure through the Belt and Road Initiative (BRI). The combination of competitive innovation among private firms and party-state-led infrastructural transformation are China's best way out of the "middle income trap," the tendency of developing countries to get stuck in the diminishing returns of their economic niche. But China's drive to break out of the niche created by its labor factor advantage means breaking into the high-tech oligopoly of the developed world.

Two aspects of China's industrial revolutions tie its production even more immediately into the regional economy and beyond. First, global value chains, in which an international linkage of producers, often sections of the same multinational corporation, are involved in making intermediate parts of a final product in different countries, now involve more than two-thirds of world trade. Pacific Asia and especially Japan are leaders in the dispersion of production across national boundaries, and high-tech production in China is the ultimate example. A 2018 study of the iPhone value chain estimated that the final assembly in China was only 3 to 6 percent of its cost, while more valuable components came from Korea, Japan, Taiwan, the United States, and Europe.[28] And the iPhone assembly factory in China, Foxconn, is owned by a Taiwanese company. In effect, "made in China" on an iPhone package means "last seen in China."

Second, China is increasingly dependent on imported resources, most notably energy. In the premodern era China was self-sufficient, and in the modern era its limited imports were mostly for final consumption

---

[28] Adam Jourdan, "Designed in California, Made in China: How the iPhone Skews U.S. Trade Deficit," *Reuters*, March 21, 2018.

rather than for production. In the early reform era China exported oil to Japan, but by the mid-1990s its imports began a steep rise. China was the sixth largest oil producer in 2020, but over the past twenty years its electricity production has risen by a factor of five. Despite growth in hydroelectric, solar, and wind power, China became the world's largest oil importer in 2017.[29] In 1990 China consumed 11 percent of the world's energy; in 2019 it consumed 21 percent, and 15 percent of global energy imports.[30] Besides energy, China has become a major importer of practically every product from producer raw materials such as iron ore and feed grain to consumer products such as bananas and Tesla cars.

Ironically, the economic integration made possible by China's regional and global integration also creates new vulnerabilities. Most obviously, China's need for raw materials creates exposures to shortages and price fluctuations. But diversification of sources and long-term contracts can reduce uncertainty. Disruptions due to politics are more problematic. China's unsuccessful attempt to punish Australia by restricting imports simply raised China's costs and encouraged Australia to diversify. The "chip war" begun by President Biden reveals a deeper vulnerability to the remaining strength of American economic and hi-tech centrality. China spends more on imported computer chips than it does on oil, and while the chips are not all made in the United States, the US is able to restrict their export.[31] The situation is somewhat similar to the old hub-and-spoke system in that there is no immediate alternative.

Relationships

The largest difference between China's regional relationships of the current era and those of the premodern era is that the earlier ones evolved through two millennia while the present ones have

---

[29] Samantha Gross, "The Global Energy Trade's New Center of Gravity," *Brookings*, September 14, 2020. www.brookings.edu/articles/the-global-energy-trades-new-center-of-gravity/

[30] Calculated from International Energy Association, *World Energy Balances Highlights 2021*. www.iea.org/data-and-statistics/data-product/world-energy-balances-highlights

[31] Chris Miller, *Chip War: The Fight for the World's Most Critical Technology* (New York: Scribner, 2022).

just arrived. Habituation into relationships takes time. Moreover, memories of the two previous eras can easily lead to misunderstanding the situation of the current one. Chinese could think that they were returning to what they imagined to have been the glories of the Chinese empire. Its neighbors could imagine their more recent and vivid past, in which new hegemonic powers pushed themselves forward and oppressed the less powerful. These lingering implicit templates of glory and power cloud the novelty of the era. In fact, the regionalization of a globalized world presented a fundamentally different situation, though parts of the past remain relevant. China's 3 Ps could indeed establish it as an active center of Pacific Asia, but only if it acknowledged the autonomy and interests of its neighbors. Ultimately, their confidence in mutual benefit must exceed their concern about asymmetric dependency. The era of Western modernization provided legacies of sovereign agency and formal equality despite the role of power in creating globalization.

Thick Connectivity

Thick connectivity differs from thin connectivity because it is a policy to maximize contact. As articulated in the BRI program, China wants to promote five goals: policy coordination, facilities' connectivity, unimpeded trade, financial integration, and people-to-people bonds.[32] However, the old idea of preventing external surprises by managing connectivity continues in a new context, but now by building relationships rather than by restraining connectivity to formal ritual. Given China's new dependency on external energy and raw materials, its policy is to control risk by investing in extraction, diversifying sources, and controlling price risk through long-term contracts. The initial bloom of BRI has worn off, but the program remains significant. In 2021 BRI activity remained at 2020 levels of $60 billion, of which $14 billion was investment and $46 billion in contracts.[33] The BRI's emphasis on infrastructure development lowers the dependency

---

[32] "Vision and Actions on Jointly Building Silk Road Economic Belt and 21st-Century Maritime Silk Road" (March 2015). https://eng.yidaiyilu.gov.cn/qwyw/qwfb/1084.htm

[33] Christoph Nedopil, *China Belt and Road Initiative (BRI) Investment Report 2021* (Shanghai: Green Finance and Development Center, Fudan University, January 2022).

of developing countries on established economies by adding new routes and possibilities of contact. The ideal of "making the world safe for China" is not one of control, as it was for imperial Japan, but rather one of risk reduction through mutually beneficial (win-win) connectivity. Mutually beneficial transactions build relationships. The thicker the relationships the less likely they are to produce undesirable surprises.

Partnerships are China's main mode of enhancing relationships. As of 2017, China had partnerships with 90 countries and five regional organizations (including ASEAN).[34] The only neighbors without partnerships were North Korea, Japan, and Taiwan. While the rather bewildering variety of partnership titles (32 different official titles have been proclaimed) are reminiscent of the creative titles offered nomadic rulers in the Tang dynasty, partnership formation is a core element of Chinese diplomacy, and quite different from American alliance formation. The basic utility of China's broad array of partnerships is to confirm relationships of mutual respect and benefit, and to do so with a mechanism that can be upgraded, from "partnership" to "strategic partnership," to "comprehensive strategic partnership," as the relationship becomes thicker.

As Georg Stüver observes, "In contrast to common arguments about alliance formation, partnerships seem unlikely to be driven by shared domestic ideologies. In fact, bilateral partnerships help to bridge ideological gaps and to enable, at least in the case of China, the respective partners' pursuit of economic gains and diplomatic preferences."[35] The best illustration of the difference between partnerships and alliances is the contrast between the Soviet alliance with Cuba and China's avoidance of a partnership with Cuba. The Soviet-Cuba alliance was based on affinity and common threat. China has avoided formalizing its friendly relationship with Cuba because a partnership would antagonize the US and thus tend to increase uncertainties and decrease inclusivity. Ironically, China would be more likely to agree to a partnership with Cuba if Cuba's relations with the US were better.

---

[34] Quan Li and Min Ye, "China's Emerging Partnership Network: What, Who, Where, When and Why," *International Trade, Politics and Development* 3:2 (2019), pp. 66–81. I thank Quan Li for updating the data to the end of 2021.

[35] Georg Stüver, "China's Partnership Diplomacy: International Alignment Based on Interests or Ideology," *The Chinese Journal of International Politics* 10:1 (2017), pp. 31–65, here p. 31.

China has a strategic partnership with Canada and a comprehensive strategic partnership with Mexico.

One of the principal advantages of partnerships over alliances is that they do not require exclusivity. Vietnam, for example, has "comprehensive strategic partnerships" with China, Russia, and India, fourteen "strategic partners," and a number of "comprehensive partners," including the United States.[36] Like the rituals of yore, the framework of partnerships provides a benevolent sleeve for the relationship, but unlike the tributary rituals they are based on equality of sovereign agency. As the example of Vietnam suggests, they are not a security alliance. Indeed, they are the opposite – Vietnam's security is enhanced by having partnerships in all directions. The intent of partnership diplomacy is to reduce the uncertainties of interaction by affirming and strengthening connectivity.

China's promotion of trade and investment is a massive and varied enterprise whose individual components are obscured rather than coordinated by the BRI. In 2020 global trade declined by 12 percent, but China's trade increased slightly and rose to 13 percent of global trade. In general, Asia did well despite the pandemic, with its trade value up by 19 percent in 2020.[37] Despite the attention attracted by BRI investments, Chinese investments are a relatively small part of investments in Southeast Asia. However, they grew twenty-fold from 2005 to 2019, and Laos and Myanmar are considered dependent on Chinese investments.[38] China's infrastructural investments, like its partnerships, are open-ended. The train to Laos only goes to China at the moment, but the goods that are shipped may be Thai products heading to Duisburg, Germany. The linkages that China is building go beyond the region and beyond specific connectivity to China. But many still worry that thick connectivity might be too thick. The difficulties in finalizing high-speed rail construction in Thailand and Malaysia are symptomatic of caution regarding commitment, but the delays also demonstrate local agency

---

[36] Alexander Vuving, "Will Vietnam Be America's Next Strategic Partner?" *The Diplomat*, August 21, 2021.
[37] World Trade Organization, *World Trade Statistical Review 2021* (Washington DC: WTO, 2021).
[38] Evelyn Goh and Nan Liu, "Chinese Investment in Southeast Asia, 2005–19: Patterns and Significance," SEARBO Policy Briefing, New Mandala, August 2021.

in executing BRI projects.³⁹ On the other hand, infrastructure development can lead to new options and new local strengths.⁴⁰

China's attention to thickening relationships is not restricted to bilateral ones. Its most impressive collective initiative has been toward Russia and Central Asia. The Shanghai Five was founded in 1996 with Russia, Kyrgyzstan, Kazakhstan, and Tajikistan, all new neighbors after the dissolution of the Soviet Union, and it has expanded since its rechristening as the Shanghai Cooperation Organization (SCO) in 2001. The SCO has evolved into a multi-faceted forum involving almost all Asian countries between Pacific Asia and the Arab Middle East. The Asian Infrastructure Investment Bank (AIIB), which began operations in 2015, has been a triumph at the global level and will be discussed in Chapter 6. Since 1990 China has been increasingly involved in ASEAN's various enterprises. China is enthusiastic about public ceremonies of friendship and promotes regional free trade associations such as the ASEAN China Free Trade Area and most recently the Regional Comprehensive Economic Partnership (RCEP), which went into effect in January 2022. However, China is cautious about regional and global organizations that might bind its policy options. Although its participation in regional organizations proves that it does not engage in strategies of "divide and rule," it avoids situations of "join and be ruled by majority rules." China's shunning of the Mekong River Commission is the best evidence of this attitude. And although China began to discuss "global governance" in 2015, it avoids United Nations conventions that might be restrictive. For example, China was one of only three states not to sign the 1997 UN Convention on the Law of the Non-Navigational Uses of International Watercourses (UNWC).⁴¹

As Barry Buzan argues, China's approach to development is fundamentally one of "peaceful rise/development," but it wavers between cold

---

[39] David M. Lampton, Selina Ho, and Cheng-Chwee Kuik, *Rivers of Iron: Railroads and Chinese Power in Southeast Asia* (Oakland: University of California Press, 2020).

[40] Linda Yin-nor Tjia, "Kazakhstan's Leverage and Economic Diversification amid Chinese Connectivity Dreams," *Third World Quarterly*, March 17, 2022. https://doi.org/10.1080/01436597.2022.2027237

[41] Hongzhou Zhang and Mingjiang Li, "China and Global Water Governance," in Hongzhou Zhang and Mingjiang Li, eds, *China and Transboundary Water Politics in Asia* (London: Routledge, 2018), pp. 219–236.

and warm alternatives.⁴² There is nothing in China's dream of national rejuvenation that requires the conquest or subjugation of its neighbors, or the defeat of the United States. As in previous eras, China sees its interest as served by peace. However, the concrete choices that it faces in its interactions are often between alternatives that either maximize its bargaining power vis-à-vis its counterpart or maximize the strategic common interests of both parties. The first alternative, the "cold" one, is tempting. Besides the benefits of hard bargaining on the issue at hand, China's position on the larger end of asymmetric relationships gives it additional weight and at the same time reduces proportionate risk. China is well-positioned to be pushy. However, cold, hard bargaining underlines the differences of interest between itself and its neighbors, and it puts them at a relative disadvantage. Their resentment limits China's ability to lead through persuasiveness and diminishes the potential for regional solidarity. Warm peaceful development, based on common interests in the relationship, sacrifices some marginal gains from bargaining but makes a strategic investment in relationships and in regional solidarity.

Asymmetric Perceptions of Recentering

Misperception is inevitable in asymmetric relationships, and it is accentuated by novelty. Mature asymmetric relationships require the mutual experience of the limits of relative power. Habituation is particularly difficult in relationships involving disputed sovereignty, as most of China's Pacific Asian relationships do. Moreover, it is complicated by the other relationships of the region, internal as well as external. For example, Cambodia's relationship with China is conditioned by its asymmetric relationships with its two neighbors, Thailand and Vietnam, as well as by the long personal relationship between Prince Norodom Sihanouk and China's top leaders.

From Above

China was admitted into the WTO in 2001, and the following year Jiang Zemin announced the beginning of a twenty-year window

---

[42] Barry Buzan, "The Logic and Contradictions of 'Peaceful Rise/Development' as China's Grand Strategy," *The Chinese Journal of International Politics* 7:4 (2014), pp. 1–40.

of "strategic opportunity" for China because of a peaceful and encouraging global environment. As Yong Deng details, China's strategy of pursuing the opportunity took a significant turn under Xi Jinping's leadership.[43] From 2012 China's economic statecraft moved from serving China's development to serving its political purposes.[44] Xi added the political dimension of his "community of common destiny" and raised his sights to establishing a "new type of major power relations" and to achieving global leadership by 2035.[45]

The tense transition from the previous era's posture of "keeping a low profile" (韬光养晦) to Xi Jinping's "striving for achievements" (奋发有为) is mirrored in a pair of articles published in 2014 by two of China's most prominent political scientists, Yan Xuetong and Qin Yaqing. Essentially, Yan argues that Xi Jinping is and should be taking the path of Buzan's cold peaceful rise. He claims that China has missed opportunities by being too concerned with the opinions of other countries and that it should pursue its own interests without hesitation. Ultimately, China should form alliances and rise to challenge the United States.[46] Qin counters the competitive triumphalism of Yan, arguing that China remains committed to cooperation and to valuing relationships above transactions.[47] Both cold and warm elements remain present in China's public posture. On the one hand, the "community of common destiny" appeals both to shared concerns and to relational interaction. On the other hand, the "new type of major power relations" is more ambiguous, since it focuses on global powers but stresses relational values such as mutual respect.[48] Regardless of the continuities in China's policies and posture, however, the region and

---

[43] Yong Deng, *China's Strategic Opportunity: Change and Revisionism in China's Foreign Policy* (Cambridge: Cambridge University Press, 2022).
[44] Ibid., p. 74.
[45] Xi Jinping, "Report to the 19th National Party Congress," October 18, 2017. www.xinhuanet.com/english/special/2017-11/03/c_136725942.htm
[46] Yan Xuetong, "From Keeping a Low Profile to Striving for Achievement," *Chinese Journal of International Politics* 7:2 (2014), pp. 153–84.
[47] Qin Yaqing, "Continuity through Change: Background Knowledge and China's International Strategy," *Chinese Journal of International Politics* 7:3 (2014), pp. 285–314.
[48] Qi Hao, "China Debates the 'New Type of Great Power Relations'," *Chinese Journal of International Politics* 8:4 (2015), pp. 349–370.

the world now look at China with more anxious eyes, and so China seems different.⁴⁹

Xi Jinping's personal grandstanding in domestic and external politics is a major change in the optics and theatrics of China's image abroad. Xi does have precedents. The First Summit of the Forum on China Africa Cooperation (FOCAC) in 2006 featured the presence of thirty-five African leaders and the announcement of $5 billion in Chinese loans. But FOCAC is on a regular three-year schedule and alternates between Beijing and Africa. Similarly, the annual leaders' meetings of the Shanghai Cooperation Organization (SCO) rotate among the capital cities of members. But the BRI has been different. Although it is an umbrella program that includes prior initiatives, the Belt and Road Forums held in 2017 and 2019 raised Xi Jinping's claim to center stage to a new level. The first forum attracted representatives from 130 countries and 70 international organizations, and the second announced $64 billion in new projects. And while multilateral meetings with formally equal partners can be rotated, the BRI is primarily a collection of China's bilateral deals with other countries. It is hard to imagine a BRI Forum outside of Beijing, let alone outside of China, and equally difficult to imagine a BRI Forum without Xi as the dominant figure. However, the 2021 Global Development Initiative will be a partnership under the umbrella of the UN and cooperating with existing regional development programs.⁵⁰

As Xi Jinping's China enjoys regional center stage and global stature, it believes it is doing so for the benefit of everyone and with the approval of all – win-win (双赢). The term originated in China's WTO negotiations in 1999, but quickly became the label of choice for China's foreign relations.⁵¹ It fits in with the core ideals of Chinese foreign policy. From the beginning China has criticized the exploitative and self-serving nature of imperialism and hegemonism, and "equality and

---

⁴⁹ Brantly Womack, "International Crises and China's Rise: Comparing the 2008 Global Financial Crisis and the 2017 Global Political Crisis," *Chinese Journal of International Politics* 10:4 (2017), pp. 383–401.
⁵⁰ Ministry of Foreign Affairs, People's Republic of China, "Wang Yi Talks about the Importance of the Global Development Initiative," September 26, 2021. www.mfa.gov.cn/ce/ceth//eng/zgyw/t1909908.htm
⁵¹ Brantly Womack, "Beyond Win–Win: Rethinking China's International Relationships in an Era of Economic Uncertainty," *International Affairs* 89:4 (July 2013), pp. 911–928.

mutual benefit" was one of the Five Principles of Peaceful Coexistence enunciated in the mid-1950s and a consistent part of China's relations with what was then called the Third World.[52] However, the problem with win–win as a regional strategy is that it is not sufficiently sensitive to the greater exposure to risk of smaller states in asymmetric relationships. The caution of smaller states is not a matter of resenting the gain of the larger – indeed, in an exchange of equal benefit the smaller side gets more in proportional terms. But risk is a more vivid concern than gain, especially since 2008. Greater asymmetry means greater exposure, and smaller states will be alert to the ambiguities of the intentions of the larger state as well as to their own degree of isolation and dependence. In order for win-win to be reassuring to the smaller side, the smaller side must be confident that its other options remain open. In this regard Xi Jinping's proposal for a regional security order based on "Asia for Asians," while particularly upsetting to the US, was also disturbing to the region.[53] The slogan has not been repeated, but many wonder if exclusivity lurks behind "win-win."

From Below

As shown in the regional opinion polls cited above, the neighbors are not complacent about China's rise. If soft power refers to the power to persuade rather than to use incentives or sanctions, then it seems to trail far behind China's economic enticements as a motive for cooperation. To suddenly have a formerly isolated and politically quite different neighbor become so important would be disquieting regardless of how it behaved. Only time would tell how long China's initial smile might last. And to be on the smaller end of an asymmetric relationship is inherently a position of greater risk as well as possibly greater opportunity. Also, China's continued growth may bring more opportunities, but it will certainly involve greater asymmetry.

Soft power is taken seriously by Chinese leadership. The first article about soft power was written in 1993 by China's leading political intellectual Wang Huning, and the importance of cultural diplomacy

---

[52] Sophie Richardson, *China, Cambodia, and the Five Principles of Peaceful Coexistence* (New York: Columbia University Press, 2010).
[53] Linda Jakobson, "Reflections from China on Xi Jinping's 'Asia for Asians'," *Asian Politics & Policy* 8:1 (2016), pp. 219–223.

was endorsed at the 16th Party Congress in 2002.[54] But it is interesting that even in the former Sinosphere, China's cultural self-promotion is treated skeptically. Perhaps it is because Korea, Japan, and Vietnam value the individuality of their cultural traditions, and they do not appreciate China's implicit appropriation of something that they have made their own. More visibly, China's tight and conservative control over its own current cultural production causes it to lag behind the creative frontier of regional and global popular culture. Similarly, China's media journalism seems constrained and not interactive compared to other sources. China's soft power seems all "power," especially economic, and no "soft."

China's neighbors are acutely aware of their conflicts of interest with China. While they appreciate the rubric of win-win, they know whose win comes first. To the extent that conflicts exist, China will push its own interests. The extreme cases are the sovereignty conflicts such as that of the South China Sea. For China to win, the others must lose. Until China accepts that the sovereignty conflicts are stalemates that must be negotiated, the neighbors have reason to be anxious about China's assertiveness. There are other issues in which China is slow to accommodate core interests of neighbors in order to favor less serious interests of its own. China is always big, sometimes not generous, and rarely altruistic. It lives in a neighborhood that cooperates cautiously and maintains its reservations.

The rising tensions between China and the United States will be discussed in the final chapter, but here we should note that it is vital for China's thick connectivity to continue with its policy of inclusive partnerships. The key value of any political community is its autonomous agency to pursue its own interests, and therefore the more alternatives the better. Not only does no neighbor want to choose sides between global rivals because the choice would cost them the valuable connection to the one not chosen, more importantly the neighbors do not want to be subordinated to the one that they would choose. Whichever power tries to force a choice, it becomes the proximate threat ipso facto. Thus China's global power mentality is a threat because it suggests the possibility to others of having to face a choice.

---

[54] Li Mingjiang, "China Debates Soft Power," *Chinese Journal of International Politics* 2:2 (2008), pp. 287–308.

China's Soft Return

Despite its rapid growth, China's rise has been remarkably undisruptive for a number of reasons. Most importantly, it grew into the existing global system, and by methods familiar to its neighbors. China was the third phase of Pacific Asian take-offs, beginning with Japan, then the "Four Tigers" – Korea, Taiwan, Singapore, and Hong Kong – and finally China. All were successful developmental states, all focused on the American market, and all invested in the rest of Pacific Asia. The "flying geese" paradigm, popular in the 1980s, pictured Japan as the leader of a V-shaped regional hierarchy of production in which the leaders invested in the labor factor advantage of the less advanced to produce for developed markets.[55] China appeared to be the least advanced, barely taking off in the 1980s, but flying along in the same direction. China's growth involved changes of scale but not of system. Moreover, until 2000 its growth relied primarily on domestic resources and increasing efficiency rather than on world resource supplies, though after 2003 China's resource imports rose faster than GDP.[56]

Another factor easing China's entry was that the door of Deng's openness policy first opened inward. First the Shenzhen Special Economic Zone (SEZ), then Guangdong Province more generally, provided an attractive investment opportunity mediated through Hong Kong's financial firms.[57] By the 1990s China's labor factor advantage was attracting massive global investment. Although the lesser geese began to worry about China breaking formation, their economies were also benefiting from Chinese products and prices. In 1997 China began to be a "significant other" to Southeast Asia, first by stabilizing the currency speculation and then by promoting the ASEAN–China Free Trade Area, formed in 2002 and fully implemented in 2010 for the more developed economies and 2015 for the less developed ones. China began its own external foreign investment in 2002, and then in 2013–14 opened the umbrella of "One Belt One Road," later

---

[55] Shigehisa Kasahara, "The Flying Geese Paradigm: A Critical Study of Its Application to East Asian Regional Development," *United Nations Conference on Trade and Development Discussion Papers* 169 (April 2004).

[56] Dan Rosen and Beibei Bao, *Broken Abacus? A More Accurate Gauge of China's Economy* (New York: Rowman and Littlefield, 2015), p. 3.

[57] Ezra Vogel, *One Step Ahead in China: Guangdong under Reform* (Cambridge, MA: Harvard University Press, 1989).

called the Belt and Road Initiative (BRI). In infrastructure construction China has flown quite far from the Japanese model and competes with the lead goose. It is not establishing an economic hierarchy, but together with its own market, it is establishing economic centrality in the regional configuration.

There are important political aspects of China's soft return. China has a stable leadership with a well-known commitment to non-interference in domestic affairs and a newer rhetoric of a community of common destiny.[58] It is an active participant in international governmental organizations, and its standing as one of the Permanent Five of the UN Security Council is its most valuable diplomatic legacy from the earlier era. It has been especially active in regional organizations since the mid-1990s. China not only participates in ASEAN-initiated programs such as Asia Regional Forum, ASEAN plus Three, East Asia Summit, and most recently the Regional Comprehensive Economic Partnership (RCEP), but it is respectful of ASEAN's role in initiating these efforts.[59] China's attention to Southeast Asia far overshadows American involvement in the region, though the region remains more concerned about China.[60] And despite the mutual bristles of the Sino-American relationship, China has generally avoided public condemnations of American policies such as the invasion of Iraq or the pullout from Afghanistan.

Stepping on Toes with Larger Feet

As China's profile has risen, there is more critical global and regional interest in its domestic politics and more concern about its relationships with "Greater China" – Hong Kong, Macau, and Taiwan. While China considers all of these internal matters and rejects external

---

[58] Wang Linggui and Zhao Jianglin, *China's Belt and Road Initiative and Building the Community of Common Destiny* (Singapore: World Scientific, 2019).
[59] Wei Ling, "Upgrading the China-ASEAN Partnership: ASEAN's Concerns, China's Responsibility and Regional Order," *China International Studies* 92 (2022), pp. 36–64.
[60] Robert Sutter and Chin-Hao Huang, "China's Growing Influence Overshadows U.S. Initiatives," *Comparative Connections* 23:3 (2022), pp. 71–78.

criticism of what it considers its internal affairs, China's complaints only increase international concern and disaffection. The greatest challenge for the party-state is its intolerance of differences, a problem that is heightened by its unrestricted political reach into society. The problem of unlimited domestic power is further complicated by China's peculiar graduated sovereignty. On the mainland, governance is unitary rather than federal, while Hong Kong and Macau are Special Administrative Regions with specified local autonomy effective until 2047 and 2049, respectively. While a diminishing number of small states recognize the Republic of China (on Taiwan) rather than the People's Republic of China, no state recognizes Taiwan as independent from China. But it is obvious that Taiwan is a quite separate self-governing democracy that has not been a functioning part of a larger China since the Japanese took over in 1895. China's greatest external challenge is peaceful reunification with Taiwan, and how it copes with that challenge has immediate and strong regional repercussions. Hong Kong and Taiwan are both major participants in the Pacific Asian economy in their own right.

China's dramatic change of cross-Strait policy in 1979, from liberation to peaceful reunification, was reasonably successful until the mid-1990s, but then Taiwan's democratization created a quite different challenge. China was attempting a smooth and peaceful end to the civil war, and until the pivot in Taiwan's domestic politics it was dealing with a mainland Kuomintang (KMT) elite in Taiwan that enforced martial law until 1987 and was also interested in acceptable reunification. But Taiwan-born Lee Teng-hui became chair of the KMT and moved domestic policy toward democratization, and cross-Strait policy away from reunification. The next two decades were volatile in both domains, but with the election of Tsai Ing-wen in 2016, the political identity of Taiwan as fundamentally distinct from the Mainland appears confirmed. The challenge for China's cross-Strait policy is no longer how to end a civil war, but whether to accommodate a different and successful political community or to subjugate it. Under Xi Jinping, China's cross-Strait policies have hardened but the overall rubric of peaceful reunification remains in place.[61] However,

---

[61] Suisheng Zhao, "Is Beijing's Long Game on Taiwan About to End? Peaceful Unification, Brinkmanship, and Military Takeover," *Journal of Contemporary China*, September 28, 2022. https://doi.org/10.1080/10670564.2022.2124349

the increasing subordination of cross-Strait policy to US–China tensions raises the risk of military action.[62] While the region is concerned about possible Chinese aggression, it is also unsettled by American brinkmanship.[63]

Like climate change, political-economic reconfiguration produces hot spots, and Hong Kong has been the most acutely affected, first positively and then negatively, by China's rise. By the late 1970s Hong Kong's light manufacturing economy was slowing down, but with China's change of policy, and especially with Guangzhou being "a step ahead" in the early 1980s, Hong Kong became the bank next to China and the front desk of the Shenzhen workshop. As a result, Hong Kong's economy grew faster than China's until 1998. However, as China's financial options diversified and its manufacturing developed its own momentum, Hong Kong's advantage was diminished and its own economy stagnated. Hong Kong did not regain its 1998 peak GDP until 2017.[64] But with land values soaring and the multidimensional pressures of mainland tourism, Hong Kong's rich got richer. Hong Kong's density of millionaires grew twice as fast as that of the US from 2005 to 2020, even though inequality was also increasing in the US.[65] 2020 was a good year in general for the world's richest people, but of the twenty wealthiest "countries" Hong Kong (ranked third) was the only one in which the rich lost wealth, and it was a global worst case.[66] Hong Kong now is a terrible place to get rich, a bad place to be rich, and not a good place to be young. In these circumstances emerged the shock of sustained massive demonstrations, failed domestic governance, and the increasingly heavy hand of Beijing, to the astonishment and horror of all.

The next category of friction with neighbors is that of conflicting sovereignty claims. Although China has settled most of its land border disputes and some of its maritime ones, the remaining disputes

---

[62] Stephen Roach, "Two Insecure Superpowers Stumble towards Collision over Taiwan," *Financial Times*, August 4, 2022.
[63] Iain Henry, "Taiwan Stirs Allies' Fear of Entrapment in Asia," *East Asia Forum*, October 9, 2022. eastasiaforum.org/2022/10/09/taiwan-stirs-allies-fear-of-entrapment-in-asia/
[64] Calculated from IMF, *World Economic Outlook*.
[65] Credit Suisse, *Global Wealth Report 2021* (Geneva: Credit Suisse Research Institute, 2021), p. 29.
[66] Ibid., p. 12.

appear to have hardened since 2008.[67] The largest and most complex sovereignty dispute concerns the South China Sea.[68] There are five overlapping claimants, and both the People's Republic of China and the Republic of China hold the China claim, with Taiwan occupying the largest feature. There is hardly an aspect of the situation that is not disputed – whether or not there are islands or merely features, whether the 2016 Arbitral Tribunal judgment is binding, whether the exclusive economic zones of continental shelves have priority over historical claims, and so forth. Despite the loud and nationalistic rhetoric on all sides, there have been no major military confrontations or claim-jumping incidents since 1988. China occupies seven features in the South China Sea; Vietnam occupies twenty-one.[69] Nevertheless, both national pride and potentially significant resources are involved, and given the nature of sovereignty disputes, any party aggrieved by the action of another party must protest publicly or risk undermining its own claim. Besides the sovereignty dimension of the dispute, the expansion of China's naval and para-naval forces raises concerns about control over shipping, although all except the US are parties to the UN Convention on Law of the Sea (UNCLOS). In any case, naval predominance was the means of sharp power in the previous era of Western modernization. There are common interests in avoiding conflict as well as interests in fisheries and enivironmental management, so if these can be teased away from the hot issues of sovereignty perhaps some cooperation might occur. There are ongoing deliberations on a Code of Conduct for the South China Sea, and if successful they might prove a watershed away from the current standoff.

The conflicting claims of China and Japan over the Diaoyutai (Senkaku) islands have little to do with the resources on the islands themselves, somewhat more to do with the consequent claims to sovereign waters and exclusive economic zones, and primarily a synecdoche of the tectonic friction between the two. As with the South China Sea, national pride has become tied to the claims, and thus concessions are politically impossible. They have become a platform for assertions

[67] Taylor Fravel, *Strong Borders, Secure Nation: Cooperation and Conflict in China's Territorial Disputes* (Princeton: Princeton University Press, 2008).
[68] Brantly Womack, "The Spratlys: From Dangerous Ground to Apple of Discord," *Contemporary South East Asia* 33:3 (2011), pp. 370–387.
[69] Carlyle Thayer, "Vietnam's Response to Chinese Encirclement," *Thayer Consultancy Background Brief*, September 1, 2022.

and responses, with China being on the assertive side since Japan is the occupier of the islands. Underlying the island confrontation is a fundamental change in the economic relationship. Now Japan needs China more than China needs Japan.[70]

An important venue of conflicting interests between China and its Southeast Asian neighbors is the Lancang-Mekong river system. There are also transboundary water problems with Kazakhstan, India, and Bangladesh. China's construction of a series of dams on the Lancang, the upper half of the Mekong, affects the river's flow to the downstream countries of Myanmar, Laos, Thailand, Cambodia, and Vietnam. The Mekong and its annual but uncertain shift in volume between the monsoon and dry seasons are absolutely central to the lives and livelihoods of most Cambodians, and the Mekong's fresh water is essential to Vietnam's rice production. Although others, especially Laos,[71] are also building major dams, China's eleven dams have a potential reservoir volume equal to the Chesapeake Bay.[72] Until recently, China's attitude toward Mekong basin water governance has been analogous to the American attitude toward UNCLOS: rhetorical support but avoidance of binding commitments.[73] However, the need for cooperation on BRI initiatives as well as greater US involvement in Mekong issues may lead to increased cooperation. Together with the maritime problems of the South China Sea, China has significant water disputes with every Pacific Asian country.

The BRI's honeymoon of official announcements and ribbon-cutting ceremonies is over, and the phases of implementation and loan repayment are less exciting and more complicated. The signature project of extending a high-speed railway from Singapore to China and from thence to Europe has had different problems in different places.[74] The train is especially important for Laos since it is landlocked, but also especially expensive. Not only did Laos go from being "landlocked to

---

[70] Takashi Sekiyama, "Rethinking the Triangle: A Japanese Perspective," in Brantly Womack and Yufan Hao, eds, *Rethinking the Triangle: Washington-Beijing-Taipei* (Singapore: World Scientific, 2016), pp. 139–156, here p. 146.
[71] Bruce Shoemaker and William Robichaud, eds, *Dead in the Water: Global Lessons from the World Bank's Model Hydropower Dam in Laos* (Madison: University of Wisconsin Press, 2018).
[72] Brian Eyler, "Science Shows Chinese Dams are Devastating the Mekong," *Foreign Policy*, April 22, 2020.
[73] Zhang and Li, "China and Global Water Governance."
[74] Lampton, Ho, and Kuik, *Rivers of Iron*.

landlinked" when the line opened in December 2021, it was China's first direct, modern rail link to Southeast Asia.[75] However, the negotiations with Thailand and Malaysia have delayed further extension, and the collapse of tourism in the wake of Covid deeply affects regional economies. More generally, the implementation of BRI projects tend to run into unanticipated problems of accommodating local interests, changes of governments, and debt repayment.

China's expanding and maturing domestic economy also generates its share of tensions, though most of these are with developed economies. China has gradually transitioned from being a deal-taker to being a deal-maker in technology transfers, due in large part to its enticing domestic market. Moreover, its "Made in China 2025" development program launched in 2015 aims to move China's production into high-tech and leading-edge areas directly competitive with developed economies. This is less of a problem for Pacific Asia because its developed economies are already integrated into regional production chains and its developing economies benefit from Chinese investment in their labor-intensive production.

A larger economic problem for neighboring countries is China's occasional use of economic leverage. The clearest example was the "Garlic Battle" with Korea in 2000.[76] China reciprocated Korean restrictions on Chinese garlic with restrictions on Korean mobile phones, and eventually a settlement was negotiated. In economic frictions such as this, the asymmetries of the relationship enable China to respond more forcefully. However, China has also used economic leverage for political purposes, though it has officially denied the quid pro quo reaction. Two important cases were the cutting back on Korean ventures in China in response to Korea's agreement to host the US military's Terminal High Altitude Area Defense (THAAD) missile detection system in 2016, and various restrictions on Philippines products because of its pursuit of arbitration over South China Sea claims.[77] While such

---

[75] Ibid., p. 93. The Kunming-Hanoi line was built by the French in 1910, and the Pingxiang-Langson connection with Vietnam involves a change of gauge.
[76] Jae Ho Chung, "From a Special Relationship to a Normal Partnership? Interpreting the 'Garlic Battle' in Sino-South Korean Relations," *Pacific Affairs* 76:3 (2003–4), pp. 549–568.
[77] Carla Freeman, "China's Periphery: A Rift Zone in U.S.-China Relations," in Anne Thurston, ed., *Engaging China: Fifty Years of Sino-American Relations* (New York: Columbia University Press, 2021).

uses of leverage occur elsewhere as well, for example against Lithuania in 2021, they are particularly sensitive within the Pacific Asian region because of the density of asymmetric interrelationships. China is not shy about expressing its disapproval of postures and actions taken by other governments, and it has considerable capacity for sanctions at its disposal. Moreover, China's netizens are shrill in their advocacy of nationalistic postures, creating an audience cost for moderation. China has a lot of weight to throw around, and if aiming at a neighbor it does not have to throw it far.

China's handling of the Covid pandemic provides an excellent illustration of the domestic systemic differences between China and its neighbors. Initially China punished domestic whistleblowers[78] and complainers, but its hyper-efficient local control and lockdowns quickly brought the spread of the disease under control and likely prevented the deaths of millions of people. China also mobilized its manufacturing to produce personal protection equipment as well as vaccines and to distribute them worldwide. But as Covid became a pandemic and more variants of Covid emerged, China's rigidity and self-isolation created a physical disconnect with the region and with the rest of the world. Many neighbors could not have acted so efficiently, and none persisted so rigidly.

A final factor adding tension to regional relationships is the increasingly belligerent and arrogant tone of Chinese diplomacy, compounded by Xi Jinping's personal concentration of decision-making. The shift from Deng Xiaoping's cautious tone was signalled by Foreign Minister's Yang Jiechi's famous utterance at a 2010 meeting in Hanoi, "China is a big country and other countries are small countries, and that's just a fact."[79] While the best-known targets of "wolf warrior" diplomacy are the United States and Australia, who have their own lupine tendencies, it is an approach that is alien to Pacific Asian diplomatic culture. The growth of Chinese nationalism in social media and in outlets such as *Global Times* increases concerns about having China in the middle of the region. Meanwhile, Xi's "top-level design" approach to foreign policy as well as to domestic policy increases the

---

[78] Most notably Li Wenliang, a doctor in Wuhan who subsequently died of the disease.

[79] Alex Palmer, "The Man Behind China's Aggressive New Voice," *New York Times*, July 7, 2021.

arbitrariness of policy. As Zhao Suisheng puts it, "Pledging loyalty to the Party with Xi Jinping as the core and declaring fealty to Xi Jinping personally, Chinese bureaucrats have performed only for the audience of the supreme leader."[80] However, as with Xi's identification with the zero-Covid policy, his personal ties with Vladimir Putin could both make Chinese policy less flexible and lower the credibility of his leadership.

Conclusion: The Era of Re-centering Regional Relationships

This chapter has detailed the characteristics of post-2008 Pacific Asia and its new configuration. Certainly, an underlying difference from the two previous eras is thick connectivity as policy and reality. But economic relationships happen within political interactions, and those have changed fundamentally from the previous eras. In contrast to the premodern era, they are interactions between political communities as well as between leaders. In contrast to the modernization era, they are regional as well as global. As a result, the management of regional relationships in an era of uncertainty poses new challenges.

The ideal of Chinese traditional diplomacy is well captured in the title of James Hevia's book, *Cherishing Men from Afar*.[81] Diplomacy was a personal and ranked relationship between (usually male) rulers. The emperor expressed his hospitality and generosity, and the visitors expressed their deference. The kowtow, with its repeated prostrations, was a graphic expression of the verticality of the relationship, embarrassing to visiting rulers at the time and unthinkable now in an era of instant media and engaged publics. China has tried to adjust its public manifestations of centrality with varying success. The most problematic are the grand meetings in Beijing, which necessarily underline the honor of meeting with Xi Jinping, the receiving of lucrative investments, and being one of many in a group photograph. At the level of individual official visits, protocol is watched carefully by both sides. For example, when Ho Chi Minh visited Beijing in 1955, Mao Zedong

---

[80] Suisheng Zhao, "Top-level Design and Enlarged Diplomacy: Foreign and Security Policymaking in Xi Jinping's China," *Journal of Contemporary China*, March 14, 2022.

[81] James Hevia, *Cherishing Men from Afar: Qing Guest Ritual and the Macartney Embassy of 1793* (Durham, NC: Duke University Press, 1995).

was coming down the steps of the Beijing Hotel to meet Ho. Ho did not want the pictures to show him on a lower step reaching up to Mao, so he called for his whole delegation to join him in greeting Chairman Mao.[82] Similarly, ten years later when tens of thousands of Chinese were gathered in his honor in Tiananmen Square to express China's solidarity with Vietnam in the war, Ho coined his signature message in his communication back to Vietnam: "Nothing is more sacred than independence and freedom."[83]

More successful are the various forms of Chinese official visits abroad, from naval port calls to goodwill trips by high officials. Until the pandemic, Chinese officials participated in an exhausting schedule of meetings abroad. Meanwhile, an increasing number of naval port calls featuring the latest ships and public welcoming ceremonies made explicit gestures of friendship, but along with an underpinning of existential experiences of China's imposing presence.[84] The presence of the Chinese navy in disputed waters has a different effect. China's most successful public diplomacy is its active participation in multilateral activities such as those of ASEAN and SCO. This implies respect for multilateral institutions, and Chinese centrality appears horizontal rather than vertical.

A second major aspect of politics of the new era is Pacific Asian regionality. Using the term "Pacific Asia" for the premodern era was awkward because the relationship was more land-based than maritime, and China's most active and occasionally overwhelming relationships were in the north, away from the Pacific. The modern era brought the individual regional components into a global framework but splintered their previous relationships. In the post-colonial era, globalism prevailed as a less formally segmented but still hub-and-spoke relationship, and China began to return to the picture only after 1980.

Regionalism is not a retreat from globalization, but rather an adjustment to the increased uncertainty of a multinodal, post-hegemonic system. Multinodal uncertainty implies flexibility as well as fluctuation. In the hub-and-spoke system in which the US is both the final arbiter and

---

[82] Personal communication from a participant.
[83] Brantly Womack, *China and Vietnam: The Politics of Asymmetry* (New York: Cambridge University Press, 2006), p. 178.
[84] John Robinson, *The Great Red Fleet – China's Port Call Diplomacy: Battlewagons as Bandwagons* (PhD dissertation, University of Virginia, 2021). https://doi.org/10.18130/6y1c-qn89

the final market, the global configuration predetermines local configurations. The "flying geese" model is an example. In the multinodal system described in the following chapter, other markets and relationships become more important, especially local ones. Pacific Asia is arguably the most open region, in part because of ASEAN's outreach, in part because of Japan's global connectivity, but also in part because China provides extra-regional connectivity as well as intra-regional stability.

The relationships of the new era are quite different from the previous one. Bilateral relationships remain the basic tie, but they are now essentially conditioned by other relationships. This is a complete change from the possessive relationship of step-mother country to colony. It is also different from the traditional era. Triangular relationships mattered then, with Korea's situation between China and Japan as the best example, but tributary relationships remained individual rather than conditional or multilateral, and without the public dimension of relationships there were fewer simultaneous interrelational effects. In the current era, relationships are public to both domestic and external audiences. For example, China's only "All-Weather Strategic Cooperative Partnership" was established with Pakistan in 2005, the year after China established its "Strategic Cooperative Partnership" with India.[85]

China's proliferation of partnerships is analogous to the proliferation of *guanxi* (relationships 关系) by individual Chinese in the reform era. In both cases the *guanxi* help reduce future uncertainty, but as the number of international (and personal) contingencies proliferate in a market environment, it is difficult to expand *guanxi* to cover every connectivity. General consistency then becomes a virtue. At the international level, rules and institutionalization become more important. Especially for a central figure such as China in Pacific Asia, or the United States at the global level, a credible posture of impartiality and fairness is a necessary framing to individual relationships. This resonates with the traditional imperial mandate to face south and to rule by virtue, but the content and circumstances are different.

The re-emergence of China's centrality in Pacific Asia is a basic feature of regional reality, but it does not determine its cohesiveness. China's economy is in the process of adjusting from its earlier strategy of catch-up maximum growth to high-tech sustainability, and its

---

[85] Quan Li and Min Ye, "China's Emerging Partnership Network," p. 69.

centrality could be undercut, though not cancelled, by missteps. More importantly, regional political cohesiveness is riven by suspicions and tensions. If China is overbearing, the neighborhood will hedge away from it, and possibly even ally against it. The challenge of successful management of regional relations is made doubly difficult by rising tensions with the United States. On the one hand, the countries of Pacific Asia will have to manage their own balances of regional and global uncertainties. On the other, the global theater tempts China to forget that it is first of all a regional center. Regional cohesiveness will be the barometer of regional diplomatic stability.

Commentary
Qin Yaqing

The chapters thus far discuss the three phases or eras of the relationship between China and the world, defined by different types of connectivity, thin, sharp, and thick. These different types of connectivity are further measured by the three structural realities, that is, presence, population, and production. The third phase, which is marked by thick connectivity, and which is the focus of Chapter 3, witnesses a soft return of China to *centrality*, with both opportunities and challenges. In addition, the three phases provide us with a major historical trajectory of China's relationship with the outside world, from centrality to de-centrality to re-centrality.

From all the chapters, the most important insight is that the world is a multinodal web of asymmetric relationships. China's re-centrality, with both opportunities and challengers, will not create a bipolar hegemon-challenger model; rather, a pattern is emerging in which the negotiated management of disparities creates a multinodal network. In particular, I quote, "States are aligned by partnerships rather than by alliances because their task of securing a variety of international prospects becomes more pressing than that of defending against a specific enemy."

I have a couple of comments, which will be around an idea I have had in mind for quite some time, that is, a world without a center or centers. The world will not center around the United States; East Asia will not center around China; and there will be no clear centers like what we used to see and perhaps are used to thinking. There are definitely larger states with more military might, economic strength, and demographic advantage, but no state will be able to be centered around. It is exactly the multinodal web of relationships that make any fixed and dominant entity as a power center impossible. Let me paraphrase the above-quoted statement, "*States are aligned by partnerships rather than by alliances because their task of securing a variety of international prospects becomes more pressing than that of centering around a specific power.*"

The overall trend is, therefore, a deep *decentralization* from a more fixed *power hierarchy* to a more fluid *relational process*. The world will be more like the city of Los Angeles, spreading with all relationships connecting different parts and partners, than that of New York, with the Fifth Avenue and the Rockefeller Center as the hallmarks and the center of the city.

Let me make several points to describe this multinodal and deeply decentered world.

First, Multinodality as the Base for World Order

A multinodal web of asymmetric relationships is a distinct feature of the world order. It reflects the decline of hegemony and an ongoing process of deep power decentralization. The twentieth century is said to be the American century, meaning that the world order is an American-led hegemonic order. But the relative decline of American hegemony is clear. The United States, still the single, most powerful state in the world, is no longer able to provide the necessary public goods alone and the world seems not to support a hegemonic order, whether it is benign or malign. The COVID-19 pandemic is a clear indicator. I think the concept of multinodality agrees with this development.

As American hegemony is in decline, and at the same time, China has become the second largest economy in the world, and especially the competition between the two countries has become quite obvious, arguments have emerged that there will be a bipolar system, together with a new cold war. In other words, there will be a world of structural power struggle for hegemony, plus ideological confrontation, so as to make two power centers possible. I don't think this is and will be true, for no single state can be a new hegemon and no member of international society will be willing to accept a hegemonic order. A multinodal world is a much better description of the world now and ahead.

But this multinodal world reflects a deep decentralization of power, refusing to accept any hegemony as the legitimate world order. China, the United States, Russia, Germany, India, and others are major powers, in terms of size, population, territory, and other power elements, but they are no longer able to be a fixed center with others *below and around*. Since all are entangled in the web of relationships, small nodes may play a leading role, as ASEAN nations have shown in the regional processes. The connectivity in a multinodal world is thick, but it is not unidimensional. A multinodal web of complex relationships, plus a multi-dimensional process of relational entanglement, makes deep decentralization possible.

The multiple nodes are live agents, active parts of and in the relational web. The world cannot go back to the old rigid, power-centered structure, and cannot go back to any form of hegemony. It is going to have more active nodes, but without a fixed center.

Second, Global Governance

Global governance is flattening. A hegemonic order makes a vertical governance model possible. It is the American institutional imperium. Pillared by American material and ideational power, institutions are established at the global level to govern the world. The League of Nations and the United Nations are both examples whose designers had in mind this vertical governance model. Rules, norms, and ways of behavior are more or less made by the system-level institutions, sustained by American material power, imbued with liberal ideas, and spreading all the way down to actors in the international system. It is also a governance model in which the hegemonic power is reluctant to encourage multilateral governance at other levels, such as the regional or mini-lateral.

A multinodal web of relationships becomes the outstanding feature of the world as the hegemonic order is declining. Governance in a multinodal system flattens, and actors at all levels are more active agents. Multiple actors including states and non-state actors, multiple levels including regions and individuals, and multiple areas such as climate change and public health, all enrich the multinodal network, defined by various kinds of relationships.

A multinodal world is almost always porous, each penetrating and cutting into others, actors, areas, and levels alike. But first of all, the traditional power centers become porous. There is no clear center that is axipetal, and any nodal actor is in a superposition of being centripetal and centrifugal, of being a leader and a follower. For example, ASEAN reflects very much a module of governance without hegemon or without a center, and it centers around no single major power. To some extent, the European Union is also governance without hegemon, though in a different way.

Third, China and Pacific Asia

China has grown fast. As Professor Womack has said, its presence is clear, within and without the Pacific Asian region. Its connectivity is thick, both within and without the region. Then we may ask a question: Is the region re-centering around China?

My answer is negative. Professor Womack has discussed in more detail the challenges China faces, the various relationships it has to deal with, and the perceptions and misperceptions brought about by the asymmetric relationships. These challenges are real and serious indeed despite the rapid growth and the obviously increased material capabilities on the side of China.

Moreover, as I have argued, no fixed power centers dominate on the relational web. It is not the most powerful single entity that dominates while others center around it; power and agency are always distributed.

Pacific Asia does not and will not center around China, just as the world is and will not center around the United States, for no fixed power center will dominate in a processual web of relationships. The traditional concept of "power center" no longer describes today's reality of the world as well as the Pacific Asia region. A web is something that provides any node on it with alternatives to turn to, with distributed agency to initiate, and with ability to connect across various webs of relationships. Taking any substantial entity as a power center does not describe the working of relational webs.

We may take a look at the region of Pacific Asia. Almost during the whole process of China's rise, ASEAN has taken the driving seat in the regional development. To some extent, in the regional web, ASEAN centrality is maintained and accepted by almost all countries concerned. China, Japan, and South Korea accepted the central role of ASEAN though any of them singly is more powerful than ASEAN nations. Later, when other major powers, including Australia, New Zealand, the United States, India, and Russia joined the Pacific Asian regional process, they also made it clear that they recognize and support ASEAN's centrality. In reality, ASEAN has mostly played a central role in regional cooperation through its open, inclusive, and process-oriented regionalism rather than through its power in the traditional sense.

However, ASEAN itself is more a process than an entity. Its activities are very often termed "process" by ASEAN itself. In some way,

ASEAN reflects more the quality of a wave-particle duality rather than a traditional entity as a power center. ASEAN centrality is not out there because it is most powerful in the region. Rather, as a process it has been always engaged in negotiating, adjusting, coordinating, and making concessions, within and without. Within the 10+6 mechanism, any of the six is more materially powerful than any ASEAN nation, and even than ASEAN as a whole, but the centrality is with ASEAN. It is a fluid, dynamic, and processual centrality rather than the most powerful entity in the region.

Thus, when we see the world as a web of relations, we may need to reconsider the concept of power and rethink about the concept of power centers. We may need to reflect on a situation where power centers are constantly moving in a dynamic process on the global multinodal web of relationships.

Conclusion

How do we understand the nodes in a multinodal world? Do we believe that those nodes that have more hard and soft power are centers of the multinodal, complex web, and other non-center nodes are moving around them? It is perhaps an easier way to understand the world and world politics. After all, we are used to it.

However, if we do not take the nodes on the web as entities as network theory usually does and if we do not take the connections between them as non-substantial backgrounds and as external to such nodes for the mere purpose of connecting them, then these nodes themselves are no longer mere entities. Rather they are simultaneously nodes and relations, enfolding and unfolding themselves in a wholeness of time and space, or the wholeness of world politics as a process. This duality and perhaps superposition of the "nodes" should overwhelm any fixed understanding of "power center," as traditional international relations theory has always done and as our common sense informs us as true.

5 | *China, Pacific Asia, and Reconfiguring a Multinodal World*

The challenge of reframing our thinking regarding Pacific Asia is in part a challenge of understanding the region's history and current trajectory. That has been the task of the first four chapters. The task of this chapter is equally grand and daunting. The interaction of China and the world, and of Pacific Asia and the world, has been dynamic in all of its parts and their relationships. The world has had to relate to a changing China, and vice versa. The world has had to relate to a changing Pacific Asia, and vice versa. Meanwhile, as we have seen in the last chapter, the relationship between China and Pacific Asia has been transformed. As with the historical dynamics, the task here is not to propose a counterintuitive view of the world order but to make its general contours into a conscious framing of our understanding of the present situation and its possibilities.

A global perspective also requires the retrospective of some global history, because this century has seen the reversal of a 500-year trend of divergence between "the West and the Rest." Another momentous global event in 2008 must be added to the four mentioned at the beginning of the last chapter, but unlike the other four (the uprisings in Tibet, the Sichuan earthquake, the Olympics, and the Global Financial Crisis) this one not only passed unnoticed at the time, but unknown at the time, because the statistics had yet to be gathered. In 2008 the GDP of the developing world, measured in terms of purchasing power parity (PPP), exceeded the GDP of the developed world for the first time since the nineteenth century.[1] The former "Rest" – here the middle-income and low-income countries – have been doing quite well in this century. Their relative decline vis-à-vis the advanced economies persisted through the 1980s, but then aggregate production took off in 2000, surpassed the "West" – here the advanced economies, wherever they are – in 2008, and is estimated by the International Monetary Fund

---

[1] Calculated from IMF, *World Economic Outlook* (2021).

(IMF) to reach 153 percent of that of the West in 2025. Population is part of the story, since the Rest have six times as many people, and therefore convergence in per capita production is much slower than convergence in aggregate production. Thus, the most general frame of our analysis of the global configuration must consider the effect of the rise of demographic power and its relationship to the incumbent power of wealth. Both China and Pacific Asia play important parts in this evolution, but they are not the whole story.

The United States and the rest of the developed world can feel the shift of the sands of economic preeminence under their feet, and they fixate on China as the threat to the prerogatives of the established order. But demographic power is broader than China, and the global hub-and-spoke configuration essential to American hegemony has been undermined by the diversification of the world economy as well as by mistakes in American leadership. China is not the challenger waiting in the wings to take over, because neither it nor anyone else can build its own hub and re-align the spokes. The hegemonic era is over. Power still matters, but it does not dominate. What that means in practice will be worked out by trial and error, but we are already in a multinodal world, one of interlinked and located actors with different capacities. As Evelyn Goh puts it in her commentary on this chapter, it is an era of "messy pluralization." Each state has as its primary diplomatic task the management of the uncertainties that a multinodal environment presents.

Pacific Asia is both a major part and a microcosm of these global developments. The relationship of China and Japan is an extreme example of the juxtaposition of demographic and incumbent power. And the region as a whole is the largest and most dynamic part of the global economy. In 2020 the production of Pacific Asia equaled that of the United States and the EU combined.[2] Pacific Asia is no longer a global periphery. It is a global forward frontier. And Pacific Asia is not simply a geographic construct. Regardless of political differences, its economies are not merely interconnected, they are interwoven in global value chains of international production. If Pacific Asia could manage its internal political challenges of cohesion, it could be a coordinated global center. But that is a big if.

---

[2] In Purchasing Power Parity. Calculated from IMF, *World Economic Outlook*.

Of course, China is a major part of the tectonic changes in the global economy. As Angus Maddison pointed out to Emperor Jia Qing at the beginning of Chapter 3, in 1820 China was one-third of the global economy, and sank to one-twentieth by 1950. But to continue Maddison's story, he expected China to climb to 23 percent of global production by 2030.[3] As of 2013 it was equal to the United States' GDP in terms of purchasing power parity (PPP), and the IMF estimates that China will be 50 percent larger than the US economy by 2023 in terms of PPP.[4] China's global significance is thus two-fold. First, China is a major presence to the rest of the world. China's ninety bilateral partnerships involve 81 percent of the world's population, and it is a major trading partner of almost every country. Its loans and investments are a small part of the global total, but are growing fast. Its example of success has the power of relevance to many developing countries.

Second, in per capita terms China is still a middle-income country, but its scale allows a sophistication of production capabilities and a capacity to concentrate resources on national projects. China's hydroelectric engineering and its space program are prominent examples. Thus, China is in a position to be a rival to the United States, although an asymmetric one, and that is the topic of the next chapter. Also, it is capable of making revisionist demands on the existing global system. China has benefited from the current international order and does not consider itself the enemy of the United States, though China is convinced that the US is trying to contain it. However, it is difficult for the developed world in general to adjust to having a less privileged position, even if it is still advantaged. It is particularly wrenching for the United States to adjust to a loss of global hegemony.

This chapter begins with a discussion of the overall change in the proportions of the global economy between the West and the Rest, and an analysis of the differences between demographic power and incumbent wealth power. The next section describes what I call the multinodal world order, one in which hegemonic control is not feasible, and therefore the management of uncertainty is the key diplomatic challenge. A multinodal situation is fundamentally different from the familiar stereotypes of Cold War bipolarity or unipolarity, and also

---

[3] Of course, Maddison could not anticipate black swans like Covid. But Maddison dealt in global millennia. He was a roc; he flew above the swans.

[4] IMF, *World Economic Outlook*.

different from European notions about balance of power. The following section describes Pacific Asia as a new central region, but not hegemonic in contrast to European centrality and American centrality in the previous era. Finally, China's global relevance is discussed. China is certainly a global presence, but its role is different vis-à-vis different regions. Despite these differences, there are common challenges of global governance in a multinodal era.

The Rise of the Rest

The distinction between "developed" and "developing" countries is useful, but the terms are misleading. Modernity is built on the idea that progress is desirable, and no political community, least of all the most "developed," would resign itself to no longer making progress. All see themselves as actively changing. But developed and developing countries certainly have had different experiences of modernity. The great divergence of global life chances between the West and the Rest that characterized the modern era was built in part from innovations in the leading countries and in part on their predatory control of others. Modernization was designed to the advantage of the West, but the post-colonial era eventually created the conditions in which the Rest could rise at a greater rate than the rate at which the West could continue to rise, though with little chance of the Rest catching up in terms of per capita production. Despite the persisting gap, the trend toward convergence of the West and the Rest has put greater weight on population differences, which favor the Rest as a whole and in particular its most populous members such as China, India, Indonesia, and Brazil. As the balance of production shifts, the importance of new markets mount, as do the revisionist pressures on global systems. While these changes pose challenges for incumbent wealthy countries and their established institutions, if managed appropriately, the advanced economies still have significant asymmetric advantages.

The Ironies of Being Left Behind

While the task of the "white man's burden" of the colonial era consisted mostly of carrying resources back to colonial masters – and even then, the natives did the carrying – the very success of modernization in the West created a concrete and tangible goal of progress for the globalized periphery. The path was not easy for the periphery, but the direction of march was clear and the West had proved that progress was possible. Moreover, the development gap attracted investment from the West, and as the more rapid rate of growth of the periphery became apparent, the Rest attracted more Western investment. Advances in communication, transportation, and finance diminished the effective distance between the developed center and the developing periphery.

The priorities of catch-up are different from the priorities of the vanguard. The vanguard faces an unknown frontier of possibilities. It must discover what to do next. Its growth priorities are therefore invention and innovation. As Simon Kuznets put it, sustained growth was possible because of "the increasing stock of tested knowledge."[5] For the ones behind, however, the priorities are to learn what has already been discovered and to concentrate on the cost per item of production rather than on its novelty. While innovation requires experimental ventures and trial and error, imitation and reduced cost of production require scale, efficiency, and public organization. The "developmental state" is a creature of catch-up.

Other differences in priorities are also important. For those in the lead, continuity is a prime value, both in terms of maintaining relative position and in terms of preserving its current quality of life. For those behind, obtainability is a more vivid concern than preservation of assets. What the West seeks to preserve is what the Rest strive to obtain. The difference in perspective affects even common concerns such as climate change. While the effects of climate change and pandemics might affect all regardless of level of development, the relative priority of these concerns and the budget of resources that must be shared with other priorities are likely to be different. Moreover, there will be the suspicion that the West is primarily interested in sustaining its relative position, and therefore it is demanding that the Rest slow down. As convergence closes the gap between the Rest and the West, perhaps shared concerns will be more vivid, but only if the West can control its fears of displacement and the Rest can control their enthusiasm for it.

[5] Simon Kuznets, "Reflections on the Economic Growth of Modern Nations," in *Toward a Theory of Economic Growth* (New York: W.W. Norton, 1965), p. 83.

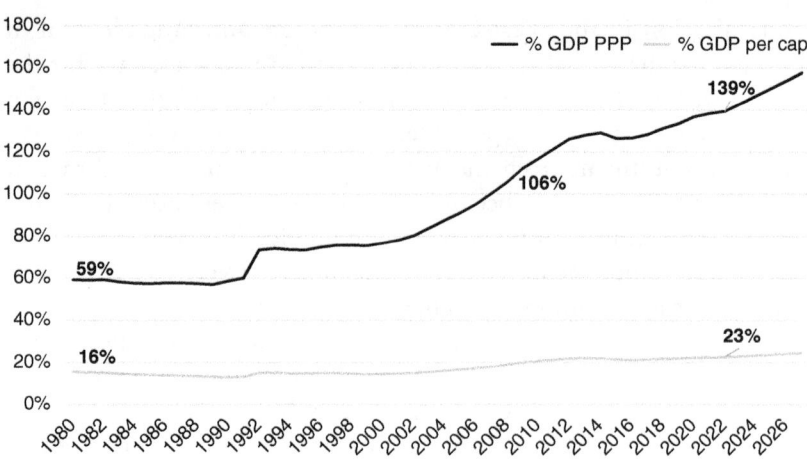

Figure 5.1 GDP of developing countries as percentage of GDP of developed countries

Demographic Power v. Wealth Power

Figure 5.1 presents the two basic facts concerning the convergence of the West and the Rest, according to IMF data and forecasts. First, in terms of aggregate production, the emerging and developing economies (EDE) surpassed the advanced economies (AE) in 2008.[6] The change has been rapid. In 1980, AEs contributed 60 percent of global GDP and others 40 percent, but, according to the IMF projection, by the late 2020s the proportions will be reversed. Of course, China is a big part of the story. China's GDP is now one-third of its group's GDP. Put another way, the Chinese economy is about half as large as the rest of the EDE combined. But even without China the Rest have been doing well. From 2000 to 2020, the EDEs minus China rose from 56 percent of AEs to 94 percent, and by 2025 it would overtake the AEs without China.

Second, the gap in per capita production is not shrinking rapidly, although it is diminishing. The percentage was stagnant until 2004, and then EDE per capita production began a slow rise. Clearly it will not come close to that of the AEs in the foreseeable future. The gap is

---

[6] The IMF divides the world economy into these two categories. The definition of the IMF's group categories is available at www.imf.org/external/pubs/ft/weo/2021/02/weodata/groups.htm.

here to stay. The reason for the difference between EDE's spectacular growth of aggregate GDP but slow growth of per capita is a proportional population shift. From 1980 to 2020 the EDE population advantage grew from 3.8 times that of AE to 6.1 times. Hence the term "demographic power" for the emerging Rest.

The implications of this data can be driven home by a 2017 Price Waterhouse forecast of the world economy in 2050.[7] It predicts that the world's five largest economies will be China, India, United States, Indonesia, and Brazil, in that order. However, the five wealthiest major economies, those with the highest per capita GDPs, will be familiar faces: United States, Germany, United Kingdom, Canada, and France. Needless to say, such projections are only best-guess amplifications of current trends. "Black swans," unanticipated events that disrupt trends, will certainly occur. Covid and its variants were the first of these black swans to arrive since that 2017 projection, and in 2022 Putin is riding an even blacker swan. However, the future, insofar as it is foreseeable, will have some economies whose prominence is founded on their population, and some wealthy economies that are the current incumbents of leading global roles but that will have to adjust to a different global configuration. Nevertheless, it is also predictable that with greater prosperity and urbanization, population growth will slow in developing countries as it has already slowed in the developed world. Aging populations are the ultimate "gray rhinos" of demographic prospects: a highly probable, but slow and neglected problem.[8] It is possible that China reached its maximum population in 2022.[9]

Demographic power and incumbent wealth power are not mutually exclusive. The United States is, after all, the third most populous country, and that is why it is more powerful than places with higher GDPs per capita like Norway and Hong Kong. Moreover, China's rise to

---

[7] Price Waterhouse, *The World in 2050* (February 2017). www.pwc.com/gx/en/research-insights/economy/the-world-in-2050.html
[8] Michele Wucker, *The Gray Rhino: How to Recognize and Act on the Obvious Dangers We Ignore* (New York: Macmillan, 2016).
[9] "中国社会科学院原副院长：2022年中国人口总量或达峰值" [Vice Director of China Social Science Academy: In 2022 China's population may reach its peak], *Caijing*, March 20, 2022. https://house.ifeng.com/news/2022_03_20-55288194_0.shtml

prominence over the last forty years was helped by a one-child policy rather than by a baby boom. And most developing countries do not have the population magnitude of China and India. Developing countries the size of Ecuador or Eritrea face prospects very different from those of Brazil or Nigeria. Nevertheless, we can differentiate national demographic and wealth power at the extremes.

There are two basic disadvantages of catch-up development that limit the salience of demographic power. The first is that the development gap is a measure of lack of resources, so developing countries are in search of capital, markets, and technology. Poverty is a measure both of what one doesn't have and what one can't borrow, but borrowing, especially borrowing denominated in dollars, can create unmanageable debt. The second is that, as developing countries close the gap, the problem of the "middle income trap" comes into view. To the extent that low labor costs drove the initial growth, rising labor costs will make it more difficult to maintain market share. Moreover, to the extent that government services are related to population size, welfare demands will be more urgent in EDE countries. And a developmental state has greater infrastructural challenges. Moreover, military needs tend to be high-tech and expensive, and difficult to produce in a small economy. All of the above imply that the central government of a developing country will have proportionally fewer resources for national projects, or that those national projects will be crowding the welfare budget more than they would in an advanced country. On the other hand, there is a scale advantage with big populations. China can develop an independent space program even though shunned by the American National Aeronautics and Space Administration (NASA); Belgium cannot.[10] And the size of the domestic market gives leverage vis-à-vis multinationals.

What can we expect of the new configuration? I predict, with an eye out for black swans and destructive rivalries, that the West will remain at the center of innovation and sophisticated services even as it loses its centrality of control and markets. The hub-and-spoke structures will fade further into the past. The big economies will be producing primarily for themselves and the rest of the world's more dispersed middle class. But the accumulated economic and social capital of the

---

[10] The 2021 Mars probe of the United Arab Emirates was impressive, but it could not be considered an independent space program.

West, as well as the inertia of established patterns and expectations, should keep it in the attractive center of global economic activities. The periphery, however, will be closer and it will be more demanding. The smaller economies are not likely to coordinate to build an alternative structure, but their individual and common demands for more shared global governance can be ignored only at the risk of causing chaos. Meanwhile all will be coping with the challenges of aging populations and environmental sustainability.

Advanced economies and the larger developing economies would likely be in a bimodal asymmetry. On the one hand, the AE would have the advantages of wealth: deployable resources, technology, and experience in central roles. But demographic power would have the advantage in goods production and markets. The AE would have to cope with the periphery's habituated resentments directed towards them, while developing countries, China especially, will have to cope with the AE's fear of displacement. The AE will be tempted toward self-isolating defensiveness, while the rising countries will be tempted to be unreasonably assertive. But there are mutual advantages in interaction, as well as common challenges that require cooperation.

A Multinodal World

The demise of the post-Cold War unipolar moment has been noted by many analysts, perhaps most trenchantly by Amitav Acharya[11] and Fareed Zakaria.[12] While some see the current moment as merely an intermission before the bipolarity of a new Cold War, many see the era beyond 2008 as a new situation of indefinite length, in which American hegemony is in question, but no one else, China included, is the replacement. The new global era has been given many names, of which the official fallback is "multipolar."[13] Acharya suggests "multiplex," Zakaria proposes "post-American," others say

---

[11] Amitav Acharya, *The End of the American World Order* (Cambridge: Polity Press, 2014).
[12] Fareed Zakaria, *The Post-American World*, Release 2.0 (New York: W.W. Norton Co, 2011). See also "Transcript: Ezra Klein Interviews Fareed Zakaria," *New York Times*, March 4, 2022. www.nytimes.com/2022/03/04/podcasts/transcript-ezra-klein-interviews-fareed-zakaria.html
[13] Brantly Womack, "Asymmetry Theory and China's Concept of Multipolarity," *Journal of Contemporary China* 13:39 (2004), pp. 351–366.

"post-Western,"[14] "polycentric,"[15] "G-zero,"[16] "polygonal,"[17] or "de-centered globalism."[18] To the extent that all these terms point to a more complex global environment that is not simply a time of chaos in between hegemons, they are improvements. They implicitly or explicitly challenge the Cold War mindset of international relations theory by imagining a situation other than a power transition between incumbent hegemon and challenger.[19] In 2014 I suggested that the term "multinodal" would be more appropriate for the global configuration.[20] Microsoft Word has stoutly resisted my term, auto-correcting it to "multimodal," and a student in Shanghai once misheard it as "multi-noodle," but I maintain that multinodal is the best label for the current world order.

"Multinodal" is the most appropriate term for a post-hegemonic world order because it points to a richer texture of active international relationships than do the others. What I mean by a multinodal world order is a configuration in which two factors, power and location, are important but not conclusive determinants of the options faced by states. Relative power still counts. The United States can sanction Iran; Iran cannot sanction the United States. But relative power does not automatically prevail. After all, Iran can develop its external relationships despite the United States. I define power as the potential for influence. As Evelyn Goh argues, influence involves inducing others to do what otherwise might not be done.[21] Influence does not necessarily involve compulsion or even rewards or sanctions. According to

---

[14] Oliver Stuenkel, *The Post-Western World: How Emerging Powers are Remaking Global Order* (Cambridge: Polity Press, 2016).

[15] Daniel Möckli, ed., *Global Trends 2012* (Zürich: Center for Security Studies ETH Zürich, 2012), pp. 7–13.

[16] Ian Bremmer, *Every Nation for Itself: Winners and Losers in a G-Zero World* (New York: Portfolio/Penguin, 2013).

[17] Nele Noesselt, "Strategy Adjustments of the United States and the European Union vis-à-vis China: Democratic Global Power Identities and Fluid Polygonal Relations," *Journal of Chinese Political Science*, March 18, 2022. https://doi.org/10.1007/s11366-022-09794-3

[18] Barry Buzan, "A World Order without Superpowers: Decentered Globalism," *International Relations* 25:3 (2011), pp. 3–25.

[19] A. F. K. Organski, *World Politics* (New York: Knopf, 1958).

[20] Brantly Womack, "China's Future in a Multinodal World Order," *Pacific Affairs* 87:2 (2014), pp. 265–284.

[21] Evelyn Goh, ed., *Rising China's Influence in Developing Asia* (Oxford: Oxford University Press, 2016), pp. 5–15.

Goh, "weaker actors may conform to the will of the stronger not only because the latter may wield greater incentives, sanctions or legitimacy, but also to further their own political or strategic agendas."[22] Of course, the potential to influence is not always exercised, and the attempt to exercise influence can be ineffective or even counterproductive. It is also important to note that the realm of international power and influence are much broader than security concerns.

The first six months of Russia's invasion of Ukraine can be used to illustrate the reality and limits of military power in a multinodal world. The fact that the Russian army could attack Ukraine with no fear of a comparable counterattack demonstrates the asymmetry of power, and Ukraine's population and economy suffered terribly. Thousands of dead, millions dislocated, partial occupation, economic collapse, inflation, and acute dependence on external aid. But Putin's assumption that power would prevail proved wrong. Ukrainian resistance prevented a takeover, Europe and NATO rallied to Ukraine's support. Politically, the results of the invasion were a more cohesive Ukraine and Europe, greater prestige for the United States, and strategic alienation of Russia from the developed world. After six months neither side has a creditable prospect of victory. Stalemate benefits neither side, but compromise appears politically impossible. Putin's attempt to compel compliance proved counterproductive in terms of influence and effectiveness.

Location is the second defining factor of multinodality. Political communities are generally more exposed to neighbors than to more distant states. Moreover, clusters of neighbors create regional patterns and the possibility of regional coordination and regional centrality. Patterns can persist because the states usually stay in place. As Goh points out, influence can have a multiplying effect if it empowers the common agendas of a region. Global connectivity does not homogenize location but it does increase options, and distance can be relativized. A distant global power is more present as a potential influence than a distant smaller power would be. But location, like power, can have perverse effects. The ancient Indian thinker Kautilya argued that neighbors were proximate threats and therefore it was prudent to ally with the states beyond them.[23] A similar sentiment is given in the

---

[22] Ibid., p. 11.
[23] Kautilya, *King, Governance and Law in Ancient India: Kautilya's Arthasastra*, Patric Olivelle, trans. (New Delhi: Oxford University Press, 2013).

long-standing saying that a powerful state should "divide and rule" its neighbors. Fortunately, these are not the only locational calculi, but it is worth remembering that regional mismanagement and the presumption of win-lose relationships can result in the opposite of cohesiveness. Two examples are the relationship of Israel to the Arab Middle East, and that of post-Soviet Russia to its near abroad.

I use the term "nodes" to indicate a state's international presence as a locus of power and connectivity. There are larger and smaller nodes, and, as we have just seen, different kinds of power, such as incumbent wealth power and demographic power. Together these nodes form a multinodal matrix of attention that is restlessly interacting. Given that there is no controlling hegemon or global governance, the interaction, while directly bilateral among sovereign actors, is shaped by complex and multi-dimensional international environments. Interactions can be coordinated by some groups, such as the EU or ASEAN, for a range of purposes. Besides mutual coordination, there are also collective reactions to regional and global powers. Thus, the multinodal global order is an asymmetric matrix of located political communities interacting with one another and sometimes collectively. And as Qin Yaqing suggests in his commentary on the previous chapter, each node is more a cluster of relational activities of all sorts, rather than a unitary actor focused on a single relationship. Nodal interactions are not like Newtonian billiard balls or Leibnitzian monads – unitary actors colliding with one another but remaining unaffected internally. Rather, they are clouds of activity themselves, and their connectivity shapes their identities and interests, analogous to atoms in quantum physics. I use the term "matrix" rather than "networks" because the roles of location and power in international relationships are quite different from personal networks.

A matrix of multinodal states is not necessarily chaotic. Power and location provide texture, and the inertia of existing relationships provides vectors toward the future. This is contrary to David Lake's claim that "in international relationships, authority hierarchies mostly rest on social contracts, in which dominant states provide political orders to subordinate states of sufficient value to offset their loss of autonomy"[24] Lake suggests a partial and conditional notion of hierarchy,

---

[24] David Lake, "Status, Authority, and the End of the American Century," in T. V. Paul, Deborah Welch Larson, and William C. Wohlforth, eds, *Status in*

which is certainly an advance over more absolute notions. However, his social contract is an unnecessary fiction.

Despite the general rise in demographic power, the key difference between the unipolar hegemonic situation and the current multinodal matrix is not an equalization of power, but a new distribution of agency. Hegemonic power is control of the system. Beyond its bilateral power advantage vis-à-vis another state, the hegemon can exclude its opponent from normal global relationships. In a post-hegemonic, multinodal situation, power still counts, but the stronger power does not control the environment of the relationship. States remain vastly different in their capacities and in their vulnerabilities. The United States, the most powerful state, can still push other countries around. But not as far, and with different results. Applying Albert O. Hirschman's classic analysis of exit and voice to global structure requires a bit of stretching, but it can illustrate the basic difference between unipolar hegemony and multinodal post-hegemony.[25] Hirschman points out the importance of exit (for instance, customers switching to a different company) as a corrective to company policy. If exit is not available, then voice – complaining and making demands – is the alternative corrective.

Hirschman is concerned with firms and with domestic politics, but we can transpose these ideas into global politics. In a unipolar, hub-and-spoke global order, the states at the spoke ends do not have an exit option. From the point of view of the hegemon, which of course is the dominant point of view, the hegemon is providing the public good of preserving the global order by gatekeeping. But for those on the system's periphery the gate implies a fence, an iron rim, and outside the rim there is only isolation. They are at the edge of the global cliff, and they cannot step backward.[26] They have voice of a sort, though not within the political system of the hegemon. Besides compliance, they can appear to comply but actually evade, using what James Scott calls the "weapons of the weak."[27] If they feel a mortal threat from the

---

World Politics (Cambridge: Cambridge University Press, 2014), pp. 246–269, here p. 252; David Lake, *Hierarchy in International Relations* (Ithaca, NY: Cornell University Press, 2009).

[25] Albert O. Hirschman, *Exit, Voice, and Loyalty: Responses to Decline in Firms, Organizations, and States* (Cambridge, MA: Harvard University Press, 1970).

[26] A bipolar hegemony would be more complicated.

[27] James C. Scott, *Weapons of the Weak: Everyday Forms of Peasant Resistance* (New Haven, CT: Yale University Press, 1985).

hegemon they can resist, but the hegemon is likely to isolate them if it cannot overcome them. Cuba has been under a continuous American embargo since 1962. Cuba has adjusted to isolation, but it has not prospered. The hegemonic system is defined by the hegemon's systemic power, even if the hegemon does not prevail in all cases. As hegemonic control deteriorates, the hegemon will be tempted to bang the gate more vigorously, but with diminishing corrective effect. But at this stage, as Adam Tooze suggests, hegemonic condemnation "is best seen not so much as an actual act of intimidation as rather a ritualistic discourse through which the guardians of norms reassure themselves and the rest of the world of who is in charge, and what the rules are."[28]

In a multinodal world there are exit options. States have many more choices in their economic and political relationships. They can shift their alignments, hedge against dependencies, and develop associations with states facing similar uncertainties and vulnerabilities. The salience of differences in relative power is reduced, though at the cost of greater systemic uncertainty. Power still matters, but it usually cannot dominate, and it might face long-term negative consequences if it tries to impose its will. Putin's invasion of Ukraine is the exception that proves the rule. States have more options outside of bilateral relations, even with global powers. Rather than a global cliff edge, there is a field of diplomatic options. Relationships flesh out a horizontal as well as a vertical dimension to the asymmetric matrix. Of course, the process of choosing which option to take can be traumatic for both domestic and international politics. Multinodal diplomacy is new territory, and it lacks the enforced guidelines of hegemonic order.

As Qin Yaqing argues, global governance is flat, but not chaotic.[29] Without hierarchy states have agency, but they face uncertainty. The dual diplomatic calculus of each state is to pursue its national interests but also to reduce uncertainty.[30] Uncertainty can take many

[28] Tooze makes the observation with reference to British economic policy by the incoming Truss administration in September 2022. Adam Tooze, "Project Fear 3.0, or the Gatekeepers and the Tories," *Chartbook* 156 (September 28, 2022).
[29] Qin Yaqing, "全球治理趋向扁平" [Global Governance Tends to be Flat], 国际问题研究 [International Studies] 5 (2021), pp. 55–72.
[30] Evelyn Goh, "The Asia Pacific's 'Age of Uncertainty': Great Power Competition, Globalisation, and the Economic-Security Nexus," *RSIS Working Paper No. 330* (Singapore: S. Rajaratnam School of International Studies, 2020).

forms: isolation, dependency, threat, resource insufficiency, and so forth. There can be forms of uncertainty, such as global warming, that are not the direct result of interactions with others, but might be better managed by cooperation. The attempt to dominate confirms the contradiction of interests not only between the powerful and its target, but between the powerful and other states who feel their own risk. Domination is a self-isolating strategy in a multinodal matrix. A central power, whether regional or global, successfully exercises strategic influence by reducing the uncertainty of others.

As Shih Chih-yu and Chiung-Chiu Huang argue, relational security requires a more complex logic than simply domination or submission.[31] For both sides, long-term stability of expectations is more important than short-term gains. Concessions are proportionately less burdensome on the larger side, and its posture of empathetic generosity can strengthen the relationship. The deference of the smaller side needs to be credible, but dependency must be resisted through oblique opposition and the expansion of other relationships. Thus, for example, Vietnam formally supports China's BRI program but is cautious about committing to specific projects, and Taiwan is a larger investor in Vietnam than is China.[32] Of course, Vietnam acknowledges that Taiwan is part of China, but Taiwan's trade and investment strengthen Vietnam's bargaining power with China as well as being valuable in their own right.

The idea of multinodality can be extended to other international networks and to non-sovereign nodes. The activities of non-governmental organizations can be seen as an additional and interactive dimension of multinodal reality, and systems of connectivity – the internet, social media, media more generally – have their own matrix textures that interact with political choices. Within states, capacity and location matter in the interrelationships of provinces and cities even though the domestic configuration is not officially hierarchical. Paris and Lyon, or California and Nevada, can be viewed as nodes in asymmetric multinodal matrices. But for present purposes the multinodal configuration of states and regions is complex enough.

---

[31] Chiung-Chiu Huang and Chih-yu Shih, *Harmonious Intervention: China's Quest for Relational Security* (Farnham: Ashgate, 2014).
[32] Chiung-Chiu Huang and Nguyen Cong Tung, "Dancing between Beijing and Taipei: Vietnam in the Shadow of the Belt and Road Initiative," *China Review* 22:2 (2022), pp. 315–339.

Not Balance of Power

The difference between a multinodal global configuration and a return of Cold War bipolarity will be addressed in the next chapter, but here it is important to distinguish the multinodal matrix from the multipolar balance of power calculi that prevailed in Europe in the modern era. Both models involve a number of large and small states, and the mission of both is the attempt to control uncertainty. As Martin Wight put it, "So long as the absence of international government means that Powers are primarily preoccupied with their survival, so long will they seek to maintain some kind of balance between them."[33] Because survival is at stake, balance of power is essentially limited to a security calculus, rather than dealing with the more general uncertainties of a multinodal matrix. And because survival depends on not being at risk to the other powers, the "certainty vacuum" of multinodality is reduced to a power vacuum. Moreover, balance of power theory is typically focused on the relationships of "great powers," those "poles," rarely more than five, that are capable of contending with one another. A power vacuum is assumed to exist when a region of small states, presumably with insignificant agency of their own, is not securely within the sphere of influence of a great power. The smaller bit players may occasionally play a triggering or a pivotal role, but the game is a great power game.

I would argue that, with one important reservation and some exceptions, national survival is not the major problem facing most states, great or small, since 2008. The exceptions are entities, such as Taiwan or Ukraine, whose claim to sovereignty or claim to territory is a matter of major dispute with a larger power. In a post-hegemonic world, most states seek to pursue their interests and reduce uncertainty by diverse means, including associating and disassociating, but they do not feel that their survival is at stake. Power is too diverse and cross-cutting to be concentrated in grand coalitions, and in any case becoming dependent on one "great power" would usually increase the long-term uncertainties of a smaller state.

The reservation concerning the irrelevance of national survival concerns nuclear war. As long as the capacity to destroy the world exists,

---

[33] Martin Wight, "The Balance of Power," in Herbert Butterfield and Martin Wight, *Diplomatic Investigations: Essays in the Theory of International Politics* (London: Allen &Unwin, 1966), pp. 149–75, here p. 174.

every state has a just concern about national survival, even if it is not a direct participant in war. However, the balance of power mentality increases the chance of globally destructive war by eliding the certainty vacuum and the power vacuum. The balance of power calculus aims at minimizing the possibility of defeat, but it accepts the possibility of nuclear war. The security dilemma created by the deterrence race creates increasing potential for destruction, though for the ostensive purpose of avoiding defeat. Given the possibility that accidents, rogue actors, escalation, incompetent leadership, and blind adventurism are all possible, the great power standoff is a mortal risk not only to the nuclear powers themselves, but to all the rest as well. Collective mortal uncertainties such as nuclear war, or global warming, are best minimized by cooperation.

Partnerships Rather than Alliances

In the previous chapter I discussed China's strategy of partnerships, but it is important to emphasize the general utility of the partnership strategy in a multinodal configuration. The common diplomatic task in an uncertain environment is to maximize reliable relationships of mutual benefit. The reduction of uncertainty in a relationship of mutual benefit is not absolute because the benefit to each side is relative to their other preferences and concerns. However, uncertainty is reduced, since each side now has reason to expect mutually convenient behavior on the part of the other side. This is the essence of partnership. A partnership between states is not a contract binding future performance, but rather a formal confirmation and encouragement of mutually beneficial interactions in a continuing relationship. To slightly rework Hirschman's framework, as it applies to multinodal diplomacy, the elements of "exit, voice and loyalty" become "exit, choice, and partnerships."

An alliance, which is a binding agreement for cooperation in specified situations, primarily in defense, is a stronger mutual commitment and thus might seem to be a better way to reduce uncertainty. However, alliances usually have an evident enemy in mind. Joining with one side in an exclusive alliance increases dependency on the alliance and reduces opportunities outside the alliance. An alliance is exclusive in principle, while a specific partnership can be one of many umbrellas that a state holds. But in a crisis even an alliance contract might not hold. Carl von Clausewitz puts it well: "Never will it happen that a state engaging on behalf of another state would take the affairs of the other as seriously as its own."[34] Moreover, after a long peace and continued political development, an alliance might become a "heritage alliance," with allies having less appetite for the original exclusive purpose of the alliance. America's allies in the Pacific all have China as their primary trading partner, as does the United States itself. This is quite a different situation from the late 1940s when the alliances were formed. Mission drift can also occur in the other direction, as demonstrated by NATO's involvement in the Balkans and in Afghanistan, Iraq, and Libya, far beyond the North Atlantic.

In contrast to the alliance mindset of the European tradition of balance of power, the diplomatic culture of Pacific Asia is one of partnerships. Perhaps the best illustration of the difference between the two approaches is the contrast between Western interpretations of Vietnam's accession to ASEAN in 1995 and the actual calculi of Vietnam and of the region. It might seem to realists that Vietnam, with its continuing fear of China and the collapse of the Soviet Union, would be desperate to ally with neighbors having similar concerns, and it would hope that the United States would come in as a balancing, great power ally. Or, from a liberal institutionalist standpoint, perhaps Vietnam would join ASEAN to increase its trade prospects. Lastly, constructivists would be happy to note that the process of accession involved a period of socialization on both sides and resulted in a new regional identity for Vietnam. A plausible thread of evidence could be produced for each of these interpretations, but the well-documented insider's account by Nguyen Vu Tung raises questions.[35]

The realist interpretation is least satisfactory, because ASEAN does not have a collective stand vis-à-vis either China or the US, and it is not a military alliance. China did not oppose Vietnam's accession to ASEAN, and it continued its good neighbor policies toward

---

[34] "Niemals wird man sehen, daß ein Staat, der in der Sache eines anderen auftritt, diese so ernsthaft nimmt wie seine eigene." Carl von Clausewitz, *Vom Kriege*, Book 8 Chapter 6A, "Einfluß des politischen Zweckes auf das kriegerische Ziel" (Berlin: Dümmers Verlag, 1832).

[35] Nguyen Vu Tung, *Flying Blind: Vietnam's Decision to Join ASEAN* (Singapore: ISEAS Publishing, 2021).

ASEAN.³⁶ While Vietnam's accession induced US normalization in the same month, Vietnam's own plans began four years earlier, and were focused on the region, not on inducing American support. As to the economic advantages of membership, the ASEAN Free Trade Area (AFTA) did open up some possibilities, but its initial effect was to expose Vietnamese industry to superior competition and to create a large trade deficit. Economic gain does not explain accession. A constructivist account would be closer to the actual process of interaction and regional rethinking, but it would not address the question of why the accession was important for Vietnam and for the region. Vietnam and its neighbors were realistic, interested in economic development, and interactive, but how and why has ASEAN become a core part of Vietnam's international identity?

The reasons for successful accession were counter-intuitive by Western standards. Membership in ASEAN was attractive to Vietnam because ASEAN is a weak institution by realist standards, inefficient by liberal standards, and not insistent on common ideologies as constructivists might imagine. Because ASEAN is consensual, rather than deliberative and decisive, it is not threatening to prospective members. And ASEAN was also not a pinnacle of economic liberalism. The founding document of AFTA, the ASEAN Free Trade Area, is nine pages long, in contrast to the 22,000 pages of the North American Free Trade Association (NAFTA) treaty. Vietnam could gradually work its way into the habits of the regional economy. As a senior Vietnamese official put it, "[joining ASEAN] is like jumping on a moving train, whose direction and pace can be negotiated and whose passengers can know more about each other as the train goes along."³⁷ And in contrast to the high threshold of common values involved in joining the EU, ASEAN's diplomatic culture is based on a process of consensus formation through incessant meetings.

By joining ASEAN, then, what did Vietnam gain? Rather than the individual certainty (or pseudo-certainty) of an alliance contract, ASEAN offered consensual modulation of shared uncertainty and the promotion of mutual benefit among neighbors. ASEAN is partnership writ large. It is based on the presumption of mutual interests among

---

³⁶ Brantly Womack, "China and Southeast Asia: Asymmetry, Leadership and Normalcy," *Pacific Affairs* 76:3 (2003–4), pp. 529–548.
³⁷ As quoted in Tung, *Flying Blind*, p. 222.

autonomous states. For both ASEAN and for Vietnam, the successful accession was part of broader inclusive policies and facilitated the successful diplomacy elsewhere. Vietnam acquired a new regional identity, but it has been an empowering one rather than an exclusive one. With the accession of Vietnam, Laos, Cambodia, and Myanmar, ASEAN became more diverse politically and economically, but also became more complete and more legitimate as a regional association.

Between the vague but not exclusive gestures of partnerships and the targeted security commitments of alliances there is a vast frontier of international arrangements. Multilateral and minilateral agreements can be viewed as collective partnerships, especially when they are not restricted to a particular set of states. The Regional Comprehensive Economic Partnership (RCEP) is a good example.[38] It does commit the members to specific policies, but it is open in principle to any state willing to join. In 2022 RCEP's members stretched from China and Japan to New Zealand, with a total population of 2.2 billion. On the alliance side of the divide, Bismarck's Reinsurance Treaty with Russia (1887–90) was interesting as a formal but minimal (and secret) alliance, providing only that Germany and Russia each would maintain a "benevolent neutrality" if either were at war with a third party. Rather than establishing an alliance, it was a security commitment aimed at preventing a counter-alliance.[39] However, after Bismarck was removed as chancellor, the non-renewal of the treaty was part of the fracturing of Europe that led to the First World War. One problem with alliances is that even if they lose their original target or purpose, their formal non-renewal would imply dissonance among the allies, and the possession of coordinated power presents a temptation to exercise it elsewhere. Hence NATO in the early 1990s did not dissolve despite the end of the Cold War and the dismembering of the Soviet Union. It then went on to discover new purposes.

Pacific Asia as a New Global Region

A 500-year-old habit is difficult to break, but Pacific Asia is no longer on the global periphery. It is *a* central region, attracting attention beyond

---

[38] "East Asia's Economic Agreement," *East Asia Forum Quarterly* 14:1 (March 2022).
[39] George Kennan, *The Decline of Bismarck's European Order* (Princeton: Princeton University Press, 1979).

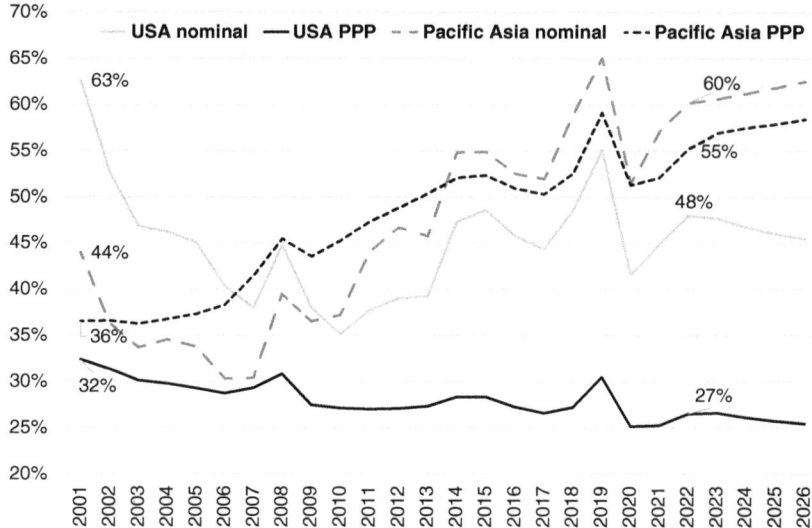

Figure 5.2 GDP of US and Pacific Asia as percentage of rest of world

itself, though not *the* central region. Pacific Asia has sufficient economic magnitude, dynamism, and coherence to be ranked with Europe and the United States as a global node, and like Europe it is a region of immediate importance to the rest of the world rather than a single central country. Given Pacific Asia's lack of political coherence, however, it is somewhere between the divisive and conflictual centrality of colonial Europe (though without colonies, fortunately) and the EU-configured coherence of contemporary Europe. Internally, Pacific Asia is itself a multinodal microcosm of global interrelationships and tensions.

Global Significance of Pacific Asia

Figure 5.2 shows the dramatic reversal in the proportional relationships of Pacific Asia and the United States to the rest of the world. In this century Pacific Asia has switched places with the US as the predominant producer vis-à-vis the rest of the world (global minus US and Pacific Asia) in terms of nominal GDP, and twice the US proportion in terms of Purchasing Power Parity (PPP). The somewhat lower PPP figure for Pacific Asia is due to the higher proportion of developing countries in the global economy if the United States is removed. It is worth noting that the production of the rest of the world is still half again that of Pacific Asia, but the change in presence of Pacific Asia is impressive.

Pacific Asia surpassed the combined PPP GDPs of the EU and the US in 2020, and was at 71 percent of their nominal GDPs. Considering that in 2001 Pacific Asia was at 55 percent and 41 percent respectively, the regional rise compared to the West is as spectacular as its rise in global terms. Within the region China grew faster than the rest. In 2001 it was one-third of the regional PPP GDP and 18 percent of the nominal, and by 2020 it had risen to 57 percent by both measures. These are changes that the region itself has yet to adjust to, let alone the rest of the world.

Pacific Asia's Economic Cohesiveness

If Pacific Asia had high GDP numbers but little internal connectivity, it would not be a region. In fact, however, its economic connectivity is triply impressive. First, the amount of intra-regional trade is high. ASEAN has become China's top trading partner, and China remains ASEAN's top trading partner in both imports and exports.[40] Japan provides another example. China is its top export destination, and eight of its top ten destinations are Pacific Asian countries.[41] Similarly, around half of Korea's total trade is within the region.

Second, and perhaps more importantly, much of the intraregional trade is the passage of intermediate products in the global value chain (GVC). More than two-thirds of international trade occurs through GVCs.[42] Based on a World Trade Organization (WTO) study of GVCs, Table 5.1 shows that China was the overwhelming top partner among Pacific Asia's top sources and targets of intermediate goods in 2015, but just as importantly for regional economic cohesion, the rest of Pacific Asia was among the top three partners more than twice as often as states outside the region. It is interesting that China's own numbers were somewhat more extra-regional, with South Korea as top partner but followed by the United States, Mexico, and Japan. However, since 2015 China's intraregional pattern has probably

---

[40] https://data.aseanstats.org/dashboard/imts.hs2
[41] www.worldstopexports.com/japans-top-import-partners/
[42] David Dollar, "Executive Summary," in *Technological Innovation, Supply Chain Trade, and Workers in a Globalized World* (Geneva: WTO, 2019), p. 1.

Table 5.1 *Top global value chain partners for Pacific Asia*

	China	PacAsia*	other	total
#1	18	1	1	20
#2	0	15	5	20
#3	2	12	6	20
total	20	28	12	60
Percent	33%	47%	20%	

*Pacific Asia minus China, Brunei, Myanmar, and Laos.
Input and output partners are combined. *Source:* Calculated from WTO, *Technological Innovation, Supply Chain Trade, and Workers in a Globalized World* (Geneva: WTO, 2019).

shifted more toward ASEAN. I also calculated the partners for a scattering of extra-regional countries,[43] and the result was that China held one-third of the top three places, but the rest of Pacific Asia was only 5 percent of the total. Most of the Pacific Asia's GVC activity is within the region.

GVC activity is more important for regional cohesiveness than trade in final products because it requires a close coordination among partners. Intraregional GVC activity in Pacific Asia exceeds intraregional activity in either North America or Europe. One reason that China's exports loom so large is that "China happens to be at the end of many Asian value chains, taking sophisticated components from Japan, the Republic of Korea, and Taiwan and assembling these into final products."[44] The pandemic bottlenecks that have created such problems in 2020 and 2021 are testimony to the interdependence of economies, though they of course also point to the need for greater resilience.[45] Moreover, the regional cohesiveness of Pacific Asian GVCs suggests that targeted "decoupling" would be very difficult.

The third dimension of regional economic cohesiveness, foreign direct investment (FDI), is less compelling because the sources are more diffuse. The region is an attractive growth prospect, and so it draws a large amount of global investment. But the region does invest in

[43] United States, Mexico, India, Germany, South Africa, and Kazakhstan.
[44] Dollar, "Executive Summary."
[45] Asian Infrastructure Investment Bank (AIIB), *Sustaining Global Value Chains* (Beijing: AIIB, 2021).

itself. In 2020 45 percent of investment in ASEAN was Pacific Asian.[46] China's investment share was only 5.6 percent, behind that of Japan and Hong Kong.[47] It is impressive that ASEAN's reinvestment in itself was equal to the shares of Japan, China, and Korea combined. Clearly sub-regional cohesiveness in Southeast Asia is important.

Pacific Asia's Problematic Political Cohesiveness

While Pacific Asia's economic cohesiveness is not sufficiently appreciated outside the region, its political divisiveness is well known. The most obvious outlier is North Korea, whose occasional missile-rattling stirs the security concerns of Northeast Asia and provides the proximate justification for American military presence in the region. Ironically, something the rest of the region has in common is frustration with North Korea, though each has its own ideas of what might be done to reduce tension. In any case, North Korea has become an isolated cyst within the region. What we will concentrate on here are the challenges regarding political cohesiveness centered on China. These begin with China's own ambiguous identity, and then the ambiguities of China's regional centrality. Finally, the relationship of China and Japan is arguably the most important bilateral relationship in the region, and the least settled.

The previous chapter discussed China's alternative policy directions of "warm" and "cold" peaceful rise – warm emphasizing reciprocity and relationship building, and cold focusing on using asymmetric leverage to maximize its gain in transactions. Both are peaceful, and both could be called "win-win," but "warm" prioritizes the relationship while "cold" prioritizes China's win in transactions. China's diplomacy is an ambiguous mixture of both, and the region's response has been a corresponding mixture of cautious cooperation and concern. Few in the region would comfortably think of themselves simply as China's friend; even fewer would comfortably think of themselves as China's enemy. The emerging global presence of Pacific Asia adds another dimension to the ambiguity of the region's political

---

[46] Calculated from *ASEAN Statistical Yearbook 2021* (Jakarta: ASEAN Secretariat, 2021), p. 159.
[47] Evelyn Goh and Nan Liu, "Chinese Investment in Southeast Asia, 2005–19: Patterns and Significance," *SEARBO Policy Briefing*, New Mandala, August 2021.

cohesiveness. The region is a central theater of global activity and its members, separately or together, are significant actors.

China's Ambiguous Identity

The rapidity and novelty of China's regional re-emergence would inevitably lead to questions about its future trajectory, but these concerns are accentuated by the domestic politics of the party-state and the unique situation of China's sovereign identity. The fundamental question regarding domestic politics is whether or not China will continue to pursue stability through centrally enforced uniformity or shift to a new phase of relaxation. The first alternative (and present direction) is necessarily more alienating to outsiders since it is an assertion of central power against difference, and outsiders are different. And although the media revolution has enabled rulers in general to become more authoritarian and personalistic, Xi Jinping seems an extreme case of power concentration and self-glorification. While his ostensive purpose is stability and further progress, Xi's physical or political mortality adds a dimension of uncertainty to his succession that promises to be both abrupt and unpredictable. Moreover, there are economic and societal limits of efficacy in enforced centralism, and these could lead to unforeseen crises, a problem already acute with the zero-Covid policies. If the policies of Xi's third term as Party Secretary simply continue the trajectory of his second term, then the hazards of personalistic dictatorship will be postponed but increased. If there are significant changes in policy content and style, then perhaps Xi can guide a soft political landing, but this is unlikely with his consolidation of power at the 20th Party Congress. Given the lack of oppositional voice in the Chinese party-state, any significant changes of direction are likely to be surprises.

Besides the unpredictability of personalized centralization, Xi's intolerance of diversity, whether ethnic, religious, or intellectual, is repugnant to the region and beyond. Although the Pacific Asian region in general is more relaxed about differences in political systems than are the United States and Europe, the contrast between China's domestic intolerance and the region's habits of toleration is cause for concern, especially as China becomes more powerful. While the region has well-earned skepticism about the civilizing or democratizing missions of global powers, it shares global concerns about human rights and about the societal and political autonomy permitted to the middle class in China.

A more proximate concern for the region, and one that reverberates globally, is the growing assertion of Beijing's control over life in Hong Kong. The promulgation of Beijing's National Security Law for Hong Kong in 2020 and its expanding enforcement is especially worrisome to Taiwan because of China's ambiguous sovereignty, but it also concerns the rest of the region and beyond because of China's crowding of Hong Kong's autonomy. In contrast to 1997, when China's support for the Hong Kong dollar was a crucial step in recovery from the Asian Financial Crisis, the turmoil in Hong Kong from 2019 followed by the heavy hand of Beijing is a reminder that ultimately Beijing asserts its own interests.

The most problematic aspect of China's ambiguous sovereignty is the cross-Strait relationship with Taiwan. This is an existential concern for Taiwan, whether or not a military crisis occurs. As Syaru Shirley Lin has argued,[48] democratization in Hong Kong and Taiwan has encouraged a public identity separate from China. But even if most Taiwanese prefer a peaceful status quo, it seems unlikely that China would give up its claim to sovereignty over Taiwan or postpone reconciliation beyond 2049, the hundredth anniversary of the founding of the People's Republic of China. The threat of military action is a concern that has become acute, but a more basic problem, in my opinion, is Beijing's lack of respect for the autonomous interests of Taiwan. This incentivizes Taipei to balance against Beijing even though that raises the risk of Beijing's intervention. Moreover, cross-Strait tension increases the concerns of the others in the region who have smaller sovereignty disputes with China.

To Beijing, its claim to sovereignty in the South China Sea is "indisputable," but to everyone else it is ambiguous and contested. The "nine dash line" is especially ambiguous as a claim and egregious in its denial of the maritime claims of others.[49] The preservation of the area's

---

[48] Syaru Shirley Lin, "Analyzing the Relationship between Identity and Democratization in Taiwan and Hong Kong in the Shadow of China," *The Asan Forum*, November–December 2021. https://theasanforum.org/analyzing-the-relationship-between-identity-and-democratization-in-taiwan-and-hong-kong-in-the-shadow-of-china/

[49] Brantly Womack, "The Spratlys: From Dangerous Ground to Apple of Discord," *Contemporary South East Asia* 33:3 (2011), pp. 370–387.

marine resources and the exploitation of its energy resources would require collaboration, but the nature of sovereignty disputes amplifies friction and attracts external involvement. While the Southeast Asian parties have a common interest in non-intervention, their asymmetric relationship with China encourages them to hedge against China's demands to exclude external participation. The dispute is a material symbol of their concern about the ambiguities of China's demands.

China–Japan as the Key Relationship

Especially from a global perspective, the management of the relationship between China and Japan is key to the success or failure of Pacific Asia's political cohesiveness. Japan is an honorary Westerner, being the most successful Asian student of both European imperialism and afterwards of American market globalism. Japan's idea of itself as a modern nation is set by these two accomplishments, and by the contrast between its success in these respects and the problems of the rest of the region, especially China. It is now proud to be a member of the "hegemonic coalition."[50] However, it is at the same time, and increasingly, an integral part of Pacific Asia. In the 1980s China's rise could be fostered by Japan in the spirit of Japan's leadership of the flying geese of Asian producers, but as China gathered momentum and showed at Tiananmen that it was not following the Western model, the relationship grew cold. China pushed patriotism by reviving memories of the Anti-Japanese War, while Japan echoed the moral superiority of the West.

Japan is not only allied with the United States, but is in a situation similar to the US vis-à-vis China. Just as China is the focus of the hegemonic nostalgia of the United States, China is the focus of Japan's status nostalgia. China's rise displaces somewhat Japan's significance for the region, though the two countries play different roles. But more deeply, Japan sees itself as the premier modern country of Pacific Asia, and China's prominence is an implicit challenge to cherished aspects of its identity as well as to its status in the regional hierarchy. And Japan is an extreme example of the problems of incumbent wealth, with a relatively stable but static economy and an aging and shrinking population.

---

[50] Fred Bergsten, *The United States v. China: The Quest for Global Economic Leadership* (Cambridge, UK: Polity, 2022), p. 10.

Meanwhile, for China the modern era was not a happy time, and the humiliation by Japan in 1895 followed by the atrocities of the war from 1931 to 1945 inform its grudge against Japan. Japan is China's most convenient target for stoking Chinese nationalism, and now China can measure its economic success by comparing it to Japan's stagnation. Japan's alliance with the United States, including the hosting of over 50,000 American military, as well as its friendship with Taiwan are major parts of the encircling constriction that concerns China. Thus, to speak of a Pacific Asian region that contains both China and Japan is a bit like describing a European region in 1930 that contains both Germany and France. The Senkaku/Diaoyu island dispute is the exposed tip of an iceberg of mutual alienation.

Nevertheless, China and Japan are close enough to appreciate their strategic importance to one another, and Japan is substantial enough not to be panicked by China's rise. As the larger power, China is in the default position of leadership in the relationship, and it is key to China's strategic interests to show respect for Japan and to collaborate with Japan on regional and global projects. A sine qua non of better relationships is for China to establish credibility that it will not change the status quo with threats of force. China's militarized assertiveness in disputed areas such as the Senkakus undercuts the emergence of a normal asymmetric relationship. If China cannot get along with Japan it will find it more difficult, if not impossible, to get along with other developed countries. China and Japan are the pivots of the region's economic cohesiveness, and the relationship with Japan will be the bellwether of Pacific Asia's political cohesiveness.

China and the World

Pacific Asia is globally important as a region, but China's global presence extends beyond its regional centrality. Its economic growth is one of the least expected and most spectacular global events of the past forty years. China's first official use of the term "overseas interests" was by Hu Jintao in 2004.[51] But China's attitude toward external

---

[51] Sun Degang, "From Fragmentation to Integration: China's Domestic Legislative and Institutional Reforms for the Protection of Overseas Interests," workshop paper, *China Protecting Its Overseas Interests* (Singapore: RSIS, 2022).

involvement changed from its earlier anti-hegemonic reticence to active encouragement under Xi Jinping. China's global engagement amplifies its presence, and its problems. In any case, China's GDP is one-third of that of the developing world in general. And according to the Lowy Institute, China now has more diplomatic offices abroad than any other country.[52] While the most obvious indicator of China's global presence is its status as a top trading partner of practically every country, its influence is broader and deeper than trade. China is not only the leading example of the great convergence of the West and the Rest, it is a leader in the convergence. And while its leadership adds to the leverage of the Rest and hence to the challenges faced by the West, it is a revisionist rather than a revolutionary challenge.

China as Developmental Alternative

China presents three different kinds of alternatives to other developing countries: as a model, as an enabler, and as leverage. It is a model of successful autonomous development, like Japan was to China and to the rest of Pacific Asia after Japan's defeat of Russia in 1905.[53] Like Japan at that time, China encourages and subsidizes students from developing countries, and those students generally have a positive experience during their studies.[54] President Tokayev of Kazakhstan, the successor of Nursultan Nazarbayev in 2019, studied in Beijing before serving in the Soviet Embassy there. Mulatu Teshome, President of Ethiopia from 2013 to 2018, received his BA and PhD from Peking University. More generally, China's success broadened the horizons of development possibilities from the colonial and American models. Although numerous alternative models had been pursued by post-colonial founding leaders over the years, none could show China's sustained success. It is difficult to define a "Beijing consensus" and China is not proselytizing a defined model, but leaders and aspirant leaders must wonder what aspects of China's policies might be applicable to their

---

[52] Lowy Institute, *Global Diplomacy Index 2019*. https://globaldiplomacyindex.lowyinstitute.org/#
[53] Ezra Vogel, *China and Japan: Facing History* (Cambridge, MA: Harvard University Press, 2019).
[54] Myungsik Ham and Elaine Tolentino, "Socialisation of China's Soft Power: Building Friendship through Potential Leaders," *China: An International Journal* 16:1 (2018), pp. 45–68.

circumstances.⁵⁵ Perhaps China's approach would be best described as "developmentalism with Chinese characteristics."

The second alternative that China presents is that of an enabler. The most obvious examples are the ubiquitous infrastructural projects sponsored under the BRI. Power plants create more reliable electrification, and roads and ports increase connectivity. China has encouraged regional as well as national projects. Although the honeymoon of easy money is over, China's projects have stimulated developmental imaginations. A successful project benefits the development of both parties. However, implementation can be problematic, and China tries to insulate its investment from defaults.⁵⁶ While China's involvement is based on a general strategic perspective of development, the implementation of specific projects affects many local stakeholders beyond the national governments, pushing and pulling in various directions.⁵⁷

China's enabling effect is much broader than specific projects. China's business strategy of 80 percent of the quality at 60 percent of the price has appeal to the world's bargain shoppers, and it opens up new vistas of opportunity to low-income consumers. By selling cheaper mobile phones and transmission networks China has provided personal communications possibilities where they had not existed before. Moreover, infrastructural projects such as roads and rails, once completed, transform the logistics options for individuals and businesses.

The third alternative that China provides is indirect. The prospect of China's involvement, and even of the "developmentalism with Chinese characteristics" more generally, adds to the external options available to developing countries, and often their customary partners improve their own offers in order to remain competitive. A good example is China's construction of a large cocoa bean processing factory at Ivory

---

⁵⁵ Joshua Cooper Ramo, *The Beijing Consensus: Notes on the New Physics of Chinese Power* (London: Foreign Policy Centre, 2004).

⁵⁶ Samantha Custer et al., *Tracking Chinese Development Finance: An Application of AidData's TUFF 2.0 Methodology* (Williamsburg, VA: AidData at William & Mary, 2021).

⁵⁷ Julie Yu-Wen Chen, "Reconciling Different Approaches to Conceptualizing the Glocalization of the Belt and Road Initiative Projects," *Globalizations*, preprint, April 20, 2022. www.tandfonline.com/doi/full/10.1080/14747731.2022.2062843

Coast in 2020.⁵⁸ Currently Ivory Coast sells two-thirds of its raw beans to European manufacturers, but it aims to do all of its own processing in the country by 2025, and then sell its value-added cocoa. Faced with a loss of profit, Swiss firms are now considering partnering with Africa for advanced production. The big and little wheels of earlier hub-and-spoke arrangements are being challenged by new capital, local producers, and new markets. China's new developmentalist hub might be termed a "hub and rim" model. It encourages developing countries to move in from the periphery of economic activity.

In general, China's attractiveness in the developing world is due to the relevance of its alternatives to their current challenges. While the general economic slowdown caused by the Covid pandemic is a sobering lesson in the risks of indebtedness, the availability of options and the encouragement of international connectivity are appreciated. China's presence to the developed world is less transformational but substantial. China's ranking as a top trading partner of both the United States and the EU is the best indicator of its importance here.

Global Presence

China is an active participant in all intergovernmental organizations (IGOs), and a founder of new ones, most significantly the Asia Infrastructure Investment Bank (AIIB). China is the second largest contributor to the UN's general and peacekeeping budgets, and supplies more troops to UN peacekeeping operations than the United States, Russia, France, and UK combined. Under Xi Jinping, China has become more active in all aspects of UN activities.⁵⁹ The AIIB is a multilateral funding agency for infrastructural investment founded at China's initiative. At the end of 2020 it had 103 members, including 79 percent of global population with 65 percent of global GDP.⁶⁰

---

[58] Anand Chandrasekhar, "Can China help African Cocoa Producers Outmanoeuvre Big Chocolate?," August 17, 2021. www.swissinfo.ch/eng/business/can-china-help-african-cocoa-producers-outmanoeuvre-big-chocolate--46862742

[59] Jeffrey Feltman, "China's Expanding Influence at the United Nations," September 2020. www.brookings.edu/research/chinas-expanding-influence-at-the-united-nations-and-how-the-united-states-should-react/

[60] www.aiib.org/en/about-aiib/index.html

There is considerable overlap between AIIB partners and BRI participants, and both reach well beyond Asia. What follows is a very brief overview of China's relationships with various global regions.

Beyond Pacific Asia, China's most impressive diplomatic accomplishment has been stabilizing relationships with Russia and Central Asia. Even though Putin's invasion of Ukraine has rendered this accomplishment a partial liability, the outcome would have been worse if China-Russia relations had become hostile in the 1990s, with Central Asia as the contested ground. The establishment of the "Shanghai Five" in 1996, which morphed into the Shanghai Cooperation Organization (SCO) in 2001, started with the minimum goal of preventing the encouragement of cross-border insurgency by neighboring states.[61] It has a consensus structure like ASEAN, and its annual summits rotate through the capitals of the members. It has grown in membership and in areas of cooperation, but its major accomplishment has been that it provides an arena of mutual respect in a region that otherwise could have been overtly competitive and unstable. Its success in this regard has led to expansion, and it now includes India, Pakistan, and Iran, with Turkey as a candidate member. Its breadth of membership limits the field of cooperation, but its inclusiveness of virtually all of Asia beyond Pacific Asia is remarkable in its own right.

The SCO's effect on Sino-Russian relations can be contrasted to the effect of NATO's expansion on Russia-Europe relations. It should be recalled that the Sino-Soviet relationship was openly hostile from the 1960s to the 1980s. Gorbachev's ill-timed visit to Beijing in May 1989, in the midst of the demonstrations at Tiananmen, was the first since Khrushchev's visit thirty years earlier, and on the eve of Soviet collapse it briefly restored both state and party relations. The new ideological distance and the sudden appearance of the weak and distressed "Stans" as independent states between Russia and China could have led to a dynamic of suspicion and hostile competition. Instead, the Shanghai Five addressed common security concerns, and its successor the SCO gradually expanded membership and the scope of cooperation.

The Sino-Russian relationship benefited from their mutual restraint in the 1990s and then from shared concerns about the United

---

[61] Jing-Dong Yuan, "China's Role in Establishing and Building the Shanghai Cooperation Organization (SCO)," *Journal of Contemporary China* 19:67 (2010), pp. 855–869.

States.⁶² A twenty-year "Treaty of Good-Neighborliness and Friendly Cooperation Between the People's Republic of China and the Russian Federation" was signed in 2002, and the close personal rapport between Putin and Xi added warmth and optics. The relationship was famously described thus by Putin and Xi at the Winter Olympics in February 2022:

> [China and Russia] reaffirm that the new inter-State relations between Russia and China are superior to political and military alliances of the Cold War era. Friendship between the two States has no limits, there are no "forbidden" areas of cooperation, strengthening of bilateral strategic cooperation is neither aimed against third countries nor affected by the changing international environment and circumstantial changes in third countries.⁶³

Since Putin's invasion of Ukraine, the above sentence that "friendship between the two states has no limits," in conjunction with the absence of an overt Chinese condemnation of the invasion, has been taken to imply an alliance between the two. A more accurate reading of China's position is given by Professor Zheng Yongnian, who points out that it would be a strategic mistake for China to ally with Russia, but on the other hand China has always criticized non-UN economic sanctions.⁶⁴ The next chapter will discuss the grander implications of the current crisis, with the crisis damaging China's economic interests as well as threatening its relations with Europe. China's interest in a resolution to the crisis is real.

China's relations with South Asia have been problematic, in part because of the inherent tensions between India and its neighbors, and in part because of hostilities and tensions between China and India dating from the 1962 border war. Despite burgeoning trade and membership in the AIIB, India feels vulnerable to China, and China's expanding relationships with India's neighbors are taken as a threat to India's primacy in South Asia. China's long-time friendly relationship with India's

---

⁶² Li Bin, "Not So Quiet in the Western Pacific," *Comparative Connections* 23:3 (2022), pp. 143–154.
⁶³ "Joint Statement of the Russian Federation and the People's Republic of China on the International Relations Entering a New Era and the Global Sustainable Development," February 4, 2022. http://en.kremlin.ru/supplement/5770
⁶⁴ "Grenzenlose Freundschaft?," interview by Xifan Yang of Zheng Yongnian. *Die Zeit*, March 18, 2022. www.zeit.de/2022/12/russland-china-beziehung-krieg-ukraine-zheng-yongnian

arch-opponent Pakistan can be contrasted with the effect of the SCO on Sino-Russian relations. The BRI's development of Gwadar port in Pakistan and China's other maritime investments in the Indian Ocean are viewed with deep suspicion in New Delhi. However, China has made official gestures to promote Pakistani-Indian reconciliation, including partnerships with both and the admission of both into the SCO.

China has been quietly involved with all parties in the Middle East and North Africa. Although China's relations with Iran draw the most attention in the United States, it has strong connections with all of Iran's putative competitors, including Israel, and with the Palestinians and Arab states as well.[65] China is now the region's largest trading partner and investor. China's investments in West Asia to North Africa in 2021 were 40 percent of China's total investments, double those in Pacific Asia.[66] As Ambassador Chas Freeman summarizes China's success in the region,

> The reality is that Arab states are both responding to the opportunities engagement with China affords them and reacting to the perceived unreliability of American protection and the fecklessness of US Iran policies by hedging their bets. Israel has its own interests and is resisting American efforts to ban projects with Chinese companies. Iranian decisions are largely reactions to the US policy of "maximum pressure," an approach with a well-established historical record of both futility and catastrophic failure and no record of success.[67]

China surpassed the United States as Africa's top trading partner already in 2009,[68] but trade is only part of a transformative relationship. China's influence as model, enabler, and leverage is most evident in sub-Saharan Africa. China supports regional efforts at cooperation and connectivity. For example, it contributed $100 million to support the development of an African Union peacekeeping force, and it is deferential to the African Union in its peacekeeping efforts. China built

---

[65] Christina Lin, "Will the Middle Kingdom Join the Middle East Peace Quartet?" *Times of Israel*, July 26, 2014.

[66] Edward White and Andrew England, "China Pours Money into Iraq as US Retreats from Middle East," *Financial Times*, February 2, 2022.

[67] Chas Freeman, "China in the Middle East: Remarks to a Panel of the Middle East Policy Council," January 21, 2022. https://chasfreeman.net/china-in-the-middle-east/

[68] Peter Wonacott, "In Africa, U.S. Watches China's Rise," *Wall Street Journal*, September 2, 2011.

the headquarters of the African Union in Addis Ababa. Its development efforts are implicitly modeled on its own experience and on similar efforts by Japan and Korea.[69] Besides the large projects, there is a dispersion of small-scale Chinese traders and enterprises.[70] Of course, at the local level the perspectives on the presence of China and the Chinese are quite diverse.[71] The global economic crisis emerging in 2022 is especially acute for poorer countries, and repayment of their debts, including those to China, has become a burning issue. All in all, the diffusion of Chinese products and the ambitions raised by major projects have increased the region's benefits of development and its traumas.

China's trade with Latin America went up almost twenty times in this century, causing dreams of new prosperity in the region. China is the top trading partner of Brazil, Chile, Uruguay, and Peru, and it has free trade agreements with Chile, Costa Rica, and Peru.[72] But China imports substantial amounts of agricultural and mineral products from Latin America, giving rise to concerns that the continent will remain only a raw materials producer.[73] The shadow over China's activities in Latin America, and especially in the Caribbean, is the allergy of the United States to external presence in the Americas. China is an observer at the US-led Organization of American States, but it is an active participant in forums of the Community of Latin American and Caribbean States (CELAC), a region-wide organization formed in 2010 that excludes the United States and Canada.[74] Xi Jinping has personally participated in their three summits. However, with or without US participation, regional organizations are not strong in Latin America.[75]

---

[69] Deborah Brautigam, *The Dragon's Gift: The Real Story of China in Africa* (New York: Oxford University Press, 2009).
[70] Peter Hessler, "Learning to Speak Lingerie: Chinese Merchants and the Inroads of Globalization," *New Yorker*, August 3, 2015.
[71] Miriam Driessen, *Tales of Hope, Tastes of Bitterness* (Hong Kong: Hong Kong University Press, 2019).
[72] Congressional Research Service, "China's Engagement with Latin America and the Caribbean," December 14, 2021. https://crsreports.congress.gov/product/pdf/IF/IF10982
[73] Juan Tokatlian, "Una nueva estrategia hacia China" [A new strategy vis-à-vis China], *La Nacion*, August 29, 2011. www.lanacion.com.ar/1401402-una-nueva-estrategia-hacia-china.
[74] Ariel Slipak, "América Latina en la estrategia del dragon" [Latin America in the dragon's strategy], *Nueva Sociedad*, February 2022.
[75] Guadalupe González et al., *Critical Juncture, Power Transition and Latin American Vacuum* (Buenos Aires: Friedrich Ebert Stiftung, 2021).

Until ASEAN took the lead in 2020, the European Union was China's largest trading partner, and China remains the EU's largest trading partner. In 2020 China was far ahead of other partners in selling to the EU, but behind the US and UK as a recipient of EU exports, a typical pattern for China's trade with advanced economies outside Pacific Asia. Major European states are members of the AIIB, and most eastern and Mediterranean European countries participate in BRI. Despite these connections, China's relations with Europe have soured since 2020 although the economic ties continue to grow.[76] There are numerous specific reasons for the downturn: pressure from the United States, China's aggressive diplomacy and human rights problems, and China's sanctioning of Lithuania for renaming its Taipei representative office. Most recently Europe is worried about China's reluctance to condemn the Russian invasion of Ukraine. As German Chancellor Olaf Scholtz points out, for Europe, the *Zeitenwende* (turning point) in attitudes towards China occurred in 2022.[77] Hitherto, the EU and Europe as a whole have been quite diverse in their opinions of China. While 80 percent of Swedes had an unfavorable view of China in 2021, 52 percent of Greeks held favorable views.[78] As the subtitle of Chancellor Scholz's article suggests, the strategic challenge for Europe is to preserve autonomy and to avoid falling into Cold War camps. However, given the particular threat posed to Eastern Europe by Putin's invasion, concerns about China's relationship with Russia are likely to counterbalance the attractiveness of China's investment projects. The more basic problem is a shift of regional attention from the marginal advantage of greater connectivity with China to the strategic challenges that China's convergence poses for Europe's interests and prerogatives.

The momentum of China's overseas development initiatives has created a considerable management burden, one that recalls why the old anti-hegemonism was shy about overseas interests. As of September

---

[76] Janka Oertel, "The New China Consensus: How Europe is Growing Wary of Beijing," Policy Brief, European Council on Foreign Relations, September 2020. https://ecfr.eu/publication/the_new_china_consensus_how_europe_is_growing_wary_of_beijing/

[77] Olaf Scholtz, "The Global Zeitenwende: How to Avoid a New Cold War in a Multipolar Era," *Foreign Affairs*, January/February 2023.

[78] Pew Research Center, "Large Majorities Say China Does Not Respect the Personal Freedoms of Its People," Pew Research Center, June 30, 2021.

2019, China held overseas assets with a net worth of US$2.2 trillion, equivalent to 13 percent of its 2020 GDP.[79] Chinese multinationals had sent half a million workers abroad, and more had ventured forth as students and entrepreneurs. To keep up with its nationals and to further its external relationships China has the world's largest array of embassies and consulates, not to mention 541 Confucius Institutes. In times of crisis, the task of protecting so many citizens abroad is large and urgent. There were around 8,000 Chinese in the Ukraine at the time of the invasion, and when Gaddafi fell, it cost China $15.2 billion to evacuate its workers from Libya.[80] To be prepared for such eventualities requires coordination and capacities for rapid deployment. However, the development and especially the forward positioning of such capabilities raise questions about China's security ambitions.

Conclusion: China, Pacific Asia, and Multinodal Governance

One of the strongest arguments for hegemony is the hegemon's responsibility and capability to provide public goods. In a post-hegemonic, multinodal world, the priority of each state is the reduction of uncertainty, and no state bears overall responsibility for provision of public goods. The question thus arises: Can there be public governance without an empowered governor? I would argue yes, but the process of enabling cooperative governance would be quite different from the top-down model of hegemonic stability.

The hegemonic approach to governance is to prevent uncertainty by means of enforced rules; a multinodal approach would control uncertainty by means of mutually beneficial relationships. It is relational because it involves commitments to cooperation by known actors that hope to give shape to an unknown future. While bilateral partnerships are the basic building blocks of multinodal governance, the relational matrixes can be extended indefinitely and can be deepened in content, although there is some tension between progress in extension and progress in depth. Taking the development of ASEAN as an example, the six original members were fortunate to have established ASEAN's identity and approach for a quarter-century before expanding to a more diverse and complete regional organization in the 1990s. ASEAN's many efforts to reach beyond Southeast Asia have the

---

[79] Sun Degang, "From Fragmentation to Integration."   [80] Ibid.

double advantage of reducing external uncertainties and strengthening regional identity. The expansion of the SCO is more problematic, though avoiding exclusivity is an important priority and its "region" does not have obvious limits.

As a microcosm of the global multinodal situation and as the leading center for economic growth, Pacific Asia has a special responsibility to take seriously the establishment of multilateral consensual governance in its region and the extension of its approach above and beyond the region. In economic terms, the establishment of RCEP and the ongoing efforts to expand the Comprehensive and Progressive Agreement for Trans-Pacific Partnership (CPTPP) are promising, and China's various initiatives, most notably BRI and AIIB, are important contributions to the stability and positive outlook of global expectations. Political consensus lags behind because its benefits are less tangible and it involves more sensitive issues. Within the region, three specific challenges are the management of the cross-Strait relationship, achieving a Code of Conduct for the South China Sea, and improving relations between China and Japan. Beyond the region, perhaps Pacific Asia can serve as an exemplar of mutually beneficial control of the uncertainties inevitably generated by global convergence.

Commentary
Evelyn Goh

It has been a great pleasure to engage with the chapters in this volume by one of my favorite original minds and scholars of East Asia. I have long admired Professor Brantly Womack's work on the structures, politics, and practices of asymmetry in international relations, especially his path-breaking book on China and Vietnam.[81] Moreover, his articles on China in the future multinodal order and US-China asymmetric parity are some of the most stimulating reads in the literature on futures thinking regarding East Asia.[82]

Over the preceding four chapters, Womack has provided a stimulating *tour d'horizon* of China's premodern centrality, de-centered modernity, and re-centering post-modernity. In the process, the lens has widened with each chapter, from the initial Sinic focus, out towards a wider look at East Asian encounters with modernity, and then at how China's resurgence in the global political economy and international relations facilitated the region regaining centrality in global affairs. In this chapter, Womack draws these strands together and looks towards the future. He analyzes the characteristics of the future order that East Asia is heading towards, and China's power, positioning, and production in this future order. In so doing, Womack offers deeply insightful, and sometimes also provocative, observations. I rise to the bait by reacting to some of the most important propositions he advances in this chapter.

The Multinodal Framework

Womack's central proposition, that the world is reconfiguring into a multinodal structure, is highly plausible and attractive, and analytically

---

[81] Brantly Womack, *China and Vietnam: The Politics of Asymmetry* (New York: Cambridge University Press, 2006).
[82] Brantly Womack, "China's Future in a Multinodal World Order," *Pacific Affairs* 87:2 (2014), pp. 265–284; Brantly Womack, "Asymmetric Parity: US-China Relations in a Multinodal World," *International Affairs* 92:6 (2016), pp. 1463–1480.

helpful. To my mind, the multinodal framework emphasizes, above all, the existence of multiple centers – or more accurately, nodes – in the international system. These nodes are the important junctures where multiple cross-cutting flows intersect, and which wield authority because they become the "control centers" of globalized connectivity. By my reading therefore, the multinodal framing is at once functional *and* structural; it emphasizes diffusion and networks of authority and relations, but at the same time acknowledges that power and power differentials still play an important part, albeit via a wider range of modes and means. This seems to capture the ongoing transitions of power and order in East Asia and the world.

Certainly, there is ongoing diffusion and fragmentation away from any single hegemon, core, or center. But I do not see us moving towards an international system with no nodes at all, or no great powers at all. I agree with Womack's observation that power asymmetries remain important, but not necessarily definitive. However, an outcome of "deep decentralization" with no international nodes appears unlikely to me – or at the very least, there will be an extremely messy and open-ended transition to get through before that.

Womack's analysis contributes to a better understanding about the nature of this ongoing transition. His multinodal framework resonates with other scholars' analyses of "deep pluralism"[83] or a "multiplex" order.[84] Elsewhere, I have described a contemporary "messy pluralization" with "more actors, more factors, more vectors" in East Asia, as we move from an order that was based on a single pillar (US hegemony centered on its hub-and-spoke relationships), to one that rests on multiple stilts.[85] This is a transition of order rather than of power *per se*. The notion of power transition focuses on the handing over of the baton from one dominant power to another, usually reluctantly and via war. In contrast, my concept of order transition is broader, encompassing "significant alterations in the common goals and values, rules of the game, and social structures of international society."[86] Order transitions may or may not involve wars, but they always entail

---

[83] Amitav Acharya and Barry Buzan, *The Making of Global International Relations* (Cambridge: Cambridge University Press, 2019).
[84] Acharya, *End of the American World Order*.
[85] Goh, "Asia-Pacific's 'Age of Uncertainty'."
[86] Evelyn Goh, *The Struggle for Order: Hegemony, Resistance and Transition in Post-Cold War East Asia* (Oxford: Oxford University Press, 2013), p. 16.

normative changes that result from bargaining and negotiation, sometimes in long-drawn-out and non-linear processes. Therefore, there is going to be a great deal of pulling, pushing, shoving, and horse-trading. We are not going to wake up one day and find ourselves in a brave new world; and it is most likely to be messy and multiply negotiated. During such a transition, what we imagine the new order to look like is vitally important, because this imaginary shapes *how* and *with whom* we are willing to negotiate or to fight, and *what* we negotiate and fight for. In this context, Womack's multinodal world is one that is attractively pluralist, offering potential agency for different actors and combinations of actors, while retaining some familiarity because it acknowledges that there will be some hubs and some spokes. This, I feel, is a vision that most pragmatic Asians can live with (and perhaps negotiate and even fight for).

Transition and Uncertainty

One of the key strengths of Womack's approach, including in this project, is his historically grounded and history-sensitive analysis. This strength becomes very evident in this chapter focusing on the contemporary and the future. The preceding chapters provide the longer-term context, an understanding of the evolution of Asia's centrality, subsequent decentering, and more recent recentering. This raises the important reminder that any analysis of contemporary Chinese politics, China's role in the world, or Sino-American relations, is necessarily premised upon uncertainty and assumptions. Quite apart from the ongoing order transition, China's modernization challenge – so key to Asia's recentering – is also still ongoing.

Wu Yu-Shan's reminder about the earlier period of "confused modernization" experienced in China and East Asia in his comments on Womack's third chapter is important. Wu suggested that China's centrality and decentering were determined by China's power, which was in turn determined by China's choice of a "(political-economic) institutional path that leads to a rapid rise in productivity and growth of the economy." Despite the incredible successes of China's post-totalitarian authoritarian modernization since the 1980s, this institutional route is still an ongoing, unforged path. The political economist Yuen Yuen Ang draws the analogy between the US's Gilded Age around 1870–1900 and current China: "…whereas the American

Progressive Era relied on democratic measures to fight crony capitalism – for example, through political activism and a 'muckraking' free press that exposed corruption – Xi is attempting to summon China's own Progressive Era through command and control. The world has yet to witness a government successfully overcome the side effects of capitalism by decree."[87]

China's modernization challenge is still going on, and with results still uncertain. To the extent that Womack's analysis relies on China's continued economic success to drive Asia's recentering, this is an assumption that requires explicit spotlighting and discussion of probability. (Just like assuming unproblematic continued US domestic stability and foreign policy capability is an assumption that increasingly needs to be spelt out and interrogated.)

Asia as the World's Economic Center of Gravity

However, there is a case to be made that Asia's recentering is building upon a regional momentum beyond China's continued economic growth and evolution, important as the latter is. The "rise of the Rest" has altered the relative distribution of global economic activity, in terms of production, consumption, and investment. But the implications for de-centering the US and the West are more severe than simply the rise of other wealthy nodes in a pattern of capitalist convergence. Indeed, we tend to focus on production when thinking about China's resurgence and East Asia's significance. However, in the medium to long term, as long as the current international consensus on varieties of capitalism holds, it is in consumption that the levers of power reside.[88]

Prior to the Covid-19 pandemic, the reorientation of global trade had already significantly reduced dependency on Western or developed consumers. According to a 2019 Bloomberg report, by 2017, 53

---

[87] Yuen Yuen Ang, "A Reckoning for the China Dream," *Project Syndicate*, September 30, 2021. www.project-syndicate.org/bigpicture/a-reckoning-for-the-china-dream

[88] For the argument that economic "value" is created primarily by consumers rather than by producers, see Philip G. Cerny, "Restructuring the State in a Globalizing World: Capital Accumulation, Tangled Hierarchies and the Search for a New Spatio-Temporal Fix," *Review of International Political Economy* 13:4 (2006), pp. 679–695.

percent of all bilateral trade in the world involved at least one emerging market, up from 38 percent in 1997. The number of countries that conducted the majority of their trade with emerging markets rose from 19 to 64 during the same 20-year period.[89] This meant that producers in developing countries had loosened their previous dependence on demand from developed markets. These producers, along with producers from developed countries, are channeling more goods, services, and employment to developing countries and emerging economies, where new consumer markets and the middle class are growing dramatically. By 2015, Asia accounted for about half of over 3 billion people globally who fell into the middle-class category, and in 2017 it was estimated that almost 90 percent of the next billion entrants into the global middle class will be in Asia: 380 million Indians, 350 million Chinese, and 210 million other Asians.[90] Put simply, the wealth of nations no longer primarily depends on Western consumption, but neither will it rely mainly upon Chinese consumers.

China: Not Just a Regional Great Power

Perhaps the most controversial claim in this chapter is the notion of "China as primarily regional vs. US as primarily global." This has been a popular notion, especially up to the early 2000s, when many still felt that Chinese power was limited and China would not become a "peer competitor" of the United States. However, if Womack's analysis of the trends in China's presence, position, and production is correct – and I think it is – then we would have to give up the hope that we can continue to regard China as confined to being mainly a regional power while retaining the US as the sole, consistently global power.

I am not sure we can have it both ways: Is Asia recentering itself in global affairs through the rise of China and the economic resurgence of the region more generally, or is it not? Could we possibly have an

---

[89] Andre Tartar and Cedric Sam, "How the Rise of Developing Countries Has Disrupted Global Trade," *Bloomberg New Economy Report*, May 7, 2019. www.bloomberg.com/graphics/2019-bloomberg-new-economy/global-trade-developing-nations/

[90] Homi Kharas, "The Unprecedented Expansion of the Global Middle Class: An Update," *Global Economy & Development Working Paper* 100, February 2017. www.brookings.edu/wp-content/uploads/2017/02/global_20170228_global-middle-class.pdf

Asia that is the political-economic center of a globalized and intensely networked world, but at the same time keep China and Asia contained within itself, within its regional bounds? This seems problematic, analytically and empirically.

Indeed, the opposite of the proposition might be true. If the United States were serious about treating China as its primary peer challenger, the US may have to become less global and more determinedly Asia-oriented, precisely because the US strategic and foreign policy establishment believes that US-China "flashpoints" are all in Asia. Therefore, if Womack's overall analysis is right, we might exactly flip their imperatives: The US problem then mainly becomes how it relates to Asia (not just Asian allies), while China, to ensure its continued prosperity, because of its global political-economic embeddedness, must deal with how it relates to the rest of the world, not just Asia. In other words, as strategic competitors, China has to become more primarily global, while the US would need to become more primary Asian.

Independent of US perceptions, the nature of China and Asia's recentering, so effectively captured by Womack in this volume, highlights China's truly global position and imperatives. China's position as a vital global node of production, investment, and consumption is well known by now. It would be worth highlighting two key aspects of this global position that are pertinent to the discussion here. First, China's centrality as a regional and global node brings with it governance requirements: whether we like it or not, Beijing is regulating the connectivity it is building, making rules and setting standards across many domains, including the terms of trade, legal frameworks, transport and communication, as well as new areas such as AI and other elements of Fourth Industrial Revolution (4IR) development and usage.[91] These areas of governance are not just regional; many have implications for evolving global practices and agreements. By growing its governance footprint, China is also developing its international role as a public goods provider. As Womack pointed out in Chapter 2, the *control* of connectivity might be more vital than connectivity in and of itself.

---

[91] See, for example, Antoine Bondaz, "Promoting 'Soft Connectivity': China's Standards-setting Reforms and International Ambitions," *Recherches & Documents* 15, September 2021. www.frstrategie.org/en/publications/recherches-et-documents/promoting-soft-connectivity-china-s-standards-setting-reforms-and-international-ambitions-2021

Second, the extent to which China is willing and able to take up global responsibilities is an increasingly crucial variable today, when messy pluralism creates the worry that we would end up with "No One's World,"[92] one in which declining, risen, challenger, or secondary powers all fail to act quickly or substantively enough to provide leadership for the ultimate global public goods. This is very clear when we think about what used to be quaintly called "non-traditional" security threats, especially climate change and pandemics. This is literally the stuff of "common destiny." As the global crises caused by these latter threats vividly demonstrate, China plays a vital role – negative and positive – in addressing the greatest global challenges of the Anthropocene. To illustrate: China is responsible for approximately 26 percent of global carbon emissions, continues to be the largest net coal consumer (accounting for 64 percent of the global total), and is a major financier of fossil fuel projects globally with over 70 percent of the world's coal power plants believed to be dependent on Chinese financing.[93] But there is a flip side to this structural power: Should China alter its coal dependency and promotion, it will have a disproportionate *positive* effect on global emissions. Hence, President Xi's carbon neutrality pledge in 2020, and the 2021 pledge to stop all further investments in coal-fired energy projects are potentially game-changing at a global level, even if it is too early to gauge how these pledges will be upheld.

Multinodality and Centrality

Let me draw the above threads back together by highlighting two of the most intriguing questions that arise from Womack's analysis. First, in this reconfigured world, which parts are multinodal, and are there some parts that are not? For instance, are we facing a Sino-centric Asia in a multinodal world? This specification is important, mainly because it harks back to my earlier concern about a tendency to want to continue bracketing Asia (and China) within sub-global

---

[92] Charles A. Kupchan, *No One's World: The West, the Rising Rest, and the Coming Global Turn* (New York: Oxford University Press, 2012).
[93] Maddy White, "China's Belt and Road Initiative: Green Leadership or Greenwashing?," *Global Trade Review*, October 14, 2020. www.gtreview.com/news/sustainability/chinas-belt-and-road-initiative-green-leadership-or-greenwashing/

confines. Assuming China's centrality – economic, cultural, and political – within Asia would also deeply circumscribe how non-Asian actors can hope to connect with, relate to, or resist, Asian societies and countries.

But by my reading, Womack's analysis pushes us towards grappling with *a multinodal Asia in a multinodal international system*. In this regard, Wang Gungwu's commentary on Chapter 2 poses the helpful reminder that, historically, China has never been a node unto itself, but rather one major node in a wider Eurasian context containing at least two other major civilizational nodes and a variety of asymmetrical polities interconnected by culture, trade, and threat. But accepting this reality in the contemporary world can pose a very significant challenge, as it requires breaking many standard international relations or strategic studies' molds and assumptions. During the recent decades in which International Relations developed as a sub-discipline, IR scholars have allowed themselves to be beguiled by the convenience of simplifying and dichotomizing under US hegemony. Womack's analysis is a powerful addition to a growing body of working on East Asia that throws down the gauntlet for scholars to conceptualize and analyze power, interdependence, culture, and change in much more subtle, diverse, and empirically rigorous ways.

Second, what is the quality of centrality in a multinodal world? This query is important not just for China, but also for the United States and their respective allies, supporters, clients, and partners. One might argue that a truly multinodal system would display very little centrality because of the sheer diffusion of power and authority across a larger number of nodes and domains. Yet I do not think it is adequate to reduce "centrality" to the idea of something dense being positioned "in the middle." This overly physical rendition underplays the multi-dimensional quality of centrality, especially in the Chinese context. Womack's emphasis on China's "presence," and Wang's exposition on the remarkable continuity at the heart of the Chinese sense of centrality, are extremely helpful in this regard. In particular, Wang's commentary stresses how China's historical centrality was grounded in its evident continuity as a unified, exceptional polity, and as being proven over time relationally vis-à-vis others in its sheer persistence, whether through defense, attack, or absorption. In the contemporary context, I would add that China's system centrality takes on a marked quality of *indispensability* – it is a crucial node that cannot be ignored, whether in economic, political, governance, or other terms. Not all roads lead to Rome in the middle as such, but China looks set to become one of the most important – if not the most important – node in a diffused system with multiple nodes of different types.

Conclusion

We urgently require new concepts and new mindsets to understand this world that Brantly Womack describes in this volume. He has performed a significant service by taking some significant steps forward in this enterprise, and I have no doubt that others will be building effectively upon his foundations. Overall, I appreciate how Womack has done a beautiful job of painting a picture without rose tints. Allow me to wield a less graceful sledgehammer to support the notion that East Asia's future is not going to be comfortable or cozy, and especially not for those who cleave to the vision of a previous US-led "liberal international order" in which the lamb lay down safely next to the tiger and dragon and all was good. Strategists in/of East Asia will have less trouble with this lack of tinting, as they have not tended to start from a cozy view of the pro-US status-quo ante in this region. Despite the centrality of the US role and its alliances, in spite of the many benefits of US hegemony, within this region, the norm has been a lack of comfort, lack of expectation of perpetual peace, contestation, the sense of being post-colonial rule-takers, and of living as asymmetrical neighbors with China. This is what drives the "pragmatic" mindsets now facing a future laden with peril and opportunity.

6 | Global Power Rivalry, Pacific Asia, and World Order

Approaching the topic of global power rivalry from analyses of grand historical dynamics and underlying regional and global economic trends, one might expect a rather deterministic attitude, but the opposite is the case. The United States, China, Pacific Asia, and the rest of the world face consequential choices. Those choices will be made by leaders and political communities acting on their perceptions. Examining the frameworks presupposed by those perceptions is important precisely because better and worse choices can be made.

As Evelyn Goh pointed out in her commentary on the previous chapter, global politics is facing an order transition rather than a power transition. The configurations, values, and uncertainties of world politics are not simply those of switching from the American hegemonic order to a Chinese hegemonic order, or of preserving a democratic world order from authoritarian threat. The nature of global interactions is changing from central order underwritten by a global power to a more diffuse matrix in which relative power still matters but cannot dominate relationships. This is what I call the multinodal world order. This major change has been peaceful and rather gradual thus far, not the result of a cataclysmic war. The most prominent part of the change has been the rise of China. But, as Putin's invasion of Ukraine has demonstrated, neither peace nor gradualness are inevitable.

The US-China rivalry is the strategic focus of world attention, and understandably so. The United States and China are one another's major challenge in terms of security and status. They occupy the center stage of the global political economy, as well as being the two major military powers. But they are not only unequal, they are asymmetric. Part of their asymmetry is that they are at different economic levels, and another is that China is nested in Pacific Asia while the United States is an established global center. China's long-term strategic success requires success in its Pacific Asian relationships, both political and economic, while long-term American success requires an inclusive approach to preserve its global influence. Because of the dangers inherent in rivalry, the mutual reduction of risk is a major challenge. Global leadership in a multinodal world requires quite different virtues and processes from hegemonic leadership. As Goh described it, it is a "messy pluralization," with "more actors, more factors, more vectors," at both the regional and global levels.

This is being written shortly after the Russian invasion of Ukraine. At best, there will be a ceasefire and settlement, and, with nuclear powers involved, the worst is difficult to contemplate. The effects of the crisis on US-China relations are also uncertain. Relations got off to a bad start with China's reluctance to explicitly condemn the invasion and with the US presumption that China was an accomplice. The ramifications of the crisis for China's relationships with Europe are not clear, and the connectivity of Europe and Asia is at stake.

Despite the uncertainties, the crisis can be taken as a stress test of the global system, and its multinodal character has thus far proved resilient.[1] Ukrainian resistance and its broad international support were clearly underestimated by Putin. Moreover, the reverberations of the conflict on global food and energy are significant. They highlight not only global market prices, but more importantly the global matrix of supply chains. Europe is hit hard by energy problems, and the Middle East is particularly dependent on Ukraine and Russian grain. While Putin may have expected European disaffection with American unipolarity to split the opposition, in fact the outrageousness of a brutal military action brought everyone together. The crisis is likely to continue to increase tensions in the US-China rivalry, but because of parity, both will suffer from zero-sum policies, and because of asymmetry, victory is not an option for either.

Asymmetric Parity

Thus far in this book the role of US-China rivalry has been underplayed in order to highlight China's changing roles and underlying continuities in Pacific Asia and trends in the overall global order since 2008. The regional vantage point was the necessary background for

---

[1] Brantly Womack, "China's New Strategic Opportunity in Europe," Al Jazeera Center for Studies, March 14, 2022. https://studies.aljazeera.net/en/analyses/china%E2%80%99s-new-strategic-opportunity-europe

putting the rivalry in context. But risk attracts attention, and more risk attracts more attention, and so global attention is certainly fixed on the United States and China, and on their relationship. Not surprisingly, the United States and China are obsessed with their relationship as well. They are in a novel situation. Neither has faced a counterpart comparable to the other. Both have the Cold War as their proximate public image of the confrontation, but from different angles. And in fact, the asymmetry of the US-China relationship gives it a fundamentally different natural dynamic from the earlier US-Soviet rivalry.

Parity in Center Court

If we apply our "3 Ps" – presence, population, and production – the United States and China together certainly qualify for center stage. They are the first and third most populous countries, with the first and second largest consumer markets. The facts of production centrality of the two global powers are as impressive as those of Pacific Asia presented in the last chapter. Together, the US and China were 42 percent of global GDP in nominal terms, 34 percent in PPP terms in 2020.[2] They are the middle third of the world economy. They are each larger economies than the next four countries combined: Japan, Germany, UK, and India. American military expenditure is three times larger than China's, but China's is larger than the next four combined: India, Russia, UK, and Saudi Arabia. It is hardly surprising that they pay attention to each other, and that the world pays attention to them. If the relationship were cohesive rather than divisive, it would certainly lead the world, as happened in the Paris climate accords in 2015.

Together, the US and Chinese military budgets are slightly over half of the world total. As a percentage of GDP, China's military budget is 1.7 percent, half that of the US and lower than all of the top ten except Japan and Germany. At 3.7 percent of GDP, the United States has a higher percentage expenditure than all of the top ten except Russia and Saudi Arabia.[3] However, military preponderance is not the same as capacity to dominate. The American withdrawal from Afghanistan illustrates the difficulty and frustration of attempting

---

[2] Calculated from IMF, *World Economic Outlook*, April 2021.
[3] Diego Lopes Da Silva, Nan Tian, and Alexandra Marksteiner, *Trends in World Military Expenditure, 2020* (Stockholm: Stockholm International Peace Research Institute (SIPRI), 2021).

control of another country by force of arms. Certainly, no one would want to be in Afghanistan's shoes, where according to the World Food Program in the winter of 2022 over half the population faced acute food insecurity and 8.7 million faced emergency food insecurity.[4] But the failure of "small wars" should provide perspective on the imaginable realities of larger ones. Afghanistan's population is somewhat smaller than the average population of China's thirty-one provinces. Beyond the risks and costs of major war itself, even the most optimistic vision of a post-war situation is unsettling. One could imagine the difficulties of a post-war American military governor of Shandong Province, with a population of 102 million, or of a Chinese military governor of Texas, with millions of guns in disgruntled private hands. We will return to the question of the risk of war between the United States and China later in this chapter, and it certainly should be taken seriously, but, fortunately, it is not inevitable.

The two global powers are the primary nodes of the multinodal configuration described in the previous chapter. Governments and businesspeople around the world watch the American stock market and Chinese production figures. Each global power has unique leverage in its asymmetric relationships with everyone else. However, neither is capable of forcing capitulation of another political community at an acceptable price to itself. Moreover, beyond the bilateral interactions of the primary nodes, the located, multinodal texture of secondary middle power and smaller nodes shapes the practical diplomatic alternatives of the primary nodes, and all are capable of their own initiatives. International relationships are the active result of negotiations and accommodations, not command and obedience. While sometimes the choices faced may echo Hegel's definition of freedom as "insight into necessity," the primal importance of autonomy undergirds sovereignty.

Parity implies that rivalry between the global powers is inevitable. They are one another's major concern. Their sense of progress or decline will be influenced by how they perceive their own change relative to the other. The vast differences in their histories and systems facilitate mutual suspicions. However, the modalities of rivalry can vary. At the soft end of rivalry, powers at parity are competitive politically as well

---

[4] Peyvand Khorsandi, "'Our Presence is Hope': US$2.6bn Needed as Winter Spells Hunger for Afghanistan," *World Food Program*, January 25, 2022. www.wfp.org/stories/our-presence-hope-us26bn-needed-winter-spells-hunger-afghanistan

as in economic terms, but they cooperate in areas of mutual interest. China's rise relative to the US changes the proportions in the relationship, but global economic development is not a fixed pie. China's construction of a high-speed rail network put it ahead of the United States in terms of public passenger transportation, but it did not remove rails from the US nor prevent the US from following suit. Indeed, one can hope that the demonstrated convenience of rail transportation in Japan, Europe, and China will stimulate similar efforts in the US. Moreover, there are opportunities for political cooperation, and connectivity can be encouraged as mutually beneficial. Beyond the bilateral interaction, soft rivalry expands the field of autonomy for the other nodes because of the active competitive interest of the primary nodes.

The hard end of rivalry assumes a zero-sum game with the other that must culminate in the end of parity. Relative gain is all that matters, so the priorities shift to preventing the progress of the other, insulating oneself from vulnerability to the other, and isolating the other. The more ideologically disposed members of President Trump's foreign policy team vigorously propound hard rivalry,[5] while the Biden team talks more softly to China but maintains a similar approach.[6] As Professor Shi Yinhong predicted at the beginning of Biden's term, the "revision [of Trump's policy] is likely to be quite partial and limited, and the confrontation and competition with China in some other areas will probably intensify."[7] Both administrations have shared the Pentagon's idea of China as a "pacing threat," justifying increasingly large and sophisticated military budgets.[8]

The "us or them" mentality tightens the global multinodal fabric between the primary nodes, but is unlikely to produce separate camps.[9] While the tightening may occasionally sharpen the leverage of intermediate powers, decisively committing to be on one side or

---

[5] Matt Pottinger, "Russia, China and the New Cold War," *Wall Street Journal*, March 18, 2022.

[6] Joergen Oerstroem Moeller, "Biden Has Inherited the Ingredients that Engendered Trump's Grand Strategy," *National Interest*, May 24, 2021.

[7] Shi Yinhong, The Recent and Predictable Future: The U.S. Posture toward China During and After the Presidential Election Campaign," *East Asian Affairs* 1:1 (2021).

[8] Fareed Zakaria, "The Pentagon is Using China as an Excuse for Huge New Budgets," *Washington Post*, March 10, 2022.

[9] Martin Wolf, "Containing China is Not a Feasible Option," *Financial Times*, February 3, 2021.

the other would entail a loss of autonomy. To become a member of a camp increases dependency on the camp leader and reduces connectivity with the other camp. Since most countries are thickly interdependent with both the United States and China, camp formation would be resisted by most. Moreover, decoupling would compound the problem of American proportional decline.

The Biden administration's strategy of economic decoupling from China has caused acute difficulties for some of China's high-tech companies in the short term, but it is likely to be harmful to American strategic interests in the longer term. Decoupling weaponizes the existing interdependence of the globalized economy; thus, its effectiveness increases the risk of interdependence with its initiator as well as with its target.[10] The strategies of "onshoring" (domestic sourcing) and "friend-shoring" (sourcing from allies) may appear to stabilize production chains, but it alienates excluded participants and therefore restricts markets and general economic resilience.[11] In the Cold War decoupling wasn't necessary, since Soviet activity in international markets was negligible. In any case, however, the uncertainty created by tension between the primary nodes will cause others to hedge their bets by retaining ties to both the US and China but also reducing their exposure to both where they can.[12] There should be many other options, since two-thirds of the global economy is outside the primary nodes.

Many American analysts take a "Goldilocks" position between hard and soft rivalry. For example, Fred Bergsten[13] argues for "conditional competitive cooperation," Kevin Rudd[14] suggests "managed strategic competition," and Joseph Nye recommends "cooperative rivalry."[15]

---

[10] Anna Gros and Demetri Sevastopulo, "Dutch Chip Toolmaker ASMI Warns of Escalating Trade Tensions," *Financial Times*, November 29, 2022.

[11] Samuel Hardwick and Adam Triggs, "Friend-shoring No Ready-made Answer to Asian Supply Chain Resilience," *East Asia Forum*, November 27, 2022. www.eastasiaforum.org/2022/11/27/friend-shoring-no-ready-made-answer-to-asian-supply-chain-resilience/

[12] Sam Fleming and Andy Bounds, "Dutch Minister Defends Trade Links with China," *Financial Times*, November 30, 2022.

[13] C. Fred Bergsten, *The United States v. China: The Quest for Global Economic Leadership* (Cambridge, UK: Polity, 2022).

[14] Kevin Rudd, *The Avoidable War: The Case for Managed Strategic Competition* (New York: The Asia Society, 2020).

[15] Joseph Nye, "The Cooperative Rivalry of US-China Relations," *Project Syndicate*, November 6, 2018. www.project-syndicate.org/commentary/china-america-relationship-cooperative-rivalry-by-joseph-s--nye-2018-11

These are quite reasonable positions given the differences of interests between the US and China and the continuing possibilities of mutual benefit. Some in China recognize the problem that China's rise poses to the United States. According to Prof. Wu Xinbo of Fudan University, "The rise of China certainly poses a complex and somewhat unique challenge to the United States."[16] But the relationship does not have to be win-lose. As Evan Feigenbaum put it, "the United States and China don't need joint approaches to pursue strategic cooperation, just mutually beneficial ones."[17] Domestic American problems such as the hollowing out of its manufacturing base and vulnerability to supply shocks encourage hedging against globalization, and additional concerns about China as a rival add a political dimension of concern.[18] While the Goldilocks position lacks the satisfying clarity of the soft and hard approaches, its ambiguity encourages negotiation. Both caution and the lack of caution can cause mistakes. An example of excessive caution was US opposition to the Asian Infrastructure Investment Bank (AIIB), which as of 2020 had AAA credit ratings and 103 members, representing 79 percent of the global population and 65 percent of global GDP. On the other hand, promotion by President Obama of the Transpacific Partnership (TPP) proved a step too far for domestic American politics, and Trump made two steps back. Now China is a candidate member of the modified version of TPP, and the US is not.

The turn toward confrontation between the US and China raises the risk of superpower confrontation, and it also affects the general texture of multinodal international relationships. Daniel Drezner points out that optimistic great powers will try to extend their general penumbra of soft power; when they are pessimistic they will concentrate on their "kinetic capabilities" – what they can do to directly improve their relative positions.[19] This is more likely to exacerbate the security dilemma, with each side trying to gain an advantage over the other. But besides the effect of pessimism on the bilateral relationship of primary

---

[16] Wu Xinbo, "The China Challenge: Competitor or Order Transformer?" *Washington Quarterly* 43:3 (2020), p. 100.
[17] Evan Feigenbaum, "Why America No Longer Gets Asia," *Washington Quarterly* 34:2 (2011), p. 31.
[18] Robert Kuttner, "Bringing the Supply Chain Back Home," *New York Review of Books*, November 18, 2021.
[19] Daniel Drezner, "The Perils of Pessimism: Why Anxious Nations are Dangerous Nations," *Foreign Affairs* 101:4 (2022), pp. 34–43.

nodes, a general atmosphere of pessimism is likely to increase reliance on existing regional relationships. For most non-primary nodes, bunching together is a likely response. In the summer of 2022, the "polycrisis" – the compounding of Covid, the war in Ukraine, recession, and inflation – is producing a general cloud of pessimism beyond superpower rivalry.[20] These intensify the global certainty vacuum, a situation that one does not want to face alone.

Underlying this discussion of parity is the assumption that neither the United States nor China is likely to collapse internally. Both possibilities have been raised by some, China since 1989 and the US since the election of Donald Trump. Gordon Chang's *The Coming Collapse of China* was published in 2001, and his Cassandra vision was updated by Michael Beckley and Hal Brands in 2022.[21] The collapse of the Soviet Union on the one hand, and the undermining of Athenian democracy by Alcibiades on the other, are evidence that such things happen. But the existing difficulties of each are not likely to lead to implosion, and implosion is even less likely to lead to elimination. Given the magnitude of each, parity of some sort is likely to remain. Perhaps the best advice regarding how to cope with regime catastrophe is given by Robert Kaplan, who suggests moderate rather than triumphalist policies by the survivor.[22] His advice is most relevant regarding Putin's Russia. As to the collapse of either the United States or China, the problem of fixating on unlikely scenarios is that it distorts the appreciation of more probable trends.[23]

Asymmetric Parity

"Asymmetric parity" is not a contradiction in terms, but there is a conceptual tension between asymmetry and parity. Parity requires a

---

[20] Adam Tooze, "Defining Polycrises: From Crisis Pictures to the Crisis Matrix," *Chartbook* 130, June 24, 2022. https://adamtooze.substack.com/p/chartbook-130-defining-polycrisis

[21] Gordon G. Chang, *The Coming Collapse of China* (New York: Random House, 2001); Michael Beckley and Hal Brands, "The End of China's Rise," *Foreign Affairs*, October 1, 2021.

[22] Robert Kaplan, "When Empires or Great Powers Fall, Chaos and War Rise," *Foreign Affairs*, October 4, 2022.

[23] See Philip Tetlock's classic, *Expert Political Judgment: How Good is it? How Can We Know?* (Princeton: Princeton University Press, 2005), pp. 144–188.

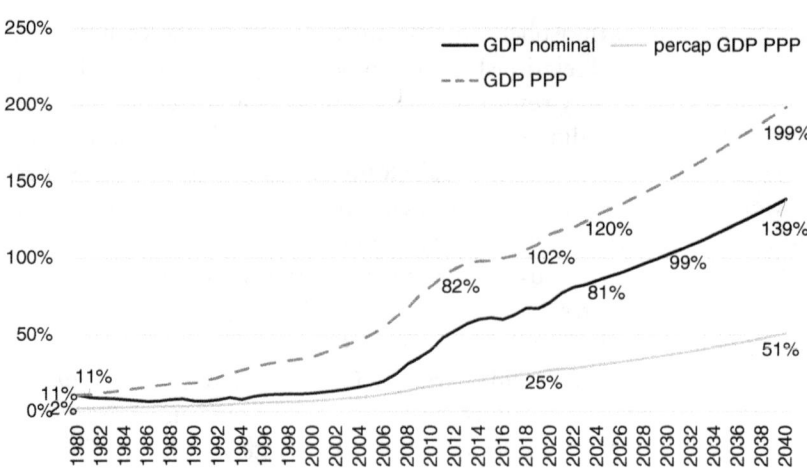

Figure 6.1 China's GDP as percentage of US GDP

rough similarity in magnitude, while asymmetry requires a significant difference in capabilities and situation, and hence difference in exposure in the relationship. The United States and China are equal enough in overall magnitude to qualify for parity. They are each important to the other, and each vulnerable to the other. But the differences between the two are more than marginal divergences in capabilities and politics.

Figure 6.1 conveys some basic realities regarding bilateral economic trends. China surpassed the United States in total GDP in Purchasing Power Parity (PPP) terms in 2016, and if we extend the IMF's estimate, China would pass the US in dollar value (nominal GDP) in 2031.[24] Of course, we have experienced the effects of Covid on the world economy, and I am writing in the shadows of the Russian black swan and of global economic uncertainty, so such extrapolations are not predictions. Fred Bergsten uses the US and Chinese growth rates for 2019 and arrives at results similar to the IMF: China's doubling of US GDP (PPP) and equal GDP (nominal) both by 2030.[25] But he cautions that

---

[24] I extended the IMF estimate by taking its estimated increments for 2026 (3.8, 3.8; 7.4, 7.3 for US, China nominal and PPP, respectively) and extending them to 2040. This is a high-end estimate for China given the likelihood of a leveling of percentage growth.

[25] Bergsten, *The United States v. China*, p. 88.

China's growth rate is likely to drop, and other economists are more pessimistic about China's short-term resilience and long-term prospects.[26] In 2022 the rest of Asia is forecast to grow faster than China for the first time since 1990, though that is partly a result of China's earlier rebound from Covid, followed by later problems that became acute in 2022.[27] In any case, as the Ukraine crisis and the 2022 Covid lockdown in Shanghai have already demonstrated, long-term extrapolations of all economies will be battered by the effects of unanticipated events. But regardless of future growth trends, China has already risen, and its current relative significance is not likely to diminish.[28] Given China's connectivity to the rest of Asia, Asia's growth is a positive influence on China's continued prospects.

The Purchasing Power Parity line of Figure 6.1 estimates the scale of Chinese production in terms of a comparable basket of consumer-oriented merchandise. Because price levels for consumer goods are usually lower in developing countries and the dollar value of non-consumer goods is usually higher, there is generally a significant gap between PPP and nominal for developing countries. As we have seen in the Chapter 4 comparison with the "poor four" of Southeast Asia, thirty years ago China was poor even by the PPP standard.[29] By 2040, China's GDP PPP is extrapolated to be twice that of the US. China's per capita GDP PPP has also risen rapidly, from 8 percent of the US in 2000 to 25 percent in 2020, and possibly to an estimated 50 percent in 2040.

The data provides underlying economic support for Goh's argument that the world is experiencing an "order transition" rather than a "power transition." Power transition theory, originating from A. F. K. Organski's general theory of world politics, has devoted itself to the study of such transitions.[30] Defining the window of power parity as equal economic mass plus or minus 20 percent, the window of parity is

---

[26] Daniel Rosen, "The Age of Slow Growth in China," *Foreign Affairs*, April 15, 2022.
[27] Edward White and Mercedes Ruehl, "China Growth to Fall Behind Rest of Asia for First Time since 1990," *Financial Times*, September 26, 2022.
[28] Shaun Breslin, *China Risen? Studying Chinese Global Power* (Bristol: Bristol University Press, 2022).
[29] A sign of how times change: the 1994 edition of *The Economist* primer on international economic measurements did not use China as one of its thirteen illustrative economies, while the 2010 edition does.
[30] A. F. K. Organski, *World Politics* (New York: Knopf, 1958).

the most likely point of major conflict.[31] But for the United States and China, that window of parity is huge. By PPP measures China entered the 80 percent power transition window in 2010 and exits at 122 percent in 2023, while in nominal terms China enters the window in 2024 and exits in 2036. So, if we combine the two measures, China has a one-year gap between the upper sill of the PPP 40 percent window and the lower sill of the nominal 40 percent window, and as of 2022 it is already halfway through a transition period lasting a quarter-century. And, if we consider the more pessimistic views of China's growth prospects, the gap is infinite, stretching between the already attained PPP parity and an unachievable nominal parity.[32] Each measure of GDP has its own problems, PPP because of its selective basket of production, and nominal because of currency exchange fluctuations, but there is a more basic problem here. There is no clear, central transition point of parity between the United States and China, because their parity is asymmetric. The ambiguities of their GDP comparisons are only the tip of the iceberg of important situational differences. As the previous chapter argued, China is the avatar of demographic power, and the United States is the avatar of incumbent wealth. And China is part of Pacific Asia, while the US is the established global power.

China's aggregate GDP growth is impressive because it is a developing and urbanizing country with a very large population.[33] Its per capita GDP PPP is only 25 percent of American per capita GDP, and is equal to the world average.[34] As a national actor it can concentrate resources on special projects, such as the space program. Scale can translate into quality. On the Global Innovation Index China ranked in twelfth place in 2021, just ahead of Japan.[35] China was the only

---

[31] Ronald Tammen and Jacek Kugler, "Power Transition and China–US Conflicts," *Chinese Journal of International Politics* 1:1 (2006), pp. 35–55, here p. 43.

[32] Bert Hoffman gives a range of estimates of nominal parity, from 2030 to never, in "How Fast Did China Grow?" a presentation at Harvard's Fairbank Center, April 27, 2022. https://fairbank.fas.harvard.edu/events/critical-issues-confronting-china-series-featuring-bert-hofman/

[33] Justin Yifu Lin, "中国经济的发展潜力、新挑战与应对 [China's Development Potential: New Challenges and Measures] (February 2022). www.36kr.com/p/1616049972241664.

[34] Calculated from IMF, *World Economic Outlook*, October 2021 and World Bank, *World Development Indicators* 2021.

[35] *Global Innovation Index 2021* (Geneva: World Intellectual Property Organization, 2021). www.globalinnovationindex.org/Home

middle-income country ranking in the top 34. Some of its localities, Shanghai, for example, are far ahead of the rest, but the national government must also satisfy the needs of four times as many people as the US population, but from the same production base. Thus, China's urgency for continued growth is greater, and its resistance to containment is more than a security concern. On the other hand, among China's many badges for "world's largest" is one for being the largest national market, and between 2020 and 2030 China's middle class is expected to add another 337 million consumers, approximately the population of the US.[36] Already in 2020 Chinese middle-class expenditures are estimated at $7.1 trillion compared to $4.7 trillion for the United States.[37] If, as Goh argued in her commentary on the last chapter, consumption is the key, then China has arrived, though, as she points out, China is only part of a larger arrival of developing country middle classes.

Besides the constraints of China's status as a developing country, the second major problem with anticipating a power transition rather than sustained asymmetric rivalry is that a post-hegemonic situation is fundamentally new. The Global Financial Crisis of 2008 marked a transition to an era in which globalization has created a situation of inequality but not dominance, and the difference between a multinodal world rather than a multipolar one is described in the previous chapter. The diversification and overlap of every country's significant relationships means that there are no natural camps of followers. Moreover, China's role in global development is not that of replacement for the United States but rather as first among the unequals of the developing world, in asymmetric parity with the US. China has a "hub and rim" pattern of partnerships, in contrast to the Cold War hub-and-spoke configuration of American alliances.

Given two primary nodes with different dynamics, rivalry between the United States and China is an inevitable part of order transition, but a key difference between power transition, with its hegemonic mindset, and order transition in a situation of asymmetric parity is that

---

[36] Homi Kharas and Wolfgang Fengler, "Which Will Be the Top 30 Consumer Markets of This Decade?" *Brookings*, August 31, 2021. www.brookings.edu/blog/future-development/2021/08/31/which-will-be-the-top-30-consumer-markets-of-this-decade-5-asian-markets-below-the-radar/

[37] Tooze, "Defining Polycrises."

power transition focuses on the point at which parity empowers the challenger, while order transition assumes a longer process of mutual adjustment, as well as the influence of the shifting realities of the global context. Order transition is not inevitable because it depends on the continuing grand trends of development since 2008. But returning to the post-Cold War "unipolar moment" that the US enjoyed from 1991 to 2008 is not an option. The world will not fit back into that box.

The positive side of asymmetric rivalry is that, because there is no necessary win/lose moment of struggle for domination, the gains that each side makes are not necessarily threats to the other side. In hegemonic rivalry the winner takes all, and therefore any gain by the rival is a threat. There can be only one king of the mountain. But if there is no mountain that can be controlled, then relative gain by the other side changes the proportions of the relationship but does not increase ultimate risk. Thus, the fundamental strategic priority in post-hegemonic rivalry should be one's own absolute gain rather than the weakening of the rival. Rivalry becomes a race rather than a fight. One does better by running faster.

Given the greater uncertainty of a post-hegemonic order, the primary nodes have a historic opportunity for collaboration. Since they do not face a win-lose confrontation over ultimate power, they could vastly increase their global influence by working together on issues of global interest. The most obvious area would be issues related to climate change, and the success of the Paris Accords demonstrated both the effectiveness of US-China cooperation and the resulting increase in prestige and influence of both countries. But there are many other areas in which both would have a mutual interest in reducing uncertainty. While other countries might worry about a "G-2" monopoly of global leadership, the difference of interest between the United States as the avatar of advanced countries and China as the avatar of developing countries implies that whatever they can agree on is likely to be close to the interests of most of the rest. In any case, a collaborative G-2 would be less risky to all than a hostile G-2. But the optics of rivalry make cooperation difficult.

The Texture of the Multinodal Matrix

Both the United States and China are tempted to fixate on their bilateral rivalry because it is for each the relationship of greatest exposure. However, given the connectivity of international relationships in a post-hegemonic world, the most effective strategy to reduce uncertainty, even for primary nodes, is to focus strategically on the texture of the general multinodal matrix. Because the rivalry is long term and the prospects of each primary node depend primarily on its own success rather than on the defeat of the other, how each relates to the rest of a complex, adaptive world system becomes the key question.[38]

The basic task of all countries, regardless of relative power, is to control uncertainty. The more powerful are tempted to control uncertainty by leveraging their predominance in order to get what they want. However, the practice of dominating transactions limits the strategic option of building relationships of mutual benefit. Power matters in a multinodal world, so it is possible to dominate transactions in asymmetric interactions. But all actors have agency, and transactional domination proves to the smaller partner that its interests are not respected. In such cases the less powerful should hedge against the more powerful. But if the more powerful promote a mutual interest, then the transaction encourages a continuing relationship of mutual advantage. If the interaction shows respect for the autonomy of the smaller side, then the transaction is not merely mutually beneficial, but the relationship acquires credibility in facing unanticipated future interactions. The strengthening of relational bonds reduces uncertainty for both sides. If instead of defining strategy as "the art of creating power,"[39] we redefine it as "the art of sustaining and increasing influence," then building relationships is the key strategic aim.

The resilience of international relationships depends on the strength of relational bonds. International reality is never simple or predictable, but the current post-hegemonic world order is more complex by an order of magnitude than a hegemonic one. Moreover, as the mutations of the Covid pandemic have demonstrated, globalization creates a global village in which there is no safe distance from a neighbor's problems. Given the complexity of global interactions and the inevitability of unanticipated crises, resilience is the key strategic virtue. It is tempting to think that a predominance of power controls one's exposure, but if the crisis is a general one, the texture of international

---

[38] Jochen Prantl and Evelyn Goh, "Rethinking Strategy and Statecraft for the Twenty-first Century of Complexity: A Case for Strategic Diplomacy," *International Affairs*, preprint, February 2022.
[39] Ibid.

relationships will be more important. If the powerful only take care of themselves, they expend their power and at the same time weaken their own relational safety net. If there are relationships founded on credible mutual interests and mutual respect, then all may cooperate in responding to the common crisis. Indeed, even if the crisis is particular to one country, the rest will treat it as a common concern, because the maintenance of relationships is a strategic concern for all. No one knows where the next black swan might land.

China's Regional Challenge

The United States and China are positioned to relate differently to the global matrix. While both are now global powers, and primary nodes of the multinodal matrix, their asymmetric parity and their locations require different relational strategies. China cannot succeed in its global relationships if it fails to normalize its relationships in Pacific Asia. If Taiwan becomes a venue of oppression and resistance, and if China's relations with Japan become irretrievably hostile, these regional problems will undercut its global presence. For its part, the United States cannot sustain its global influence if it insists on exclusive hierarchical relationships. There is an inevitable tension in the bilateral relationship, but how that relationship plays out will depend on the more general strategic success or failure of each.

China is central to a region that itself has become key to the economy of a globalized world. The asymmetry between China and its neighbors creates the opportunity for influence but at the same time the possibility of alienation. This is a continuing challenge. Each increase in China's influence increases regional dependency on the region's China-centered configuration. Dependency is tolerable only if the region is confident that its autonomy and its extra-regional relationships will be respected. Normalcy in an asymmetric relationship requires respect for the agency of the smaller side. The smaller side's autonomy can be buffered by regional solidarity and by a diversity of other relationships. However, everyone will remain watchful of the actions of the center. Verbal reassurances of benevolent respect that run contrary to perceptions of encroachment will lower the credibility of the center. The rational regional strategy for China is to maintain its resilience by strengthening its regional structure and by improving its extra-regional relationships.

The startling lack of positive or even neutral attitudes toward China in Pacific Asia, detailed in Chapter 4, point to a fundamental problem in China's external relations. While it is convenient for China to attribute the low ratings to unfamiliarity with Chinese culture and to misunderstandings of current events, and therefore to invest in Confucius Institutes and media outlets, Pacific Asia is the area with the longest exposure to China and therefore with the greatest background understanding. The basic problem is not lack of information but rather that China is at the same time a source of opportunity and a disruptor of status quo expectations. It has yet to provide a reassuring vision of its *status ad quem*, its desired future status quo.[40] Confronting a global order in which it was first excluded and then marginalized, it is hardly surprising that China is a revisionist power. But the unanswered concern of others is whether China plans to serve only its own interest, or to contribute to an order more appropriate and reliable for everyone. China's rhetoric of a "community of common destiny" and its investments in empowering infrastructure are positive, but it must demonstrate convincingly that it is willing to provide the transparency and conformity to mutual constraints that a rules-based international order requires. China's recent domestic politics have not been reassuring. Its reluctance to condemn Russia's invasion of Ukraine is also worrying. Thus far, its neighbors do not feel actively threatened by China, but they are not confident about the future.

The statecraft appropriate to China's new centrality differs fundamentally from that of its traditional centrality. Thin connectivity managed relationships that were peripheral to both parties by keeping the formal relationship private between rulers, and at arm's length. As described in Chapter 2, "officialism," the hypocrisy of hierarchy, was essential both to China's pretense of control and to providing cover for the actual agency of neighbors. Now with thick connectivity, neither the pretense of hierarchy nor traditional officialism are appropriate. Fortunately, China's own experience in the "century of humiliation" was a sobering experience of the shadow side of hierarchy. The "Five Principles of Peaceful Coexistence" and the general condemnation of hegemony grounded a rhetoric based on equality and respectful solidarity that has been essential to China's soft ascent to centrality.

[40] Brantly Womack, "China and the Future Status Quo," *Chinese Journal of International Politics* 8:2 (2015), pp. 115–137.

However, as China has become more powerful, it is more tempted to use its asymmetric advantage to pressure partners, and as it has done so, officialism has re-emerged in a new form, as the hypocrisy of the more than equal. Actions are taken, such as the banning of banana imports from the Philippines during the 2016 dispute over arbitration in the South China Sea, or the prohibition of Lithuanian imports in the 2021 crisis over the naming of the Taiwan representative office, but either the actions are officially denied or their connection to the current crisis is denied. Unlike the old officialism with its rituals of hierarchy, the new officialism is secretive about the use of power. They are similar in that both confirm the cynicism of observers, but in an era of thick connectivity there are many more occasions and many more observers.

Fortunately, China's new officialism is only occasional. It does not hide a dark plot of re-establishing hierarchy, but only the occasional yielding to the temptation to kick the counterpart under the table when an interaction is not going well. The general pattern of economic cooperation and the rhetoric of thick connectivity have been successful in establishing bonds of mutual interest, as have the infrastructural projects under the umbrella of the Belt and Road Initiative (BRI). China's reputation among elites in Southeast Asia improved slightly in 2021, probably because of its help with Covid.[41] But the tone of regional relationships would be much improved by greater openness. China's occasional officialism lends credibility to critical external speculation by undermining its own credibility. Moreover, unadmitted sanctions are unpredictable. Ultimately, normal asymmetric relationships require time, but clarity and consistency increase confidence.

Despite the general progress of China's regional relationships, there are challenges that face it with the possibility of self-containment. If China makes any neighbor feel that the risks of continued engagement with China are greater than its benefits, and that a choice between risk and engagement must be made, then China has begun a process of self-containment. If China pressures other neighbors to side against the defecting neighbor, it will accelerate the process. China's regional centrality would turn from a positive centrality driven by opportunity

---

[41] *The State of Southeast Asia Survey Report 2022*, February 16, 2022 (Singapore: ASEAN Studies Centre at ISEAS Yusof Ishak Institute, 2022). www.iseas.edu.sg

to a negative one driven by fear. While this is unlikely, the issues of relations with Taiwan, sovereignty in the South China Sea, and relations with Japan all have the potential for cascading alienation. It is possible to imagine a de-regionalization of Pacific Asia, not because of global decoupling, but because of fear of China. If the region, or significant regional actors, were to balance against China rather than merely diversifying regional relationships and hedging against dependence, then it is hard to imagine the continued strengthening of China's global role. Russia and Central Asia do not have the demographic or economic mass to substitute for Pacific Asia. China's relationships with other regions are still fairly distant, geographically and politically, and it is hard to imagine that if China's politics alienated Pacific Asia that it would nevertheless attract others. It would seem more likely that China's negative centrality would create self-containment. While its domestic scale and momentum would guarantee its continued status as a major demographic power, militarization would displace externally-related economic growth. China isolated itself in the Ming and Qing dynasties, but to do so in this century would demonstrate a disastrous failure of political leadership. Even a recent study sympathetic to the caution of the Ming and Qing dynasties notes that "Failing to emancipate the mind by following the old ways, clinging to the shortcomings and not advancing with the times, and sticking to the rules without the courage to reform will lead to the exhaustion of national strength, social stagnation, and the people's lack of livelihood."[42] Putin has reminded us that fundamental mistakes of leadership are possible.

The Global Challenge of the United States

Despite its loss of hegemonic status, the strategic strength of the United States remains its global leadership. The global configuration constructed by the United States, and around the United States, over the past seventy years is the default practice of global order. In a world that has become more uncertain, the familiarity of the US-centered

---

[42] 中国历史研究院课题组 [Research Group of the Chinese Academy of History], "明清时期'闭关锁国'问题新探" [A New Investigation of the "Closed Country" System of the Ming and Qing Eras], 历史研究 [Historical Studies] 3 (2022), p. 19.

order and its existing structures makes its continuation everyone's least uncertain prospect. In addition, the American "3 Ps," presence, population, and production, to which we could add "prosperity" as a fourth, encourage bilateral connectivity. To be like Cuba, North Korea, Afghanistan, or Iran, to be cut off from the United States, is to suffer loss of opportunities and to risk broader global isolation. Even Cuba, which has survived sixty years of US embargo and has the overwhelming sympathy of the rest of the world,[43] continues to suffer severe deprivation.

While every country, including China, would like to tweak the existing global system to their advantage, no country, including China, would like to replace it with a totally different system. In the few areas where China has incumbency advantages, most notably in the composition and prerogatives of the Permanent Five members of the UN Security Council, it is not eager for change. China is interested in changing aspects of the system where established practices do not allow it the influence that it feels is appropriate to its status. But as far as the general international system is concerned, China is revisionist rather than revolutionary, and global rather than isolated. As Xi Jinping put it at Davos in 2017, "Whether you like it or not, the global economy is the big ocean that you cannot escape from."[44]

Revisionism is opposed by the United States not because adjustments and improvements cannot be made, but because the US conceives of the global order as its sphere of influence. According to Chas Freeman's definition, spheres of influence "are assertions of an exclusive right to supervise or participate in deciding the alignments and affairs of another nation or nations in relation to still others either in general or in specific domains… Spheres of influence demand deference and restrict the geopolitical or geo-economic freedom of maneuver of the countries or regions within them."[45] A sphere of influence is necessarily

---

[43] For twenty-nine straight years the UN General Assembly has condemned the US blockade of Cuba and its extraterritorial sanctions on third country relationships. The condemnation vote in 2021 was 184 in favor, 3 abstentions, and 2 opposed (US and Israel). https://news.un.org/en/story/2021/06/1094612

[44] Xi Jinping, "Jointly Shoulder Responsibility of Our Times, Promote Global Growth," January 17, 2017. www.china.org.cn/node_7247529/content_40569136.htm

[45] Chas Freeman, "About Spheres of Influence," March 2022. https://chasfreeman.net/about-spheres-of-influence

hegemonic, serving the interests of the state whose sphere it is. It is not surprising, therefore, that the term was first used during the European division of Africa at the Congress of Berlin in 1884–5. The earliest American claim to a sphere of influence was the Monroe Doctrine in 1823, and was extended to the "free world" during the Cold War. With the collapse of the Cold War the United States assumed a global sphere of influence. There is a shifting array of enemy states that are sanctioned and excluded, and the US demands obedience from the rest to its policies regarding the enemies. But the problem with maintaining the American global sphere of influence in a post-hegemonic world is that it has become unmanageable. Spheres of influence "are now generating more instability and conflict than they confine."[46]

The basic strategic challenge for the United States is adjusting from hegemonic centrality to multinodal centrality. What the United States faces at the global level is like what the European imperial powers faced with decolonization. In both cases the end of domination did not mean the end of relationships, or, in many cases, even the end of centrality. The relationships remain asymmetric, but the options of both sides change. Coercion becomes more difficult, and the agency of the periphery becomes more active and its options more diffuse. Continuity can be maintained if it can be legitimized by mutual interest and consent. The Commonwealth of Nations, the successor of the British Empire, is perhaps the most successful post-colonial configuration, attracting even states like Mozambique, which was never a British colony and has Portuguese as its official language. But a smooth adjustment is probably psychologically and politically impossible for the former hegemonic power. It wasn't easy for the European colonial powers either. The temptation is to continue to pull the strings of hierarchy to see if they still work, and to fear that the loss of coercive power means the loss of influence altogether. Moreover, statesmanlike downscaling is not likely to be as popular at home as boasts and promises to make America great again. No hegemon has ever made a graceful exit, though some have adjusted more easily than others.

Long-term, post-hegemonic American centrality requires inclusiveness. The key to the long peace since the Second World War was not the defeat of Germany and Japan. Germany had managed to go to war again in twenty years after its previous defeat, and both countries

[46] Ibid.

after 1945 soon proved that they could rise again. Nor was the containment of the Soviet Union the key to American success in the Cold War. Stalin's domination of Eastern Europe in 1947 was the key to galvanizing European resistance. Peaceful change was made possible by American open and respectful treatment of defeated enemies, the establishment of international organizations based on sovereignty, and the openness across the Berlin Wall spearheaded by Willy Brandt's *Ostpolitik*. Meanwhile the sobering experience of world war, respect for the strength shown by Soviet resistance to Hitler, and the specter of nuclear weapons gave a visceral urgency to peaceful solutions. Peace, aided by Gorbachev, allowed the Soviet Union to collapse. Unfortunately, Russia was not treated with respect after the collapse, nor did it behave prudently vis-à-vis its neighbors new and old, and thus mutual resentment adds fuel to Putin's current revanchist actions and to Europe's reawakened solidarity. Putin is the Anti-Gorbachev, attempting to force the reversal of Russia's fate, and proving thereby that Gorbachev was for Russia much the lesser of two evils.

What does inclusiveness require in a post-hegemonic world? Each of the previous three American presidents could illustrate part of the answer. Barack Obama was eloquent about inclusiveness, and his discourse won him the Nobel Peace Prize. The implicit premise of Donald Trump's withdrawal from global leadership was that hegemony could not be maintained by the United States alone. Joe Biden's revitalization of alliances is based on the conviction that isolation is not a viable strategy. Global centrality requires global rhetoric, recognition of the limits of maintaining hegemony, and respect for other states in a post-hegemonic context. Unfortunately, the US policy continuities since 2008 include a zero-sum approach to competition with China, militarization, and heavy reliance on sanctions.

Ironically, the Cold War mentality that is predominant in Washington implies dysfunctional strategic aims and encourages self-isolation. To take China as the implacable enemy automatically cedes other American enemies, Russia and Iran, at present, to China's side, and it worries allies. American allies and others welcome US presence and support, both as a good in itself and as a counterweight to dependency on China. However, pressure to decouple from China is not welcome. Over the decades the allies, especially in Pacific Asia, have evolved away from being frontier encampments against threatening enemies. Countries like Thailand and Philippines are legacy allies, not cheerful camp followers. Japan and South Korea are more worried about North Korea, and the US and China share that worry.[47] The second highest regional concern in Northeast Asia is the tension between the US and China. In Southeast Asia only 11 percent of those in an elite poll thought that their countries must choose between the US and China.[48]

In a multinodal political economy the use of sanctions is a temptation that should be resisted. Sanctions originated in the First World War as "economic total war," designed to punish enemy populations in order to get them to overthrow their princes.[49] After the Second World War it became a convenient tool especially for the United States to pressure regimes and leaders, a kind of "weaponized interdependence."[50] As President Trump put it, "Trade wars are good, and easy to win."[51] At present one-quarter of the world's population is estimated to be under some form of sanction.[52] As Nick Mulder has documented in his global history of sanctions, sanctions rarely have the intended political effect, but can produce perverse effects.[53] League of Nations sanctions brought Hitler and Mussolini together and encouraged their autarky. A deeper problem with a sanctions strategy in a multinodal context is that sanctions are instruments of coercion, directly towards targets, and indirectly, through secondary sanctions, towards allies. Treating allies as dependent clients and targeting the populations of other countries are likely to produce disaffection with the United States.

Economic decoupling is another policy option that is likely to be dysfunctional in the long term. The supply chain disruptions induced by Covid and Putin's invasion have demonstrated the importance of economic resilience, but going beyond resilience to decoupling from China is likely to be self-isolating for the United States. While the US can cut

---

[47] "Top Ten Risks Threaten a Peace in Northeast Asia," Genron, February 2021. www.genron-npo.net/en/opinion_polls/archives/5570.html
[48] *The State of Southeast Asia Survey Report 2022*.
[49] Nick Mulder, *The Economic Weapon: The Rise of Sanctions as a Tool of War* (New Haven, CT: Yale University Press, 2022).
[50] Ibid., p. 295.
[51] Donald J. Trump, Twitter post, March 2, 2018, at 5:50 am. Cited in ibid.
[52] Idriss Jazairy, "Unilateral Economic Sanctions, International Law, and Human Rights," *Ethics & International Affairs* 33:3 (2019), pp. 291–302.
[53] Mulder, *The Economic Weapon*.

off computer chips, developing the capacity to produce sophisticated chips is the kind of visible developmental target that China can pursue to its own advantage. China has been prohibited from joint space activities with NASA since 2011, but has managed to make progress on its own. By contrast, if the United States must replace low-tech manufactures from China, its labor and retooling costs are likely to be higher, limiting external markets and adding to inflation at home. Meanwhile the US would be restricting or tainting its own brands in a middle-class market already half again the size of its own.[54] The underlying risk of both decoupling and sanctions is that they reduce the salience of the dollar as the primary global currency. A good deal of the strength of the dollar is the absence of alternatives, and both decoupling and sanctions increase global interest in fiscal resilience.

The American tendency toward economic illiberalism and the Chinese trend toward political illiberalism are the most visible global storm clouds. Mutual animosity makes for unlikely cooperation on global issues. The self-righteous indignation of each toward the other encourages the hawkish entrenchment of both. However, despite the specter of two global powers locked in a zero-sum confrontation, it is not likely to result in global Cold War camps. The prudent response of other countries would be to buffer their exposure to global power tensions by developing their regional (in the case of Pacific Asia, regional minus China) relationships rather than to join one side or the other. After all, two-thirds of the global economy is outside the global powers. The net long-term effect of zero-sum global rivalry would therefore be the reduction of the salience and influence of the conflicted global center.

Risk Reduction

Three factors affect the sense of mutual risk between the United States and China. The first, well described by Graham Allison, is the "Thucydides trap."[55] The incumbent power fears the challenge of the rising power. This is somewhat different from the power transition theorists because there is greater weight on the psychology of the

---

[54] Adam Tooze, "China, Africa and a New, 'Two World' Divide?" *Chartbook* 143 (August 19, 2022).

[55] Graham Allison, *Destined for War: Can America and China Escape Thucydides's Trap?* (Boston, MA: Houghton Mifflin, 2017).

incumbent. Coping with the rise of China has been particularly difficult for the United States because of the interlude of unipolarity created by the end of the Cold War. The absence of a peer competitor encouraged a narcissistic satisfaction of superiority coupled with concern about controlling the eventual rise of challengers. Behind Madeleine Albright's proud claim of being "the indispensable nation" lurked Samuel Huntington's dark sketch of the inevitable and total clash of civilizations. From 1992 American security was not tied to collective deterrence or to mutual risk reduction with a rival, but rather to preventing the rise of any potential challenger to American supremacy.[56] The assumption was that the United States should be capable of defeating anyone, anywhere, without significant loss on the battleground and at no risk to itself. The American ideal of its own security is absolute. The experience of the Persian Gulf War and the air war in Kosovo/Serbia fit this ideal. No other country has the luxury of assuming that it should be invulnerable simply by reason of its own power, and with the ebbing of hegemony, neither does the United States.

The second factor is the necessary antinomy between regional power and global power. China has a tremendous logistical advantage in dealing with crises along its coast, and it has modernized its armed forces. While this situation does not put the United States mainland at risk, except by way of escalation, it challenges the American ideal of absolute security and it puts at risk American allies and its commitments to them. There is no clear line of demarcation possible between a region and the rest of the globe, and in any case an incomplete hegemonic global power is a contradiction in terms.

The third factor is more intangible, and one that increases real risk by reducing sensitivity to it. Both the United States and China have strong urges to do well in their rivalry, and weak memories of the unpredictable and catastrophic effects of major war. By contrast, when the Cold War began, both the US and the Soviet Union had the recent visceral experience of the costs of war and a vivid awareness of the strength of the other side. Neither wanted war to happen again because they knew what war was. The calculus of both was military deterrence, not military victory. The present calculus of both sides is still deterrence, but each is pushing its marginal advantages rather

---

[56] Patrick Tyler, "U.S. Strategy Plan Calls for Insuring No Rivals Develop," *New York Times*, March 8, 1992.

than focusing on risk reduction. The situation is reminiscent of the rivalry between Great Britain and Germany between 1890 and 1914. As the memories of the Napoleonic wars became faint, the pursuit of antagonistic rivalries made war possible again. Henry Kissinger notes that the long peace of the nineteenth century saw a gradual "shift in emphasis from legitimacy to power."[57] It was seventy-five years from the Congress of Vienna to the removal of Bismarck in 1890, and seventy-five years from the beginning of the Cold War to the present. The collective caution engendered by disaster fades, and the narrow pursuit of national advantage in a win-lose framework can create unanticipated, entangling risks.

Military Dangers

The most adrenaline-raising factor in the US-China relationship is the risk of direct damage by the other side, and rightly so. Not only are both nuclear powers with large and modern militaries, they are also on the technological frontiers of cyber war and theft,[58] and of space weaponization. They have the capacity for mutually assured destruction as well as mutually assured disruption. Their capacities for lose-lose interactions are limitless, and the collateral damage to the rest of the world could be limitless as well.

Decisive victory by either side is not a strategic option. However, the Blitzkrieg capacity of both sides leads to the pursuit by the other of hypervigilance for counter-attack, and the escalation of hypervigilance leaves a decreasing space for correctible error in detection or interpretation. While American experts have wondered whether various advances in Chinese weaponry have created a "Sputnik moment," and therefore a challenge that the US must meet by improving its military technology, everyone should be more concerned about a new "Cuba moment," when in 1962 the US and the Soviet Union were on the brink of nuclear war because of the placement of Soviet missiles in Cuba.[59] War is possible, but not victory.

---

[57] Henry Kissinger, *World Order* (New York: Penguin, 2014), p. 73.
[58] The US and China are ranked first and second on the Cyber Power Index, with the US considerably ahead. Julia Voo et al., *National Cyber Power Index 2020*. www.belfercenter.org/publication/national-cyber-power-index-2020
[59] Edward Luce, "The Return of the 20th Century's Nuclear Shadow," *Financial Times*, April 28, 2022.

Victory requires the destruction or submission of the other side while remaining intact oneself.

While war is the acute form of military risk, militarization is also a strategic risk for both sides. Military establishments and their associated industries have privileged access to government attention and resources, and de-militarization is quite difficult. Moreover, both the military establishment and the media can benefit from the amplification of national outrage and fear. Military budgets are an invisible opportunity cost to the rest of government and to its tax base. The best example of the self-defeating effects of militarization was the Soviet Union. In the 1980s, as the economy stagnated, Soviet military expenditures per capita grew to three times those of the US with one-third of its rival's GDP. But militarization did not simply take a larger share. The Soviet security state pervaded all of society, stifling innovation. The Soviet Union demonstrated that militarization can itself become a security threat. And Putin has demonstrated that militarization can become part of a country's political culture.

Mutual Risk Reduction

If rivalry is protracted, victory is impossible, and mutual risk is real, then mutual risk reduction is the only viable security strategy. In the Cold War, the Cuban Missile Crisis provided a sobering lesson in mutual risk, and afterwards the US and the Soviet Union began a series of negotiations in order to reduce the likelihood of mutually assured destruction. The Strategic Arms Limitation Talks (SALT) began in 1969 and led to the SALT treaty in 1972. The United States withdrew from the treaty in 2002.

Mutual risk reduction is more complex but no less necessary in an asymmetric rivalry. If absolute security is impossible, then security requires agreement. The problem with waiting to come to this realization until another Cuba moment arrives is that this crisis might resemble August 1914 more than the tense but brief and ultimately peaceful stand-down in October 1962. The possibilities of third-party entanglements, miscalculations and escalations are present, and added to them are the split-second reaction times of modern weaponry. Measures to mitigate the risk of major war would start with crisis communication protocols and regular military-to-military contact, but that is only the beginning.

Beyond the grand risks of major war, there are other forms of hostile action for which absolute invulnerability is not an option. Given the interdependent complexity of modern society and increasing reliance on electronic communication and control, there are new targets for hostile action. Moreover, there are new methods of attack that do not require a high level of technical sophistication. Drones and cyber-attacks are two of the most prominent examples. These can be used in conjunction with major war, but they are also well within the reach of smaller powers and even non-state actors. The United States has made profligate use of both drones and cyber-attacks, but strategically the primary nodes have a common interest – as does the rest of the world – in mitigating mutual risk. Since other countries are potentially victims and agents of such actions there is good reason for a general control regime that would be defined in terms of prohibited actions and be binding on all, including on the United States and China. In a post-hegemonic world no country should be beyond international law, and the primary nodes should be leaders in developing legal regimes beneficial to all, and binding on all.

Global Leadership in a Multinodal World

Is the domination of a hegemon required for world order? If so, the world is in a bad way, because it is beyond hegemons, not between them. If order requires hegemons, the best we can hope for is purgatory, the worst is hell. Given that the coordinated pursuit of global goods is still necessary, that power and capabilities are unevenly distributed, and that domination, global or partial, is not a strategic option, what can be done? What are the principles of global leadership in a multinodal world? Is an order transition possible, or, as the habits of the last hegemony fade, do we face a descent into entropy?

Principles of Multinodal Order

If we assume autonomous actors, the first principle of order must be cooperation. Cooperation must replace hegemonic command and obedience. Cooperation is not contrary to the idea of self-help, but it assumes that for some purposes, helping oneself requires coordination with others who are also helping themselves. While collective action can involve problems of free riders, hold-outs, and so forth, collective order can be less complicated. At the simplest level, a common interest reacting to a common situation can produce macro-patterns of behavior. A school of a million sardines reacts to a shark attack as a collective body, not because of communication, but because each fish swims toward the middle when threatened, and each senses threat when others swim toward the middle. If we add human attributes of communication, intelligence, and foresight, of course we get more confusion, but there is also the possibility of more complex patterns of corporate behavior. Cooperation is not the sacrifice of one's interests and volition to the group, but rather the recognition that one's interests can overlap with those of others, and that if one desires a certain outcome then acting in concert can be more effective than acting impulsively.

If cooperation is necessary, respect is required. At the sardine level, common response to a common situation is all that is required. Among sardines, respect need not rise above the behavioral premise that other sardines are not a threat and will react similarly. More complex coordination requires different behavior from different actors in the group. Achieving differentiated coordination requires both a persuasive overall picture of what is to be achieved and an appreciation of the particular situation and interests of the potential participants. Persuasion is not the only motivator of complex coordination; rewards and sanctions – "hard power" – remain useful in multinodal systems. But the agency of each actor must be respected. If a state is pushed too hard, or pushed against its interests, or put in a situation that denies its agency, then hedging is likely and defection is possible. The coordinator has become shark-like.

In an asymmetric matrix all are not equal in capabilities or in exposure to risk. Therefore, the texture of multinodal order is uneven, not because the larger commands the smaller, but because effective coordination must correspond to existing patterns of resources and to differences in international attention. Hence there are central configurations, such as that of China in Pacific Asia or the United States globally. It is prudent for a smaller power to show deference to the asymmetric configuration as long as the general order serves its interests and does not threaten its autonomy. Thus, deference in a multinodal order is not simply recognition of a power differential, it is based on performance. Earned deference requires both the effectiveness of configured coordination and respect for the interests and autonomy of all participants.

Challenges Facing the Primary Nodes

Global leadership in a situation of binary asymmetric rivalry is not easy. For the United States, the Cold War habits die hard. The temptations are to fixate on China as the enemy, to presume that allies will follow orders, and to reduce the strategic mission of diplomacy to the task of negating China. For China, the temptation is to assume that every country should be as complacent about China's rise as China itself is, and therefore cooperative and uncritical in its relations with China. The contradiction between the implicit American assumption that "if China wins, we lose," and the Chinese assumption that "if China wins, everybody wins," promises not only bilateral friction but problems of global leadership as well. The incompatibility of these tendencies has all but eliminated bilateral cooperation even on such obvious common concerns as pandemic prevention and climate.

The United States and China face different challenges of tolerating diversity. For the United States, the major problem is acknowledging the diversity of systems. The presumption that the United States represents the apex of political development, conjoined with the only path to economic prosperity, has been challenged by the rise of China and the continued strength of its party-state. However, the US is still in denial about the implications of a successful Chinese party-state. On the one hand, Washington takes credit for China's rise within the liberal world order; on the other, it considers the Communist Party of China illegitimate because it does not conform to American political standards. Besides pre-empting the possibility of bilateral cooperation, these attitudes alienate the parts of the world's population that are impressed with China's accomplishments and more critical of American politics.

China's diversity challenge is the toleration of diversity below the system level. China's suppression of domestic diversity alienates outside observers and lends credibility to systemic critiques. The diversity challenge most relevant to China's regional and global leadership is that of the eventual arrangements for "Greater China," the Mainland, Hong Kong, Macau, and especially Taiwan. The Basic Law of Hong Kong and of Macau set fifty-year terms for current arrangements that end in 2047 and 2049 respectively, and it is hard to imagine that the current ambiguity of the relationship between Beijing and Taipei will persist beyond 2049, the hundredth anniversary of the end of the rest of the Chinese civil war. Given that all four are successful economic and political communities, any peaceful constitution of Greater China would have to be a meta-constitution respecting the already existing systems. This approach was suggested by Deng Xiaoping's "one country, two systems" formula from 1983, but the exercise of central control in Hong Kong in 2021 calls into question its further relevance. Cross-Strait developments over the next twenty-five years will be watched closely by neighbors and beyond.

Beyond the Primary Nodes

The unlikelihood of general G-2 coordination of global leadership is not good news for world order, but it does not spell chaos. The success of existing global international governmental organizations such as the UN, World Bank, and International Monetary Fund gives them some autonomous momentum, and the same is true of less comprehensive organizations such as the Organization for Economic Cooperation and Development (OECD) and the various multilateral development banks such as the Asia Development Bank. All of these provide structures of connectivity that include the primary nodes but do not depend on them.

Even more significant are regional organizations such as the European Union, the Association of Southeast Asian Nations (ASEAN), the African Union, the Economic Community of West African States (ECOWAS), the Community of Latin American and Caribbean States (CELAC), and the Shanghai Cooperation Organization (SCO). Regionalization is a consequence of global uncertainty since 2008, and regional organizations have become more important. Typically, they do not seal themselves off, but rather reduce uncertainty by pooling exposure. In general, they are supported by both the US and China.

The success of initiatives taken by ASEAN to encourage regional order have been especially impressive. ASEAN is the embodiment of the principles of cooperation and respect, and as a result it has earned deference. Beginning with the ASEAN Regional Forum (ARF) in 1994 and culminating in the Regional Comprehensive Economic Partnership (RCEP), effective January 2022, ASEAN has been the regional leader in inclusivity. RCEP is now the world's largest trading bloc. Also impressive was New Zealand's efforts with the Transpacific Partnership (TPP). After the US defection, the endeavor is now progressing with Japan's support as the Comprehensive and Progressive

Agreement for Trans-Pacific Partnership (CPTPP), with China as a candidate for membership. It is quite a contrast to the camps of the Cold War that now the primary nodes are competing to participate in regional initiatives initiated by others. In that competition China is currently far ahead, but with a change of policy the US could catch up.

Besides governmental efforts, the activities of non-governmental organizations, philanthropies, and individuals have added significantly to the texture of multinodal relationships. They have increased transparency, often unwelcome by the governments involved, they have focused attention in new areas of concern, and they have directly assisted in alleviating humanitarian crises. Their involvement is enhanced by the global thickening of electronic communication. Connectivity is not beyond government influence, but it is beyond government control. Multinodality is now multidimensional.

Conclusion: What If?

The purpose of this book has been to explore the grand framework of history, current dynamics, and prospects of a new world order, one that has evolved gradually but decisively from the familiar one. The new order features a newly central regional actor in a major region dedicated to inclusivity. Both China and Pacific Asia remember their histories, but remember them differently, and therefore it is necessary to start at the beginning with regional history rather than national histories. Some background in their histories is especially necessary for outsiders, since previous world history has focused on the West. The commentary by the eminent historian Wang Gungwu served as a reminder that the regional history of Pacific Asia is larger than Pacific Asia itself, since the nomadic north and west were primary concerns of China, and remain important today. And the Taiwanese political scientist Wu Yu-Shan pointed out the importance of power in Western globalization of Asia, and the continuing importance of power in the current era. The histories are crucial not because the next step is determined by the previous one, but rather the opposite. China, Pacific Asia, and the rest of us stand at the threshold of a new era, and it is important to know where we have been, before analyzing where we are. Otherwise, we cannot confront our default assumptions.

Since 2008, China has emerged as the central economic and political concern of Pacific Asia. The factors of its previous, premodern centrality – presence, population, and production – have re-emerged in a new form, and they have global reverberations as well as regional ones. But China has not gathered the region to itself and shut the door, nor does it want to. Pacific Asia's core value is its inclusivity, and China can prosper as a regional center only if it advances that value. If it cannot prosper as a regional center, it cannot succeed as a global power. China has been successful thus far in economics; politically there are still major challenges ahead. As a result of its internal coordination and global alacrity, Pacific Asia is now the world's largest economic region. A China-centered region has itself become a global center of attention.

The well-known international relations theorists Qin Yaqing and Evelyn Goh reach a similar point about the current situation, but from different angles. Qin criticizes the notion of centers because a multinodal world is composed of horizontal relationships rather than vertical ones. As ASEAN's agency in regional organization demonstrates, centrality is an outcome of successful relational management rather than the corollary of power. Goh also sees an expanded field of actors, but one in which relative power counts but is not decisive. China does not have an exclusive sphere of influence in Pacific Asia; rather, China has been an enabler of an enhanced global role for the region.

The global implications of the arrival of China and of Pacific Asia are profound. The United States remains at the center of the familiar global political, economic, and security configuration, but it is not in control. Just as China is not the command center of Pacific Asia, and Pacific Asia is not the command center of the world economy, the United States should no longer think of itself as in charge of world politics, nor should it imagine that it can slide back into the captain's chair. The corner has been turned on 500 years of divergence between "the West and the Rest," and China is only the most prominent example of a new power of demography. We are now in a multinodal world in which power matters, but it influences rather than commands. But it is a "post-hegemonic" world rather than simply a "non-hegemonic" one, and so the process of transition from hegemony is one of trial and error.

With the rise of China and the continuing centrality, if not control, of the United States, the rivalry between the two is a key characteristic of the current era. It is a long-term rivalry in which each has different strengths and neither can replace the other. In the best of worlds, they would collaborate in global leadership, but the nature of rivalry makes that unlikely. Fortunately, the lack of a controlling power has enabled many smaller powers to make significant contributions toward advancing a mutually beneficial world order, though there is still far to go.

While the book involves extrapolation from current dynamics, it is not a prediction. The gloomiest possibility is quite real: thermonuclear war. The direct victims of a hypothetical nuclear war between India and Pakistan are estimated at 27 million, and in a full-scale war between the United States and Russia at 360 million. But with indirect effects on climate the toll of the latter could climb to 5.3 billion within two years.[60] That would be a game-changer beyond anything that I have described. There are less catastrophic possibilities of lose-lose confrontation that could also make a learning curve more crooked. The only thing that is not possible is victory, the decisive domination through military defeat of the United States over China, or of China over the United States. Unfortunately, the pursuit of victory and the deterrence of defeat remain the fundamental security preoccupations, especially in the United States. Either the US or China could fail, or both could, but failure would be essentially an own goal by either, or by both.

The cautiously optimistic expectation of future developments would be a learning curve in which tactical mistakes by both rivals and the continued advances by everyone else would lead to more realistic and cooperative strategies. Multinodality would prove itself to be real and also functional. This is in the spirit of French philosopher Alain's remark, "it is the sea herself who fashions the boats, choosing those that function and destroying the others."[61] However, even the sea itself is not beyond our destructive capabilities, and if we do not learn, we are all in the same boat.

---

[60] François Diaz-Maurin, "Nowhere to Hide," *Bulletin of the Atomic Scientists*, October 20, 2022.

[61] As quoted in D. S. Rogers and P. R. Ehrlich, "Natural Selection and Cultural Rates of Change," *Proceedings of the National Academy of Sciences* 105:3416–3420 (2008), p. 3417. "Alain" was the pseudonym of Émile Chartier (1868–1951). His students included Raymond Aron and Simone Weil.

Bibliography

Acharya, Amitav (2014). *The End of American World Order*. New York: Polity.
Acharya, Amitav and Buzan, Barry (2019). *The Making of Global International Relations*. Cambridge: Cambridge University Press.
Acharya, Amitav and See Seng Tan, eds, (2008). *Bandung Revisited: The Legacy of the 1955 Asian-African Conference for International Order*. Singapore: NUS Press.
Allison, Graham (2016). *Destined for War: Can America and China Escape Thucydides's Trap?* Boston, MA: Houghton Mifflin.
Ang, Yuen Yuen (2021). A Reckoning for the China Dream. *Project Syndicate*, September 30. Available at: www.project-syndicate.org/bigpicture/a-reckoning-for-the-china-dream.
Asian Infrastructure Investment Bank (2021). *Sustaining Global Value Chains*. Beijing: AIIB.
Avery, Martha (2003). *The Tea Road: China and Russia Meet across the Steppe*. Beijing: China International Press.
Ba, Alice (2009). *(Re)Negotiating East and Southeast Asia*. Stanford, CA: Stanford University Press.
Barker, Randolph (2011). The Origin and Spread of Early-Ripening Champa Rice: Its Impact on Song Dynasty China. *Rice* 4, pp. 184–186.
Beard, Mary (2015). *SPQR: A History of Ancient Rome*. New York: Liveright Publishing.
Bergsten, C. Fred (2022). *The United States v. China: The Quest for Global Economic Leadership*. Cambridge, UK: Polity.
Bland, Ben, Laksmana, Evan and Kassam, Natasha (2022). *Indonesia Poll 2021: Charting their Own Course*. Sydney: Lowy Institute.
Bondaz, Antoine (2021). Promoting "Soft Connectivity": China's Standards-Setting Reforms and International Ambitions. *Recherches & Documents* 15. Available at: www.frstrategie.org/en/publications/recherches-et-documents/promoting-soft-connectivity-china-s-standards-setting-reforms-and-international-ambitions-2021.
Brautigam, Deborah (2009). *The Dragon's Gift: The Real Story of China in Africa*. New York: Oxford University Press.

Bremmer, Ian (2013). *Every Nation for Itself: Winners and Losers in a G-Zero World*. New York: Portfolio/Penguin.
Breslin, Shaun (2013). *China and the Global Political Economy*. Basingstoke: Palgrave Macmillan.
Breslin, Shaun (2022). *China Risen? Studying Chinese Global Power*. Bristol: Bristol University Press.
Brook, Timothy (2013). *Mr. Selden's Map of China: The Spice Trade, a Lost Chart, and the South China Sea*. London: Profile.
Buzan, Barry (2011). A World Order without Superpowers: Decentered Globalism. *International Relations* 25:3, pp. 3–25.
Buzan, Barry (2014). The Logic and Contradictions of "Peaceful Rise/Development" as China's Grand Strategy. *The Chinese Journal of International Politics* 7:4, pp. 1–40.
Buzan, Barry and Goh, Evelyn (2020). *Rethinking Sino-Japanese Alienation: History Problems and Historical Opportunities*. New York: Oxford University Press.
Buzan, Barry and Wæver, Ole (2003). *Regions and Powers: The Structure of International Security*. Cambridge: Cambridge University Press.
Calder, Kent (2019). *Super Continent: The Logic of Eurasian Integration*. Stanford, CA: Stanford University Press.
Cerny, Philip G. (2006). Restructuring the State in a Globalizing World: Capital Accumulation, Tangled Hierarchies and the Search for a New Spatio-Temporal Fix. *Review of International Political Economy* 13:4, pp. 679–695.
Chandrasekhar, Anand (2021). Can China Help African Cocoa Producers Outmanoeuvre Big Chocolate? *SWI swissinfo.ch*, August 17. Available at: www.swissinfo.ch/eng/business/can-china-help-african-cocoa-producers-outmanoeuvre-big-chocolate--46862742.
Chaudhury, Nirad (1951). *The Autobiography of an Unknown Indian*. London: Macmillan.
Chen, Julie Yu-Wen (2022). Reconciling Different Approaches to Conceptualizing the Glocalization of the Belt and Road Initiative Projects. *Globalizations*, preprint, April 20. Available at: www.tandfonline.com/doi/full/10.1080/14747731.2022.2062843.
Chung, Jae Ho (2003–4). From a Special Relationship to a Normal Partnership? Interpreting the "Garlic Battle" in Sino-South Korean Relations. *Pacific Affairs* 76:3, pp. 549–568.
Church, Sally (2005). Zheng He: An Investigation into the Plausibility of 450-ft Treasure Ships. *Monumenta Serica* 53:1, pp. 1–43.
von Clausewitz, Carl (1832). *Vom Kriege*. Berlin: Dümmers Verlag.
Congressional Research Service (2021). China's Engagement with Latin America and the Caribbean. December 14. Available at: https://crsreports.congress.gov/product/pdf/IF/IF10982.

Crawley, Roger (2015). *Conquerors: How Portugal Forged the First Global Empire*. New York: Random House.
Credit Suisse (2021). *Global Wealth Report 2021*. Geneva: Credit Suisse Research Institute.
Custer, Samantha et al. (2021). *Tracking Chinese Development Finance: An Application of AidData's TUFF 2.0 Methodology*. Williamsburg, VA: AidData at William & Mary.
Dardess, John W. (2010). *Governing China 150–1850*. Indianapolis, IN: Hackett.
Declaration between Great Britain and France with Regard to the Kingdom of Siam and Other Matters (1896). Signed in London, January 15.
DeLong, J. Bradford et al. (2022). *Slouching towards Utopia: An Economic History of the Twentieth Century*. New York: Basic Books.
Diaz-Maurin, François (2022). Nowhere to Hide. *Bulletin of the Atomic Scientists*, October 20.
Dollar, David (2019). *Executive Summary: Technological Innovation, Supply Chain Trade, and Workers in a Globalized World*. Geneva: World Trade Organization.
Driessen, Miriam (2019). *Tales of Hope, Tastes of Bitterness*. Hong Kong: Hong Kong University Press.
East Asia Institute and Genron NPO (2021). *The 9th Korea-Japan Joint Public Opinion Poll*. Seoul: East Asia Institute. Available at: www.eai.or.kr/new/en/project/view.asp?code=54&intSeq=20810&board=eng_event&keyword_option=&keyword=&more=.
East Asia's Economic Agreement (2022). *East Asia Forum Quarterly* 14:1, March.
Elkins, Caroline (2022). *Legacy of Violence: A History of the British Empire*. New York: Knopf.
Elvin, Mark (2010). The Environmental Impasse in Late-Imperial China. In Brantly Womack, ed., *China's Rise in Historical Perspective*. Boulder, CO: Rowman and Littlefield.
Esherick, Joseph (2010). China and the World: From Tribute to Treaties to Popular Nationalism. In Brantly Womack, ed., *China's Rise in Historical Perspective*. Boulder, CO: Rowman and Littlefield.
Eyler, Brian (2020). Science Shows Chinese Dams are Devastating the Mekong. *Foreign Policy*, April 22.
The Ezra Klein Show (2022). Ezra Klein Interviews Fareed Zakaria. *New York Times* podcast, March 4. Available at: www.nytimes.com/2022/03/04/podcasts/transcript-ezra-klein-interviews-fareed-zakaria.html.
Fairbank, John King, Coolidge, Martha Henderson, and Smith, Richard J. (1995). *H. B. Morse: Customs Commissioner and Historian of China*. Lexington: University Press of Kentucky.

Feigenbaum, Evan (2011). Why America No Longer Gets Asia. *The Washington Quarterly* 34:2, pp. 25–43.
Feltman, Jeffrey (2020). China's Expanding Influence at the United Nations. Brookings Institution report. Available at: www.brookings.edu/research/chinas-expanding-influence-at-the-united-nations-and-how-the-united-states-should-react/.
Fletcher, Joseph (1982). The Biography of Khwush Kipäk Beg (d. 1781) in the Wai-Fan Meng-Ku Hui-Pu Wang Kung Piao Chuan. *Acta Orientalia Academiae Scientiarum Hungaricae* 36:1-3, pp. 167–172.
Fravel, Taylor (2008). *Strong Borders, Secure Nation: Cooperation and Conflict in China's Territorial Disputes*. Princeton: Princeton University Press.
Freeman, Carla (2021). China's Periphery: A Rift Zone in U.S.-China Relations. In Anne Thurston, ed., *Engaging China: Fifty Years of Sino-American Relations*. New York: Columbia University Press.
Freeman, Chas (2022a). China in the Middle East: Remarks to a Panel of the Middle East Policy Council, January 21. Available at: https://chasfreeman.net/china-in-the-middle-east/.
Freeman, Chas (2022b). About Spheres of Influence. Available at: https://chasfreeman.net/about-spheres-of-influence.
French, Patrick (1994). *Younghusband: The Last Great Imperial Adventurer*. London: Harper.
Genron (2021). Top Ten Risks Threaten a Peace in Northeast Asia. February. Available at: www.genron-npo.net/en/opinion_polls/archives/5570.html.
Gerstl, Alfred (2022). *Hedging Strategies in Southeast Asia: ASEAN, Malaysia, Philippines, and Vietnam and their Relations with China*. London: Routledge.
Gibbon, Edward (1776). *History of the Decline and Fall of the Roman Empire*, vol. 1. London: Strahan and Cadell.
Gilpin, Robert (1981). *War and Change in World Politics*. Cambridge: Cambridge University Press.
Goh, Evelyn (2013). *The Struggle for Order: Hegemony, Resistance and Transition in Post-Cold War East Asia*. Oxford: Oxford University Press.
Goh, Evelyn, ed., (2016). *Rising China's Influence in Developing Asia*. Oxford: Oxford University Press.
Goh, Evelyn (2020). The Asia Pacific's "Age of Uncertainty": Great Power Competition, Globalisation, and the Economic-Security Nexus. *RSIS Working Paper No. 330*. Singapore: S. Rajaratnam School of International Studies.
Goh, Evelyn and Liu, Nan (2021). Chinese Investment in Southeast Asia, 2005–19: Patterns and Significance. *SEARBO Policy Briefing*, Australian National University.

González, Guadalupe, Mónica Hirst, Carlos Luján, Carlos Romero, and Juan Gabriel Tokatlian. (2021). *Critical Juncture, Power Transition and Latin American Vacuum*. Buenos Aires: Friedrich Ebert Stiftung.
Gross, Samantha (2020). The Global Energy Trade's New Center of Gravity. *Brookings*, September 14. Available at: www.brookings.edu/articles/the-global-energy-trades-new-center-of-gravity/.
Gu, Xiaosong and Womack, Brantly (2000). Border Cooperation between China and Vietnam in the 1990s. *Asian Survey* 40:6, pp. 1042–1058.
Ham, Myungsik and Tolentino, Elaine (2018). Socialisation of China's Soft Power: Building Friendship through Potential Leaders. *China: An International Journal* 16:1, pp. 45–68.
Hao, Qi (2015). China Debates the "New Type of Great Power Relations." *Chinese Journal of International Politics* 8:4, pp. 349–370.
Henry, Iain (2022). Taiwan Stirs Allies' Fear of Entrapment in Asia. *East Asia Forum*, October 9. Available at: www.eastasiaforum.org/2022/10/09/taiwan-stirs-allies-fear-of-entrapment-in-asia/.
Hessler, Peter (2015). Learning to Speak Lingerie: Chinese Merchants and the Inroads of Globalization. *New Yorker*, August 3.
Hessler, Peter (2020). Life on Lockdown in China. *New Yorker*, March 23.
Hessler, Peter (2022). China's Reform Generation Adapts to Life in the Middle Class. *New Yorker*, January 3.
Hevia, James (1995). *Cherishing Men from Afar: Qing Guest Ritual and the Macartney Embassy of 1793*. Durham, NC: Duke University Press.
Hirschman, Albert O. (1970). *Exit, Voice, and Loyalty: Responses to Decline in Firms, Organizations, and States*. Cambridge, MA: Harvard University Press.
Hoffman, Bert (2022). How Fast Did China Grow? Presentation at Harvard's Fairbank Center, April 27. Available at: https://fairbank.fas.harvard.edu/events/critical-issues-confronting-china-series-featuring-bert-hofman/.
Huang, Chiung-Chiu and Shih, Chih-yu (2014). *Harmonious Intervention: China's Quest for Relational Security*. Farnham: Ashgate.
Huang, Chiung-Chiu and Tung, Nguyen Cong (2022). Dancing between Beijing and Taipei: Vietnam in the Shadow of the Belt and Road Initiative. *China Review* 22:2, pp. 315–339.
Ikenberry, John (2001). *After Victory: Institutions, Strategic Restraint, and the Rebuilding of Order after Major Wars*. Princeton: Princeton University Press.
Ikenberry, John (2011). *Liberal Leviathan: The Origins, Crisis, and Transformation of the American World Order*. Princeton: Princeton University Press.
International Energy Association (2021). *World Energy Balances Highlights 2021*. Available at: www.iea.org/data-and-statistics/data-product/world-energy-balances-highlights.

International Monetary Fund (2021). *World Economic Outlook*. Available at: www.imf.org/en/Publications/WEO/Issues/2021/03/23/world-economic-outlook-april-2021.

International Monetary Fund (2022). *Annual Report 2022: Crisis upon Crisis*, October 6. Available at: www.imf.org/external/pubs/ft/ar/2022/english/.

Jakobson, Linda (2016). Reflections from China on Xi Jinping's "Asia for Asians." *Asian Politics & Policy* 8:1, pp. 219–223.

James, Deborah and Schrauwers, Albert (2003). An Apartheid of Souls: Dutch and Afrikaner Colonialism and its Aftermath in Indonesia and South Africa. *Itinerario* 27:3-4, pp. 49–80.

Jazairy, Idriss (2019). Unilateral Economic Sanctions, International Law, and Human Rights. *Ethics & International Affairs* 33:3, pp. 291–302.

Joint Statement of the Russian Federation and the People's Republic of China on the International Relations Entering a New Era and the Global Sustainable Development (2022). February 4. Available at: http://en.kremlin.ru/supplement/5770.

Jourdan, Adam (2018). Designed in California, Made in China: How the iPhone Skews U.S. Trade Deficit. *Reuters*, March 21.

Kang, David (2003). Getting Asia Wrong: The Need for New Analytical Frameworks. *International Security* 27:4, pp. 57–85.

Kang, David (2007). *China Rising: Peace, Power, and Order in East Asia*. New York: Columbia University Press.

Kant, Immanuel (1903). *Perpetual Peace, A Philosophical Essay*. Translated by M. Campbell Smith. London: George Allen and Unwin.

Kaplan, Robert (2022). When Empires or Great Powers Fall, Chaos and War Rise. *Foreign Affairs*, October 4.

Kasahara, Shigehisa (2004). The Flying Geese Paradigm: A Critical Study of Its Application to East Asian Regional Development. *United Nations Conference on Trade and Development Discussion Papers* 169.

Katzenstein, Peter (2005). *A World of Regions: Asia and Europe in the American Imperium*. Ithaca, NY: Cornell University Press.

Kautilya (2013). *King, Governance and Law in Ancient India: Kautilya's Arthasastra*. Translated by Patrick Olivelle. New Delhi: Oxford University Press.

Kelley, Liam (2005). *Beyond the Bronze Pillars: Envoy Poetry and the Sino-Vietnamese Relationship*. Honolulu: University of Hawaii Press.

Kennan, George (1979). *The Decline of Bismarck's European Order*. Princeton: Princeton University Press.

Kennedy, James C. (2017). *A Concise History of the Netherlands*. Cambridge: Cambridge University Press.

Kharas, Homi (2017). The Unprecedented Expansion of the Global Middle Class: An Update. *Global Economy & Development Working Paper*

100. Available at: www.brookings.edu/wp-content/uploads/2017/02/global_20170228_global-middle-class.pdf.
Kharas, Homi and Fengler, Wolfgang (2021). Which Will Be the Top 30 Consumer Markets of This Decade? *Brookings*, August 31. Available at: www.brookings.edu/blog/future-development/2021/08/31/which-will-be-the-top-30-consumer-markets-of-this-decade-5-asian-markets-below-the-radar/.
Khorsandi, Peyvand (2022). "Our Presence is Hope": US$2.6bn Needed as Winter Spells Hunger for Afghanistan. *World Food Program*, January 25. Available at: www.wfp.org/stories/our-presence-hope-us26bn-needed-winter-spells-hunger-afghanistan.
Kipling, Rudyard (1899). The White Man's Burden: The United States and the Philippine Islands. *McClure's Magazine*, February.
Kissinger, Henry (2014). *World Order*. New York: Penguin.
Koppes, Clayton (1976). Captain Mahan, General Gordon, and the Origins of the Term "Middle East." *Middle Eastern Studies* 12:1, pp. 95–98.
Kosumas, Wimonkan (2000). *Half a Hegemon: Japan's Leadership in Southeast Asia*. PhD dissertation. University of Virginia.
Kroeber, Arthur (2016). *China's Economy: What Everyone Needs to Know*. Oxford: Oxford University Press.
Kuik, Cheng-Chwee (2021). Getting Hedging Right: A Small-State Perspective. *China International Strategy Review* 3, pp. 300–315.
Kuik, Cheng-Chwee (2022). Shades of Grey: Riskification and Hedging in the Indo-Pacific. *Pacific Review*, September 9. Available at: https://doi.org/10.1080/09512748.2022.2110608.
Kumar, Krishan (2021). *Empires: A Historical and Political Sociology*. New York: Polity.
Kupchan, Charles A. (2012). *No One's World: The West, the Rising Rest, and the Coming Global Turn*. New York: Oxford University Press.
Kurlansky, Mark (2003). *Salt: A World History*. New York: Penguin.
Kuttner, Robert (2021). Bringing the Supply Chain Back Home. *New York Review of Books*, November 18.
Kuznets, Simon (1965). *Toward a Theory of Economic Growth*. New York: W.W. Norton.
Ladds, Catherine (2016). China and Treaty-Port Imperialism. In *The Encyclopedia of Empire*. New York: Wiley-Blackwell. Available at: https://doi.org/10.1002/9781118455074.wbeoe079.
Lake, David (2009). *Hierarchy in International Relations*. Ithaca, NY: Cornell University Press.
Lake, David (2014). Status, Authority, and the End of the American Century. In T. V. Paul, Deborah Welch Larson, and William C. Wohlforth, eds, *Status in World Politics*. Cambridge: Cambridge University Press, pp. 246–269.

Lampton, David M., Ho, Selina, and Kuik, Cheng-Chwee (2020). *Rivers of Iron: Railroads and Chinese Power in Southeast Asia*. Oakland: University of California Press.

Lattimore, Owen (1988 [1940]). *Inner Asian Frontiers of China*. Hong Kong: Oxford University Press.

Lenin, V. I. (1917). All Power to the Soviets! *Pravda* 99, July 18. Available at: www.marxists.org/archive/lenin/works/1917/jul/18.htm.

Li, Bin (2022). Not So Quiet in the Western Pacific. *Comparative Connections* 23:3, pp. 143–154.

Li, Mingjiang (2008). China Debates Soft Power. *Chinese Journal of International Politics* 2:2, pp. 287–308.

Li, Quan and Ye, Min (2019). China's Emerging Partnership Network: What, Who, Where, When and Why. *International Trade, Politics and Development* 3:2, pp. 66–81.

Lin, Christina (2014). Will the Middle Kingdom Join the Middle East Peace Quartet? *Times of Israel*, July 26.

Lin, Justin Yifu (2022). 中国经济的发展潜力、新挑战与应对 [China's Development Potential: New Challenges and Measures]. February. Available at: www.36kr.com/p/1616049972241664.

Lin, Shangli (1997). 国内政府间关系 [Domestic Intergovernmental Relations]. Hangzhou: Zhejiang Renmin Chubanshe.

Lin, Syaru Shirley (2021). Analyzing the Relationship between Identity and Democratization in Taiwan and Hong Kong in the Shadow of China. *The Asan Forum*, November–December. Available at: https://theasanforum.org/analyzing-the-relationship-between-identity-and-democratization-in-taiwan-and-hong-kong-in-the-shadow-of-china/.

Lopes Da Silva, Diego, Tian, Nan, and Marksteiner, Alexandra (2021). *Trends in World Military Expenditure, 2020*. Stockholm: SIPRI.

Lowy Institute (2019). *Global Diplomacy Index 2019*. Available at: https://globaldiplomacyindex.lowyinstitute.org/#.

Luce, Edward (2022a). The West is Rash to Assume the World is on its Side over Ukraine. *Financial Times*, March 24.

Luce, Edward (2022b). The Return of the 20th Century's Nuclear Shadow. *Financial Times*, April 28.

Luo, Guanzhong (1995). *Three Kingdoms*. Translated by Moss Roberts. Beijing: Foreign Languages Press.

Maddison, Angus (1971). *Class Structure and Economic Growth: India and Pakistan since the Moghuls*. New York: Norton.

Maddison, Angus (2001). *The World Economy: A Millennial Perspective*. Paris: OECD. Available at: www.oecd-ilibrary.org/economics/the-world-economy_9789264189980-en.

Maddison, Angus (2007). *China's Economic Performance in the Long Run*. 2nd ed. Paris: OECD.

Maddison Project Database 2020. Available at: www.rug.nl/ggdc/his toricaldevelopment/maddison/releases/maddison-project-database-2020?lang=en.

Mao, Zedong (1958). Introducing a Co-operative. In *Selected Works of Mao Zedong*, vol. 8. Available at: www.marxists.org/reference/archive/mao/selected-works/volume-8/index.htm.

Mill, John Stuart (1861). *Considerations on Representative Government*. Available at: www.gutenberg.org/files/5669/5669-h/5669-h.htm#link2HCH0018.

Miller, Chris (2022). *Chip War: The Fight for the World's Most Critical Technology*. New York: Scribner.

Ministry of Foreign Affairs, People's Republic of China (2021). Wang Yi Talks about the Importance of the Global Development Initiative. September 26. Available at: www.mfa.gov.cn/ce/ceth//eng/zgyw/t1909908.htm.

Möckli, Daniel, ed., (2012). *Global Trends 2012*. Zürich: Center for Security Studies ETH Zürich.

Morris, Ian (2010). *Why the West Rules—For Now*. New York: Farrar, Strauss, and Giroux.

Morse, H. B. (1908). *The Trade and Administration of the Chinese Empire*. London: Longmans, Green and Co.

Mote, Frederick (1999). *Imperial China 900–1800*. Cambridge, MA: Harvard University Press.

Mulder, Nick (2022). *The Economic Weapon: The Rise of Sanctions as a Tool of War*. New Haven, CT: Yale University Press.

Naughton, Barry (1988). The Third Front. *China Quarterly* 155, pp. 351–386.

Naughton, Barry (2018). *The Chinese Economy: Adaptation and Growth*. 2nd ed. Cambridge, MA: MIT Press.

Nedopil, Christoph (2022). *China Belt and Road Initiative (BRI). Investment Report 2021*. Shanghai: Green Finance and Development Center, Fudan University.

Ngo, Vinh Long (1991). *Before the Revolution: The Vietnamese Peasants under the French*. New York: Columbia University Press.

Nguyen, The Anh (2001). Attraction and Repulsion as the Two Contrasting Aspects of the Relations between China and Vietnam. In *China and Vietnam: Historical Interactions. An International Symposium*. Hong Kong: Hong Kong University Press.

Nguyen, Vu Tung (2021). *Flying Blind: Vietnam's Decision to Join ASEAN*. Singapore: ISEAS Publishing.

Nie, Hongping Annie (2019). *The Selden Map of China: A New Understanding of the Ming Dynasty*. Oxford: The Bodleian Library.

Noesselt, Nele (2022). Strategy Adjustments of the United States and the European Union vis-à-vis China: Democratic Global Power Identities and

Fluid Polygonal Relations. *Journal of Chinese Political Science*, March 18. Available at: https://doi.org/10.1007/s11366-022-09794-3.

Nye, Joseph (2018). The Cooperative Rivalry of US-China Relations. *Project Syndicate*, November 6. Available at: www.project-syndicate.org/commentary/china-america-relationship-cooperative-rivalry-by-joseph-s--nye-2018-11.

Oerstroem Moeller, Joergen (2021). Biden Has Inherited the Ingredients that Engendered Trump's Grand Strategy. *National Interest*, May 24.

Oertel, Janka (2020). *The New China Consensus: How Europe is Growing Wary of Beijing*. Policy Brief, European Council on Foreign Relations.

Organski, A. F. K. (1958). *World Politics*. New York: Knopf.

Palmer, Alex (2021). The Man Behind China's Aggressive New Voice. *New York Times*, July 7.

Peng, Sujian (2022). China's Population is Set to Shrink for the First Time in Sixty Years. *World Economic Forum*. Available at: www.weforum.org/agenda/2022/07/china-population-shrink-60-years-world/.

People's Republic of China (2018). *Constitution of the Peoples' Republic of China*, as amended in 2018. Available at: https://english.www.gov.cn/archive/lawsregulations/201911/20/content_WS5ed8856ec6d0b3f0e9499913.html.

Perdue, Peter (2005). *China Marches West: The Qing Conquest of Central Eurasia*. Cambridge, MA: Harvard University Press.

Perdue, Peter (2015). The Tenacious Tributary System. *Journal of Contemporary China* 24:96, pp. 1002–1014.

Pew Research Center (2021). Large Majorities Say China Does Not Respect the Personal Freedoms of Its People. Pew Research Center, June 30. Available at: www.pewresearch.org/global/2021/06/30/large-majorities-say-china-does-not-respect-the-personal-freedoms-of-its-people/

Pew Research Center (2022). How Global Public Opinion of China Has Shifted in the Xi Era. Available at: www.pewresearch.org/global/2022/09/28/how-global-public-opinion-of-china-has-shifted-in-the-xi-era/

Platt, Stephen (2012). *Autumn in the Heavenly Kingdom: China, the West, and the Epic Story of the Taiping Civil War*. New York: Random House.

Platt, Stephen (2018). *Imperial Twilight: The Opium War and the End of China's Last Golden Age*. New York: Knopf.

Polachek, James M. (1992). *The Inner Opium War*. Cambridge, MA: Harvard Council on East Asian Studies.

Polo, Marco (2016). *The Travels*. Translated by Nigel Cliff. New York: Penguin.

Pottinger, Matt (2022). Russia, China and the New Cold War. *Wall Street Journal*, March 18.

Prantl, Jochen and Goh, Evelyn (2022). Rethinking Strategy and Statecraft for the Twenty-First Century of Complexity: A Case for Strategic Diplomacy. *International Affairs* preprint, February.

Price Waterhouse (2017). *The World in 2050*. Available at: www.pwc.com/gx/en/research-insights/economy/the-world-in-2050.html.

Pritchett, Lant and Summers, Lawrence (2014). Asiaphoria Meets Regression to the Mean. *Mossavar-Rahmani Center Faculty Working Paper No. 2014-04*. Cambridge, MA: National Bureau of Economic Research.

Qin, Yaqing (2014). Continuity through Change: Background Knowledge and China's International Strategy. *Chinese Journal of International Politics* 7:3, pp. 285–314.

Qin, Yaqing (2018). *A Relational Theory of World Politics*. Princeton: Princeton University Press.

Qin, Yaqing (2021). 全球治理趋向扁平 [Global Governance Tends to be Flat], 国际问题研究 [*International Studies*] 5, pp. 55–72.

Ramo, Joshua Cooper (2004). *The Beijing Consensus: Notes on the New Physics of Chinese Power*. London: Foreign Policy Centre.

Rawski, Evelyn (2010). Chinese Strategy and Security Issues in Historical Perspective. In Brantly Womack, ed., *China's Rise in Historical Perspective*. Boulder, CO: Rowman and Littlefield, pp. 63–88.

中国历史研究院课题组 [Research Group of the Chinese Academy of History] (2022). 明清时期"闭关锁国"问题新探' [A New Investigation of the "Closed Country" System of the Ming and Qing Eras], 历史研究 [*Historical Studies*] 3, pp. 4–21.

Resolution of the CPC Central Committee on the Major Achievements and Historical Experience of the Party over the Past Century (2021). *Xinhua*, November 16.

Rice University (2017). Reconsidering the Sinosphere. Available at: https://sinosphere.rice.edu/panels/.

Richardson, Sophie (2010). *China, Cambodia, and the Five Principles of Peaceful Coexistence*. New York: Columbia University Press.

Roach, Stephen (2022). Two Insecure Superpowers Stumble towards Collision over Taiwan. *Financial Times*, August 4.

Robinson, John (2021). *The Great Red Fleet – China's Port Call Diplomacy: Battlewagons as Bandwagons*. PhD dissertation. University of Virginia. Available at: https://doi.org/10.18130/6y1c-qn89.

Rogers, D. S. and Ehrlich, P. R. (2008). Natural Selection and Cultural Rates of Change. *Proceedings of the National Academy of Sciences* 105:3416–3420, p. 3417.

Rosen, Daniel (2022). The Age of Slow Growth in China. *Foreign Affairs*, April 15.

Rosen, Daniel and Bao, Beibei (2015). *Broken Abacus? A More Accurate Gauge of China's Economy*. New York: Rowman and Littlefield.
Rudd, Kevin (2020). *The Avoidable War: The Case for Managed Strategic Competition*. New York: The Asia Society.
Scholtz, Olaf (2023). The Global Zeitenwende: How to Avoid a New Cold War in a Multipolar Era. *Foreign Affairs*, January/February.
Scott, James C. (1985). *Weapons of the Weak: Everyday Forms of Peasant Resistance*. New Haven, CT: Yale University Press.
Sekiyama, Takashi (2016). Rethinking the Triangle: A Japanese Perspective. In Brantly Womack and Yufan Hao, eds, *Rethinking the Triangle: Washington-Beijing-Taipei*. Singapore: World Scientific, pp. 139–156.
Shenzhen Statistical Yearbook 2016 (2016). Shenzhen: Shenzhen Statistics Bureau.
Shi, Yinhong (2021). The Recent and Predictable Future: The U.S. Posture toward China during and after the Presidential Election Campaign. *East Asian Affairs* 1:1. Available at: https://doi.org/10.1142/S2737557921500017.
Shieh, Shawn and Deng, Guosheng (2011). An Emerging Civil Society: The Impact of the 2008 Sichuan Earthquake on Grass-Roots Associations in China. *The China Journal* 65 (January), pp. 181–194.
Shoemaker, Bruce and Robichaud, William, eds, (2018). *Dead in the Water: Global Lessons from the World Bank's Model Hydropower Dam in Laos*. Madison: University of Wisconsin Press.
The Shoo King, or the Historical Classic (1846). Translated by W. H. Medhurst. Shanghai: Mission Press.
Slipak, Ariel. (2022). América Latina en la estrategia del dragón [Latin America in the dragon's strategy]. *Nueva Sociedad*, February.
Smith, Paul J. (1991). *Taxing Heaven's Storehouse: Horses, Bureaucrats, and the Destruction of the Sichuan Tea Industry, 1074–1224*. Cambridge, MA: Harvard University Press.
Smith, Richard J. (1978). *Mercenaries and Mandarins: The Ever-Victorious Army in Nineteenth Century China*. Millwood, NY: KTO Press.
The State of Southeast Asia Survey Report 2022 (2022). Singapore: ASEAN Studies Centre at ISEAS Yusof Ishak Institute. Available at: www.iseas.edu.sg.
Stuenkel, Oliver (2016). *The Post-Western World: How Emerging Powers are Remaking Global Order*. Cambridge, UK: Polity Press.
Stüver, Georg (2017). China's Partnership Diplomacy: International Alignment Based on Interests or Ideology. *The Chinese Journal of International Politics* 10:1, pp. 31–65.
Sun, Degang (2022). From Fragmentation to Integration: China's Domestic Legislative and Institutional Reforms for the Protection of Overseas Interests, workshop paper, *China Protecting Its Overseas Interests*. Singapore: RSIS.

Sutter, Robert (2022). China's Growing Influence Overshadows U.S. Initiatives. *Comparative Connections* 23:3, pp. 71–78.

Sutter, Robert and Huang, Chin-Hao (2022). China's Growing Influence Overshadows U.S. Initiatives. *Comparative Connections* 23:3, pp. 71–78.

Swettenham, Frank (1907). *British Malaya: An Account of the Origin and Progress of British Influence in Malaya*. London: Lane.

Tammen, Ronald and Kugler, Jacek (2006). Power Transition and China–US Conflicts. *Chinese Journal of International Politics* 1:1, pp. 35–55.

Tartar, Andre and Sam, Cedric (2019). How the Rise of Developing Countries Has Disrupted Global Trade. *Bloomberg New Economy Report*, May 7. Available at: www.bloomberg.com/graphics/2019-bloomberg-new-economy/global-trade-developing-nations/.

Tawney, R. H. (1932). *Land and Labour in China*. New York: Harcourt Brace.

Taylor, Keith Weller (1983). *The Birth of Vietnam*. Berkeley: University of California Press.

Tetlock, Philip (2005). *Expert Political Judgment: How Good is it? How Can We Know?* Princeton: Princeton University Press.

Thayer, Carlyle (2022). Vietnam's Response to Chinese Encirclement. *Thayer Consultancy Background Brief*, September 1.

Tjia, Linda Yin-nor (2022). Kazakhstan's Leverage and Economic Diversification amid Chinese Connectivity Dreams. *Third World Quarterly*, March 17. Available at: https://doi.org/10.1080/01436597.2022.2027237.

Toer, Pramoedya Ananta (1980–88). *The Buru Quartet*. Various translators and publishers.

Tokatlian, Juan (2011). Una nueva estrategia hacia China [A new strategy vis-à-vis China]. *La Nacion*, August 29. Available at: www.lanacion.com.ar/1401402-una-nueva-estrategia-hacia-china.

Tooze, Adam (2022a). Defining Polycrisis: From Crisis Pictures to the Crisis Matrix. *Chartbook* 130, June 24.

Tooze, Adam (2022b). China, Africa and a New, "Two World" Divide? *Chartbook* 143, August 19.

Tooze, Adam (2022c). Project Fear 3.0, or the Gatekeepers and the Tories. *Chartbook* 156, September 28.

Trump, Donald J. (2018). Twitter post, March 2, 5:50 am.

Tuchman, Barbara (1978). *A Distant Mirror: The Calamitous 14th Century*. New York: Knopf.

Tyler, Patrick (1992). U.S. Strategy Plan Calls for Insuring No Rivals Develop. *New York Times*, March 8.

中国社会科学院原副院长：2022年中国人口总量或达峰值 [Vice Director of China Social Science Academy: In 2022 China's population may reach its peak] (2022). *Caijing*, March 20. Available at: https://house.ifeng.com/news/2022_03_20-55288194_0.shtml.

Vision and Actions on Jointly Building Silk Road Economic Belt and 21st-Century Maritime Silk Road (March 2015). Available at: https://eng.yidaiyilu.gov.cn/qwyw/qwfb/1084.htm.

Vogel, Ezra (1989). *One Step Ahead in China: Guangdong under Reform.* Cambridge, MA: Harvard University Press.

Vogel, Ezra (2019). *China and Japan: Facing History.* Cambridge, MA: Harvard University Press.

Voo, Julia et al. (2020). *National Cyber Power Index 2020.* Available at: www.belfercenter.org/publication/national-cyber-power-index-2020.

Vuving, Alexander (2021). Will Vietnam Be America's Next Strategic Partner? *The Diplomat,* August 21.

Wang, Gungwu (1998). Ming Foreign Relations: Southeast Asia. In Denis Twitchett and Frederick Mote, eds, *The Cambridge History of China, Vol. 8: The Ming Dynasty, 1368–1644, Part 2.* Cambridge: Cambridge University Press.

Wang, Gungwu (2019). *China Reconnects: Joining a Deep-Rooted Past to a New World Order.* Singapore: World Scientific.

Wang, Linggui and Zhao, Jianglin (2019). *China's Belt and Road Initiative and Building the Community of Common Destiny.* Singapore: World Scientific.

Wang, Zhenping (2013). *Tang China in Multi-Polar Asia: A History of Diplomacy and War.* Honolulu: University of Hawaii Press.

Wee, Sui-Lee et al. (2021). When the Biggest Spenders Aren't Coming Back Any Time Soon. *New York Times,* December 5.

Wei, Ling (2022). Upgrading the China-ASEAN Partnership: ASEAN's Concerns, China's Responsibility and Regional Order. *China International Studies* 92, pp. 36–64.

Wen, Zha (2022). Leader Security and Hedging in the Era of Great Power Rivalry: Responses of the Philippines and Singapore. *China International Security Review.* Available at: https://doi.org/10.1007/s42533-022-00111-4.

White, Edward and England, Andrew (2022). China Pours Money into Iraq as US Retreats from Middle East. *Financial Times,* February 2.

White, Edward and Ruehl, Mercedes (2022). China Growth to Fall behind Rest of Asia for First Time since 1990. *Financial Times,* September 26.

White, Maddy (2020). China's Belt and Road Initiative: Green Leadership or Greenwashing? *Global Trade Review,* October 14. Available at: www.gtreview.com/news/sustainability/chinas-belt-and-road-initiative-green-leadership-or-greenwashing/.

Whitmore, John (1968). *The Development of the Le Government in 15th Century Vietnam.* PhD dissertation. Cornell University.

Whitmore, John (1970). The Thai-Vietnamese Struggle for Laos in the Nineteenth Century. In Nina Adams and Alfred McCoy, eds, *Laos: War and Revolution*. New York: Harper, pp. 53–66.
Whitmore, John (1997). Literati Culture and Integration in Dai Viet, c. 1430–c. 1840. *Modern Asian Studies* 31:3, pp. 665–687.
Wight, Martin (1966). The Balance of Power. In Herbert Butterfield and Martin Wight,eds, *Diplomatic Investigations: Essays in the Theory of International Politics*. London: Allen & Unwin, pp. 149–175.
Wills, Jack (2012). Functional, Not Fossilized: Qing Tribute Relations with Đại Việt (Vietnam) and Siam (Thailand), 1700–1820. *T'oung Pao*, Second Series, 98:4/5, pp. 439–478.
Wolf, Martin (2021). Containing China is Not a Feasible Option. *Financial Times*, February 3.
Womack, Brantly (2003–4). China and Southeast Asia: Asymmetry, Leadership and Normalcy. *Pacific Affairs* 76:3, pp. 529–548.
Womack, Brantly (2004). Asymmetry Theory and China's Concept of Multipolarity. *Journal of Contemporary China* 13:39, pp. 351–366.
Womack, Brantly (2006). *China and Vietnam: The Politics of Asymmetry*. New York: Cambridge University Press.
Womack, Brantly (2008). China as a Normative Foreign Policy Actor. In Nathalie Tocci, ed., *Who is a Normative Foreign Policy Actor? The European Community and its Global Partners*. Brussels: Centre for European Policy Studies, pp. 265–299.
Womack, Brantly (2011). The Spratlys: From Dangerous Ground to Apple of Discord. *Contemporary South East Asia* 33:3, pp. 370–387.
Womack, Brantly (2013). Beyond Win–Win: Rethinking China's International Relationships in an Era of Economic Uncertainty. *International Affairs* 89:4, pp. 911–928.
Womack, Brantly (2014). China's Future in a Multinodal World Order. *Pacific Affairs* 87:2, pp. 265–284.
Womack, Brantly (2015). China and the Future Status Quo. *Chinese Journal of International Politics* 8:2, pp. 115–137.
Womack, Brantly (2016a). Asymmetric Parity: US-China Relations in a Multinodal World. *International Affairs* 92:6, pp. 1463–1480.
Womack, Brantly (2016b). *Asymmetry and International Relationships*. New York: Cambridge University Press.
Womack, Brantly (2017). International Crises and China's Rise: Comparing the 2008 Global Financial Crisis and the 2017 Global Political Crisis. *Chinese Journal of International Politics* 10:4, pp. 383–401.
Womack, Brantly (2022). China's New Strategic Opportunity in Europe. *Al Jazeera*, March 14. Available at: https://studies.aljazeera.net/en/analyses/china%E2%80%99s-new-strategic-opportunity-europe.

Womack, Brantly, ed., (2010). *China's Rise in Historical Perspective.* Boulder, CO: Rowman and Littlefield.
Womack, Sarah (1995). The Remakings of a Legend: Women and Patriotism in the Hagiography of the Tru'ng Sisters. *Crossroads: An Interdisciplinary Journal of Southeast Asian Studies* 9:2, pp. 31–50.
Womack, Sarah (2003). *Colonialism and the Collaborationist Agenda: Pham Quynh, Print Culture, and the Politics of Persuasion in Colonial Vietnam.* PhD dissertation. University of Michigan. Available at: www.proquest.com/openview/28a0b6b265daaf4b63facb33200e7c8e/1?pq-origsite=gscholar&cbl=18750&diss=y.
Wonacott, Peter (2011). In Africa, U.S. Watches China's Rise. *Wall Street Journal,* September 2.
Wong, Diana (2013). Introduction: The New Chinese Migration to Southeast Asia. *Asian and Pacific Migration Journal* 22:1, pp. 1–6.
Wong, R. Bin (2001). Entre monde et nation: les régions braudéliennes en Asie. *Annales. Histoire, Sciences Sociales* 56:1, pp. 5–41.
Woodside, Alexander (1971). *Vietnam and the Chinese Model: A Comparative Study of Vietnamese and Chinese Government in the First Half of the Nineteenth Century.* Cambridge, MA: Harvard University Press.
Woodside, Alexander (1998). Territorial Order and Collective-Identity Tensions in Confucian Asia: China, Vietnam, Korea. *Daedalus* 127:3, pp. 191–220.
Woodside, Alexander (2006). *Lost Modernities.* Cambridge, MA: Harvard University Press.
Woodside, Alexander (2007). The Centre and the Borderlands in Chinese Political Theory. In Diana Lary, ed., *The Chinese State at the Borders.* Vancouver: University of British Columbia Press, pp. 11–28.
World Bank (2021a). *World Development Indicators.* Available at: https://datatopics.worldbank.org/world-development-indicators/.
World Bank (2021b). Why #OneSouthAsia? Available at: www.worldbank.org/en/programs/south-asia-regional-integration/trade.
World Intellectual Property Organization (2021). *Global Innovation Index 2021.* Geneva: World Intellectual Property Organization. Available at: www.globalinnovationindex.org/Home.
World Trade Organization (2019). *Technological Innovation, Supply Chain Trade, and Workers in a Globalized World.* Geneva: WTO.
World Trade Organization (2021). *World Trade Statistical Review 2021.* Washington DC: WTO.
Wu, Xinbo (2020). The China Challenge: Competitor or Order Transformer? *Washington Quarterly* 43:3, pp. 99–114.
Wucker, Michele (2016). *The Gray Rhino: How to Recognize and Act on the Obvious Dangers We Ignore.* New York: Macmillan.

Xi, Jinping (2017a). Jointly Shoulder Responsibility of Our Times, Promote Global Growth. Speech delivered January 17. Available at: www.china.org.cn/node_7247529/content_40569136.htm.

Xi, Jinping (2017b). Report to the 19th CPC National Congress. Speech delivered October 18. Available at: www.xinhuanet.com/english/special/2017-11/03/c_136725942.htm.

Yan, Xuetong (2014). From Keeping a Low Profile to Striving for Achievement. *Chinese Journal of International Politics* 7:2, pp. 153–184.

Yang, Xifan (2022). Grenzenlose Freundschaft? Interview with Zheng Yongnian. *Die Zeit*, March 18. Available at: www.zeit.de/2022/12/russland-china-beziehung-krieg-ukraine-zheng-yongnian.

Yong, Deng (2022). *China's Strategic Opportunity: Change and Revisionism in China's Foreign Policy*. Cambridge: Cambridge University Press.

Yu, Keping (2009). Culture and Modernity in Chinese Intellectual Discourse. In *Democracy is a Good Thing*. Washington: Brookings, pp. 93–113.

Yuan, Jing-Dong (2010). China's Role in Establishing and Building the Shanghai Cooperation Organization (SCO). *Journal of Contemporary China* 19:67, pp. 855–869.

Zakaria, Fareed (2011). *The Post-American World*, Release 2.0. New York: W.W. Norton Co.

Zakaria, Fareed (2022). The Pentagon is Using China as an Excuse for Huge New Budgets. *Washington Post*, March 10.

Zhang, Hongzhou and Li, Mingjiang (2019). China and Global Water Governance. In Hongzhou Zhang and Mingjiang Li, eds, *China and Transboundary Water Politics in Asia*. New York: Routledge, pp. 219–236.

Zhao, Suisheng (2022a). Top-level Design and Enlarged Diplomacy: Foreign and Security Policymaking in Xi Jinping's China. *Journal of Contemporary China*, March 14.

Zhao, Suisheng (2022b). Is Beijing's Long Game on Taiwan About to End? Peaceful Unification, Brinkmanship, and Military Takeover. *Journal of Contemporary China*, September 28. Available at: https://doi.org/10.1080/10670564.2022.2124349.

Zhuang, Guotu (2021). The Overseas Chinese: A Long History. *Unesco Courier*. Available at: https://en.unesco.org/courier/2021-4/overseas-chinese-long-history.

Zhuang, Guotu and Wang, Wangbo (2010). Migration and Trade: The Role of Overseas Chinese in Economic Relations between China and Southeast Asia. *International Journal of China Studies* 1:1, pp. 174–193.

Zuo, Mandy (2021). China Plans to Put Children Off Studying Abroad as More Pupils Head Overseas at Younger Ages. *South China Morning Post*, February 17.

Index

Acharya, Amitav, 89, 161
Afghanistan, 137, 170, 202, 218
Africa, 67, 69, 81, 86, 133, 183, 186, 219
agency, 9, 28, 43, 64, 121, 127, 129, 151, 165, 166, 168, 183, 214, 219, 227
  asymmetric, 42, 64
  distributed, 151
  multinodal, 213
  premodern, 215
Albright, Madeleine, 223
Albuquerque, Alfonso de, 68–70, 78
Alcibiades, 207
alliances, 42, 90, 116, 128, 129, 132, 148, 169, 172, 185
Allison, Graham, 222
American globalism, 90, 96
Ang, Yuen Yuen, 193
Arthur Kroeber, 33
ASEAN Regional Forum (ARF), 92
Asia Infrastructure Investment Bank (AIIB), 183
Asia Pacific Economic Cooperation (APEC), 5
Asian Financial Crisis (1997), 24, 99, 103, 178
Asian Infrastructure Investment Bank (AIIB), 130, 183, 190, 206
Association of Southeast Asian Nations (ASEAN), 10, 22, 43, 91–93, 104, 117–121, 128, 130, 136, 137, 145, 146, 149–152, 164, 170–172, 174–176, 189, 216, 229
  members of, 5
  not a NATO, 92
asymmetry, 29, 33–37, 53, 72, 73, 134
  bimodal, 161
  colonial, 93
  misperception, 35, 37, 131, 151

Augustus, 67
Australia, 121, 143, 151

balance of power, 168–169
Ban Gu, 60
Bandung Conference, 99
Bangladesh, 141
Beckley, Michael, 207
Beijing consensus, 181
Belt and Road Initiative (BRI), 41, 125, 127, 129, 130, 133, 137, 141, 142, 167, 184, 190, 216
Bergsten, Fred, 13, 179, 205, 208
Biden, Joe, 115, 204, 205, 220
Bismarck, Otto von, 172
black swans, 155, 159, 160
Brands, Hal, 207
Brandt, Willi, 220
Brazil, 156, 159
Breslin, Shaun, 3, 209
Brookings Institution, 122
Brunei, 121
Burma, 43, 91
Buzan, Barry, 130, 132

Calder, Kent, 5
Cambodia, 81, 82, 89, 91, 119, 121, 131, 134, 141, 172
Central Asia, 6, 73, 75, 86, 130, 184, 217
centrality
  of attention, 29
  as configuration, 23, 28, 30
  critique of, 151
  as cultural hierarchy, 23, 26–28
  elements of. *See also* three Ps
  as hegemony, 23–25
  regional, 37, 115
  resilience, 74
certainty vacuum, 116, 168, 169, 207

Index

Champa, 57, 60
Chiang Kai-shek, 85, 109
China
  a regional power, 6
Clausewitz, Carl von, 170
Cold War, 205
Cold War mentality, 220
colonialism, 17, 28, 43, 64, 79, 83, 90, 110
Commonwealth of Nations, 219
community of common destiny, 132, 137, 215
Community of Latin American and Caribbean States (CELAC), 187
Comprehensive and Progressive Agreement for Trans-Pacific Partnership (CPTPP), 190
Confucian-Legalist state, 73
Confucius Institutes, 189
connectivity, 40–42
  forced, 105
  sharp, 17, 43, 77, 79, 80, 83, 93, 95, 104, 110, 121
  thick, 18, 113, 127, 129, 135, 144, 148, 215, 216
  thin, 16, 17, 46, 60, 64, 69, 70, 104, 110, 127
Covid-19, 115, 194
Cuba, 128, 166, 218
Cultural Revolution, 97, 112
cycles of imperial power, 39, 68, 105

Dardess, John, 48
decoupling, 3, 7, 123, 175, 205, 217, 221
demographic deficit, 101
demographic dividend, 101
demographic power, 20, 21, 154, 159, 161, 164, 165, 210, 217
Deng, Yong, 132
Deng Xiaoping, 6, 18, 24, 27, 91, 97, 99, 103, 111, 119, 124, 143, 229
developmental state, 110, 157, 160
Drezner, Daniel, 206
Dutch East Indies, 82

Egypt, 65, 66, 68
England, 94
Ethiopia, 181
European Union, 150, 162, 188, 229

Factory Asia, 5
Fairbank, John King, 98
Feigenbaum, Evan, 206
Five Principles of Peaceful Coexistence, 43, 134, 215
flying geese, 136, 146, 179
Fort Bayard, 85
Forum on China Africa Cooperation (FOCAC), 133
Freeman, Chas, 186, 218
French Indochina, 82, 83
Fujian, 17, 51, 103

gain, relative and absolute, 67, 212
geming (revolution), 88, 99
Germany, 85, 90, 94, 129, 149, 159, 172, 202, 219, 224
Gibbon, Edward, 67
Gilpin, Robert, 39
global decentralization, 149
Global Development Initiative (2021), 44, 133
Global Financial Crisis (2008), 2, 13, 24, 114, 116, 133, 153
global governance, 150, 166, 197
  hegemonic, 189
  multinodal, 189
Global Innovation Index, 210
Global leadership, 228
global power, 7
global value chains, 96, 125, 154, 174–175
globalization, 8, 78, 88, 90, 96, 97, 99, 104, 105, 127, 145, 211, 230
  American, 89
  forced, 10
  post-hegemonic, 8
  with regions, 117
  segmented, 24, 33
Goh, Evelyn, 3, 21, 35, 154, 162, 163, 191, 200, 201, 209, 211, 231
Goldilocks position, 206
Gorbachev, Mikhail, 184, 220
gray rhinos, 159
Great Leap Forward, 101, 103
Great Wall, 17, 46, 50, 74, 100
Greater China, 5, 119, 137, 228
Greater East Asia Co-Prosperity Sphere, 88
Guangdong, 17, 136

Guangxi, 47
guanxi (relationships), 146

Habituation, 38, 127, 131
Han Wudi, 47
hedging, 117
Hegel, Georg Wilhelm Friedrich, 45, 203
hegemonic stability theory, 89
hegemony, 25, 105, 111, 149, 150, 154, 161, 165, 189, 192, 215, 220
  American, 88, 149
  hegemonic rivalry, 212
  U.S., 107, 111, 116, 198, 223
Hevia, James, 144
Hirschman, Albert O., 165, 169
Hồ Chi Minh, 2, 144
Hồ Quý Ly, 53
Hong Kong, 19, 44, 58, 85, 99, 110, 114, 119, 124, 136, 137, 139, 159, 176, 178, 187, 228
Hu Jintao, 180
Huang, Chiung-Chiu, 167
hub-and-spoke order, 89, 96, 99, 115, 145, 154, 165, 183
Huntington, Samuel, 223

imperium, 24, 42
India, 6, 7, 43, 46, 49, 57, 69, 78, 83, 89, 94, 101, 141, 146, 149, 151, 156, 159, 163, 184, 185, 202, 232
Indonesia, 69, 81, 82, 86, 91, 119, 121, 156, 159
Indo-Pacific, 5, 6, 117
Industrialization, 108
International Monetary Fund (IMF), 13
international relationships, 9, 35, 162, 164, 206
  post-hegemonic, 116
  resilience, 213
Iran, 184, 186
Iwakura Mission, 87

Japan, 11, 20, 28, 35, 46, 49, 57–59, 61, 63, 64, 69, 72, 74, 77, 78, 80, 81, 85, 87, 88, 90, 92, 93, 96, 98, 102, 103, 109, 110, 116, 118–120, 124–126, 128, 135, 136, 140, 146, 151, 154, 172, 174–176, 179–181, 187, 190, 202, 204, 210, 214, 217, 219, 221, 229
  status nostalgia, 179

Kang, David, 27
Kant, Immanuel, 80
Kaplan, Robert, 207
Kautilya, 163
Kazakhstan, 130, 141, 181
Kelley, Liam, 62
Kiakhta, Treaty of, 102
Kiautschou Bucht, 85
Kipling, Rudyard, 78
Kissinger, Henry, 224
Korea, 28, 48, 56, 57, 59, 63, 68, 72, 74, 77, 81, 87, 88, 90, 97, 135
  Garlic Battle, 142
  North, 89, 92, 120, 128, 176, 218, 221
  South, 11, 91, 93, 96, 110, 111, 120, 125, 136, 151, 174, 187, 221
Kuomintang (KMT), 87, 109, 110, 138
Kuznets, Simon, 157

Lake, David, 164
Laos, 81, 82, 89, 119, 121, 129, 141, 172
Latin America, 187
Lattimore, Owen, 49, 51
Lê Lợi, 54, 55, 59, 62
Lee Teng-hui, 138
Lenin, Vladimir I., 96
Libya, 189
life chances, 94, 100, 106, 156
Lithuania, 188
Looty the dog, 85
Lowy Institute, 181

Macartney, George, 63
Macau, 5, 44, 137, 228
Maddison, Angus, 31, 77, 83, 84, 155
Made in China 2025, 142
Mahan, Alfred Thayer, 4
Malaysia, 81, 91, 119, 129, 142
Manchuria, 88
Mao Zedong, 24, 85, 98, 109, 144
Marco Polo, 80
Marshall Plan, 90
Mediterranean, 65, 66, 70, 76
  as space, not place, 66
Mekong, 60, 130, 141
messy pluralization, 154, 192, 201

Index

Mexico, 129, 174
middle income trap, 125, 160
Mill, John Stuart, 78
misperceptions, 151
modernization, 12, 23, 33, 77, 78, 81, 87, 88, 91, 93, 96, 102, 104, 109–111, 127, 144
  American, 89
  colonial, 82, 84, 94, 157
  confused, 111, 193
  four routes, 18, 108, 109
  ongoing, 193
modernizing authoritarianism, 109–112
Mongolia, 102
Morris, Ian, 31, 64, 86
Morse, H. B., 98, 102
Mote, Frederick, 62
Mozambique, 219
multinodal Asia, 198
multinodal world order, 8, 13, 20, 21, 43, 88, 145, 146, 148–150, 152–156, 161–169, 173, 189, 191–193, 197, 198, 200, 201, 203, 204, 206, 211, 213, 219, 221, 226, 227, 230, 231
  location, 163
  matrix, 164
  nodes, 20, 164
  power, 162, 213
  primary nodes, 203, 214
  principles, 226
mutual risk reduction, 225
Myanmar, 81, 119, 121, 129, 141, 172

Nan Yue, 47
Nanjing Massacre, 98
National Aeronautics and Space Administration (NASA), 160
Naughton, Barry, 124
Nerchinsk, Treaty of, 57, 102
New Zealand, 151, 172, 229
Nguyễn Trãi, 59
Nguyen Vu Tung, 170
nine dash line, 178
Nixon, Richard, 99
nomadic mobility, 60–62
nomads, 73
North Atlantic Treaty Organization (NATO), 90, 92, 93, 163, 170, 172, 184

nuclear war, 168, 224, 232
Nye, Joseph, 205

Obama, Barack, 206, 220
officialism, 57, 58
  new, 216
one country, two systems, 19, 229
Opium War, 3, 9, 52, 57, 81, 84, 86, 102
Orange Chinese Communist Threat, 3
order transition, 3, 21, 200, 209, 211, 212, 226
  explained, 192
Organski, A. F. K., 209
Overseas Chinese, 86, 99, 123

Pacific Asia
  definition of, 5
  regionality, 145
  splintering, 81
Pakistan, 7, 146, 184, 186, 232
Paris Accords, 212
partnerships, 135, 146, 148, 155, 170, 172, 189, 211
  China's, 128
  collective, 172
  contrast to alliances, 128, 169–172
  non-exclusive, 129
Peace of Westphalia (1648), 42
Pearl River Delta, 124
People's Liberation Army, 101
Perdue, Peter, 63
Perry, Matthew, 81, 87
Philippines, 81, 91, 93, 119, 121, 142, 216, 220
Phoenicians, 66
polycrisis, 207
Portugal, 68–70
post-hegemonic world order, 8, 21, 116, 145, 162, 165, 168, 189, 211–213, 219, 220, 226
post-2008 Three Ps, 118
  population, 122
  presence, 118
  production, 124
power transition, 3, 21, 107, 162, 192, 200, 209, 211, 222
power vacuum, 116, 168, 169
Putin, Vladimir, 5, 144, 163, 185, 220

Qin Yaqing, 19, 56, 115, 132, 148, 164, 166, 231

Regional Comprehensive Economic Partnership (RCEP), 92, 130, 137, 172, 190, 229
regional order, 117, 229
  de-regionalization, 216
  inclusive, 195
  open, 117
Regionalism
  inclusive, 145
Republic of China, 75
rise of the Rest, 3, 194
Rome, 24, 65, 67, 68
Rudd, Kevin, 205
rural revolution, 98, 100
Russia, 57, 102, 172, 184
Russian revolution, 75, 96
Russo-Japanese War, 98

sanctions, 221
sardines, 227
Scholz, Olaf, 188
Scott, James, 165
security dilemma, 169, 206
self-containment, 216
Senkaku Islands, 140
Shanghai Cooperation Organization (SCO), 6, 184
Shanghai Five, 130, 184
Shenzhen, 114, 136, 139
Shi Yinhong, 204
Shih Chih-yu, 167
Shimonoseki, Treaty of, 98
Siam, 57, 77, 81, 82, 97
Singapore, 81, 83, 88, 91, 92, 110, 120, 121, 136, 141, 216
Sino-French War, 98
Sinosphere, 26, 27, 37, 42, 46, 48, 55, 59, 62, 68, 135
soft power, 28, 78, 96, 134, 152, 206
South China Sea, 44, 135, 140–142, 178, 216, 217
  Code of Conduct, 140, 190
Southeast Asia, 5, 10, 23, 43, 46, 61, 64, 81, 83, 86, 91–93, 97, 99, 103, 120, 123, 129, 136, 137, 142, 171, 176, 216, 221

Soviet Union, 89, 90–92, 130, 170, 172, 207, 220, 223–225
spheres of influence, 218
status ad quem, 215
strategic opportunity, 132
Stüver, Georg, 128
Sun Yat Sen, 87, 100, 109

Taiping Heavenly Kingdom, 84
Taiwan, 7, 19, 20, 44, 81, 88, 91, 98, 109–111, 119, 125, 128, 136–139, 167, 168, 178, 180, 214, 216, 217, 228
  cross-Strait, 109, 138, 139, 178, 190
Tawney, R. H., 100
Terminal High Altitude Area Defense (THAAD), 142
Thailand, 81, 91, 93, 97, 119, 129, 131, 141, 142, 220
Three Ps, 30, 39, 40, 46, 75, 78, 96–98, 127
  after 2008, 19
  interrelated, 33
  Population, 31, 49
  post 2008, 116
  Presence, 31, 46
  Production, 32, 51
  U.S., 218
  U.S.-China, 202
Three Ps reversed, 96
  non-population, 100
  non-presence, 97
  non-production, 102
Thucydides, 41, 59, 68, 107, 222
  trap, 3
Tiananmen, 99, 179, 184
tianxia (all under heaven), 27, 46, 96
Tibet, 52, 56, 86, 113, 153
Tooze, Adam, 166
Toyotomi Hideyoshi, 58
Transpacific Partnership (TPP), 206
treaty ports, 81, 85, 98
tribute system, 17, 37, 39, 42, 62, 63, 74
Trump, Donald, 115, 204, 206, 207, 220, 221
Tsai Ing-wen, 138
Turkey, 184

Index

U.S.-China rivalry, 8, 200, 201
  asymmetric rivalry, 212
  parity, 203–207
Ukraine, 163, 168, 184, 185, 188, 189, 200, 201
  Russian invasion of, 1, 8
UN Convention on Law of the Sea (UNCLOS), 140
United Nations, 90, 130, 150
United States
  as global power, 7

Vietnam, 28, 35, 36, 41, 46–48, 53–55, 57 61, 68, 69, 72–74, 81–83, 89–93, 97, 99, 101, 119, 121, 123, 131, 135, 140, 141, 145, 167, 170, 171, 191
  American war, 2
  Ming occupation, 53
  partnerships, 129

waifan 外藩, 42
Wang Gungwu, 17, 46, 71, 88, 198, 230
Wang Huning, 134
Washington Consensus, 99
Wei Xiang, 55
West and the Rest, 106
  agency denied, 104

  convergence, 13, 153, 158
  divergence, 94, 156
Westernization, 104
  forced configuration, 104
Westphalian system, 108
Wight, Martin, 168
win-win, 36, 128, 133, 135, 176
wolf warrior, 143
World Bank, 13
World Trade Organization (WTO), 103
Wu Xinbo, 206
Wu Yu-Shan, 18, 78, 107, 193, 230

Xi Jinping, 19, 24, 44, 132, 133, 138, 143, 144, 177, 181, 183, 187, 218
  Taiwan policy, 7
Xinjiang, 46, 86, 113

Yan Xuetong, 132
Yang Jiechi, 143
Yellow River, 72
Younghusband, Francis, 86

Zakaria, Fareed, 161
Zeitenwende, 188
Zhang Zhidong, 78
Zhao Suisheng, 144
Zheng He, 54, 68, 69
Zheng Yongnian, 185

Printed in the USA
CPSIA information can be obtained
at www.ICGtesting.com
LVHW012237190923
758761LV00009B/334